Quick
Fixes
for EVERYDAY
FEARS

Quick Fixes

Fixes

for EVERYDAY FEARS

How to Manage Everything from
Fear of Change to Fear of Flying

Michael Clarkson

KEY PORTER  BOOKS

To my wife, Jennifer Clarkson (nee Vanderklei), who has been anything but a quick fix for me. Her love, dedication and humor, as well as her perseverance through life's pain and her celebration of its pleasures, have provided me and all of our family with inspiration and comfort. And to my granddaughter Skye, with the hope and expectation that her generation will learn to deal more productively with fear.

National Library of Canada Cataloguing in Publication

Clarkson, Michael, 1948-
   Quick fixes for everyday fears: how to manage everything from fear of change to fear of flying / Michael Clarkson.

ISBN 1-55263-238-5

1.Fear. 2.Self-actualization (Psychology) I.Title.

BF575.F2C53 2004   152.4'6   C2003-907013-1

THE CANADA COUNCIL | LE CONSEIL DES ARTS
FOR THE ARTS | DU CANADA
SINCE 1957 | DEPUIS 1957

ONTARIO ARTS COUNCIL
CONSEIL DES ARTS DE L'ONTARIO

The publisher gratefully acknowledges the support of the Canada Council for the Arts and the Ontario Arts Council for its publishing program. We acknowledge the support of the Government of Ontario through the Ontario Media Development Corporation's Ontario Book Initiative.

We acknowledge the financial support of the Government of Canada through the Book Publishing Industry Development Program (BPIDP) for our publishing activities.

Key Porter Books Limited
70 The Esplanade
Toronto, Ontario
Canada M5E 1R2

www.keyporter.com

Text design: Jack Steiner
Electronic formatting: Jean Lightfoot Peters
Printed and bound in Canada

04 05 06 07 08 09 6 5 4 3 2 1

CONTENTS

PART *1: An Introduction to Fear*
What Fear Is 2
Where Our Fears Come From 10
Coping with Fear 15
How This Book Is Organized 22
The Awareness Quiz 24

PART *2: General Fears*
Fear of the Unknown 28
Fear of Not Having Control 30
Fear of Change 32
Fear of Taking Chances 34
Fear of Responsibility 36
Fear of Confrontation or Conflict 38
Fear of Not Being Loved 40
Fear of Intimacy or Love 42
Superstition or Fear of the Supernatural 44
Fear of Religion 46
Fear of Destiny 48

PART *3: Physical Fears*
Fear of Flying 52
Fear of Terrorism 54
Fear of Being Mugged 56
Fear of Getting Involved in an Emergency 58
Fear of Blood (and Blood Injury) 60
Fear of Death 62
Fear of Illness or Pain 64
Fear of Doctors or Dentists 66
Fear of Aging 68
Sexual Fears 70
Fear of Enclosed Spaces 72
Fear of Heights 74
Fear of Falling 76
Fear of Travel 78
Fear of Driving 80
Fear of Dogs and Animals 82

Fear of Snakes and Spiders   84
Fear of Water and Swimming   86
Fear of Loud Noises   88
Fear of Weather   90

PART *4: Fears of the Ego*
Fear of Embarrassment   94
Fear of Failure   96
Fear of Making Mistakes   98
Fear of Success or Happiness   100
Fear of Criticism   102
Fear of Rejection   104
Fear of Getting a Compliment   106
Fear of What Others Think   108
Fear of Invasion of Territory or Privacy   110
Fear of Losing Status   112
Fear of Oneself   114
Fear of Showing Emotions   116
Fear of Having a Photo Taken   118
Fear of Choking in Sports   120

PART *5: Fears at Home*
Fear and Stress in Children   124
Fear for Your Children's Safety   126
Fear of Your Children Leaving Home   128
Fear of Becoming a Parent   130
Fears for Your Marriage/Partnership   132
Fear of Family Get-Togethers   134
Fear of a Break-in   136
Fear of Delivering Bad News   138
Fear of Disorder or Untidiness   140
Fear of Solicitors and Telemarketers   142
Worry at Night and Sleeplessness   144
Fear of Being Alone   146
Fear of the Dark   148

PART *6: Fears in Social Settings*
Fear of People   152
Fear of Panic Attacks in Public   154
Fear of Public Speaking   156
Fear of Crowds   158
Fear of Strangers   160
Fear of Other Races   162
Fear of Singing or Dancing   164
Fear of Dating   166
Fear of the Opposite Sex   168
Fear of Commitment   170
Fear of Ending a Romantic Relationship   172
Fear of Homosexuality   174

PART *7: Fears at School*
Fear of School   178
Fear of the First Day of School   180
Fear of Appearing Stupid   182
Fear of Exams   184
Fear of Teachers   186
Fear of What Friends Think   188
Fear of Cliques   190
Fear of Your Appearance   192
Fear of Bullies   194
Fear of Not Having or Getting a Job   196

PART *8: Fears at Work*
Stress at Work   200
Financial Fears   204
Fear of a Job Interview   206
Fear of Downsizing   208
Fear of Retirement   210
Fear of Technology   212
Fear of Asking for a Raise or Promotion   214
Dealing with Deadline Pressure   216
Fear of the Boss   218
Fear of Quitting   220
Fear of Firing an Employee   222
Fear of Harassment   224
Fear of Competition   226

PART *9: Serious Worries and Ways to Relax*
     Serious Worries   230
     How to Relax   232
     How to Cope with Pressure   234
     How to Deal with Stress   235
     How to Deal with Anger   237
     When Nothing Works   239
     When You Don't Fear Enough   240
     Other Phobias   242

Acknowledgments   243
Index   245

*An
Introduction
to Fear*

What Fear Is

If you are like me, you have a number of fears and worries. I like to think of myself as relatively well adjusted, and yet I don't like going to the doctor or the dentist—to the point of occasionally avoiding visits. Sometimes I worry about what people think of my work, or even of me as a person. I still worry about my children even though they are now adults. Other times, I can't sleep at night because my mind is filled with images of things that might happen, or of things that didn't work out the way I wanted them to.

As I interview people for my books on fear management and travel as a professional speaker, I'm finding that people of all ages and backgrounds are also feeling fear. In addition to our personal fears, global problems also worry us: conflicts in the Middle East, threats of terrorism and an uncertain economy, and health concerns such as AIDS, SARS and the West Nile virus.

And yet, as I research the fascinating subject of fear, I'm realizing that it's quite all right to be afraid and to worry. Without fear, we would not be motivated to excel at work or in relationships, and we would not watch out for cars as we crossed the street. Without worry, we would not plan effectively to meet challenges at work and at school. Indeed, without fear, we would not feel the satisfaction or the adrenaline buzz of overcoming a challenge. And as nations, we would not rally to meet global problems.

Fear is our survival instinct, our number one primal emotion, even more primal than love, which I consider more of a long-term spiritual resource. Ever since our species appeared on earth, fear has helped us overcome tremendous challenges posed by the environment, by predators and by fire. But, alas, as we have evolved from cave people into more complex thinkers, fear has taken some strange twists and turns. Sadly, it has taken on forms that are often counterproductive. We have developed more fears than we ever had—fear of failure, fear of loss of control, fear of change and, particularly, fear of what others think about us. We view far too many things and situations as threats.

As a relatively new species, we do not deal particularly well with our fears. Under pressure or in emergency situations, most people perform worse than they normally would. Worry is even more of a nuisance—one study at the University of Wisconsin showed that only 8 percent of worries are legitimate; the other worries are a waste of time, energy and resources. As individuals, we allow phobias—exaggerated fears of specific things or situations—to cause ongoing disruptions in our lives. The American Psychiatric Association estimates that 10 to 13 percent of the population suffers from a phobia. The number of people who suffer from specific fears that are not quite phobias is much higher. In too many cases, fears hold people back from going for their dreams or living a fulfilling life. "Fear defeats more people than any other one thing in the world," wrote Ralph Waldo Emerson.

We deal poorly with fear for a number of reasons. For one, we are still hardwired like our cave ancestors, but society protects us too much from fearful situations, preventing us from getting used to our feelings of anxiety and learning how to deal with them. Furthermore, for most of our species' time on the planet, our average life span was 18 years. Little wonder that we're still having trouble getting used to growing into our 50s and 60s and beyond—and the emotional wisdom that this experience can bring.

Sometimes we are not fully aware of what our fears are, or what is causing our anxiety. We just know that something is wrong. In this book, we will try to identify your fears and give you ways you can deal with them. In some cases, we will even suggest ways for you to use them to your advantage. This book is primarily about everyday worries and phobias. Although it is entitled *Quick Fixes for Everyday Fears*, there are no quick fixes for some of the more serious phobias. You might have to see a doctor or therapist for those, or perhaps take medication (see "When Nothing Works" in Part 9).

There are basically three types of fear:

- **Worry**—a medium- to long-term fear, mostly about things that might happen or that have occurred in the past
- **Specific phobia**—fear about certain things or circumstances, such as fear of flying. A specific fear is considered a phobia if it becomes irrational and prevents us from doing things such as getting on a plane
- **Emergency fear**—a sudden threat that sets off our nervous system, such as a mugger or a deadline at work

To deal with these fears, nature has provided us with what I call the *fear defense system*. It is complex, with components that are psychological, emotional and physical. The first stage of fear is psychological—we interpret the world around us and identify what we believe are threats. Let's say we decide that the threat is downsizing at work. Then the second stage kicks in, the emotional response—whether to react with fear, anger, grief or another emotion. Let's say you respond with fear; you are afraid that you will be laid off, and that would spell financial trouble for you and your family. The third and physical stage releases what I call *fear energy*, a rush of powerful hormones, such as adrenaline, dopamine, endorphins and cortisol, which are dispatched from your brain throughout your body to give you added energy, strength and focus to deal with the threat. The fear defense system also gives you an inner emotional drive, a long-range determination to meet the threat.

Your fear defense system has two basic parts: the *emergency fear system* (which some people refer to as the sympathetic nervous system), which deals with sudden emergencies, and the *worry system*, which deals with long-term threats. These two branches of the fear defense system are related psychologically, emotionally and physically, and yet they sometimes call upon different hormones, or fear energy, to do their work—for example, the emergency fear system heavily relies on adrenaline, while the worry system has cortisol as one of its main fuels. Specific fears and phobias tap into the powers of the worry system.

Worry, emergency fear, and specific fears and phobias often interact with one another. Worry over a job interview can set off your emergency fear system, which can make you start to tremble or sweat. And a phobia can trigger symptoms of the two other types of fear.

This book focuses on specific fears and phobias, although worry and emergency fear often come into play. Let's take a closer look at all three fears.

Worry

Worry is perhaps our greatest resource, yet it can also lead to our greatest failures. Worry occurs when we think intensely about things that have happened to us or to those around us, or when we ponder what may transpire in the future. Even without global concerns such as terrorism and the economy, people find lots of things to fret about—an upcoming event in their lives, their job, their family situation or their relationships. Worry can lead to anxiety, tension, stress, nail biting, sleeplessness, illness, poor performance and the scuttling of a person's confidence or dreams. Some people fear thinking too much (phronemophobia). And yet there is a brilliant benefit to worry: "healthy" worriers become motivated, energized and even excited, and they plan efficiently. They are the ones who get the job done. Effective worry manifests itself in terms of planning and taking action against a genuine threat or challenge.

Where does worry come from? Unbelievably, the average person has 66,000 thoughts per day, two-thirds of them negative. The University of Wisconsin research shows that of the things people worry about, 40 percent are about things that never occur, 30 percent are about things from the past, 12 percent are needless concerns about health, 10 percent are petty and miscellaneous cares, and only 8 percent are legitimate concerns. In other words, most worry is wasted, even counterproductive, energy. We are equipped to deal quite effectively with the legitimate 8 percent because the worry system employs an elaborate network of hormones and resources to help us improve our planning and boost our energy to carry out tasks.

Effective worry can increase achievement. In researching the 500 most influential people in history, in science, business, sports, politics and other fields, I found that the majority of them came from a dysfunctional, or at least a challenged, home environment, but they learned to harness their insecurities to meet challenges on their way to the top. Less than 5 percent of the 500 came from what would be considered a well-adjusted, two-parent family. (Of course, most people from dysfunctional homes live unproductive lives, but that is the subject for another book.)

A close relative of worry is anxiety—often described as ambiguous worry, an uneasy free-floating feeling, sometimes accompanied by tension. Anxiety is from a Latin word meaning "worried about the unknown." It can be triggered by an upcoming event, by a buildup of stress or pressure, or by a person's fear of a certain situation. Sometimes it appears as a type of messenger, indicating unresolved conflicts or issues. People may not even know what is causing their anxiousness, but it can affect their ability to act or deal with everyday occurrences. In severe cases, they may feel dizzy, out of breath, sweaty or numb. They may even have heart palpitations or fear they are having a heart attack or going crazy. Anxiety can sometimes be produced by pain, such as what we experience when we have a migraine headache.

Anxiety is a common feeling affecting almost everyone to some degree. Each year, doctors write billions of prescriptions worldwide for anti-anxiety treatments! Psychologists believe there is more anxiety these days because people have not had time to react to the faster pace of society, especially to technological changes. Some people are genetically prone to anxiety; others are anxious because of traumatic events, insecure childhoods or uncertain present circumstances. Anxiety disorders are the leading mental health problem among American women and second only to alcohol and drug abuse among men. About 10 percent of Americans (up to 30 million people) suffer from panic attacks, phobias and other anxiety disorders.

Specific Phobia

A phobia is a worry that is out of control. "Phobia" was originally a Greek word, and thus words connected with it are usually Greek, such as claustrophobia (the fear of being in a tight space). Most psychologists believe there are three types of phobias:

- **Situational phobia** (fear of snakes, airplanes, heights, etc.)
- **Social phobia** (fear of looking inadequate in others' eyes or becoming embarrassed, such as in public speaking)
- **Agoraphobia** (fear of being away from a safe place, usually home, or panicking in public)

A specific fear is considered a phobia if it is out of proportion to the danger, if you become preoccupied with it, or if it interferes with your life. Phobias are often fueled by the imagination and a tendency to expect the worst. If you constantly avoid a situation, such as a medical checkup, because of your fear, then you have a phobia.

But you may have specific fears without them reaching the phobic stage. If you are squeamish about blood and still have blood work done occasionally at the hospital, you have a specific fear. If you always avoid it, you have a full-fledged phobia (hemophobia). If you are afraid of drowning and yet continue to swim, you have a fear of water. If you avoid the water, then you have a phobia (hydrophobia). Either way, you may want to do something to lessen your specific fears and your phobias, and that's where this book comes in. Don't overreact, though; most people with specific fears or phobias are otherwise healthy psychologically.

It's common for people to have phobias in areas in which they have little control, such as flying, or in areas of unpredictability, such as thunderstorms. Many phobias are complex and interrelated. For example, you may think you have a fear of being a passenger in a car because of the potential of physical harm, but looking deeper, you may also fear loss of control (to the driver) or what the driver thinks of you because you are relinquishing that control. Some fears mask deeper fears; for instance, a person who cringes at the thought of retirement may actually be afraid that death lies around the corner.

Where do phobias come from? They may be genetic (phobics tend to have at least one phobic parent), they may have their source in a traumatic experience, or they may have been taught by parents or learned from watching friends or even extreme cases in the media. Fears of specific things, such as animals or crowds, tend to run in families. Phobias are often more intense when a person is depressed.

Neuroscientist Joseph LeDoux believes that only recently in human history has fear taken such pathological forms as phobias, obsessive-compulsive behavior, panic disorders, anxiety, mental illness and post-traumatic stress disorder. All the more reason to study and understand fear better.

Emergency Fear

We all feel the symptoms of emergency fear—up to 40 times a day. It comes in a wide variety of forms, including tension, anxiety, distress and, on the good side, an increase in strength, speed and concentration. Some people feel and even invoke this fear energy more than others; they are considered to be "adrenaline sensitive" because of their chemical hardwiring.

Your emergency fear system activates automatically to help you deal with sudden threats in a variety of circumstances—when you are startled by a stranger who suddenly appears around the corner, for example, or when you are under the pressure of a deadline at work. In a split second, your mind and body go through a whole series of changes to deal with the threat: your heart pumps out more blood, your pain threshold increases, and powerful hormones such as adrenaline and endorphins are released to give you added power and focus. There are various levels of change, depending on the severity of the threat, or what you think of the threat. Some bodily systems can shut down as blood is sent from the fingers and the abdomen to the larger muscles, leaving you trembling, with a sinking feeling in your gut. At its peak, this response is known as *fight or flight*, which sometimes leads to near miracles as people produce feats of strength to overcome life-threatening situations.

The emergency fear system is as old as man and was intended to help us survive against harsh living conditions, predators and warring tribes. Some people have been able to adapt its powers to work, business and school, but these days it is largely outdated and counterproductive because we do not have nearly as many physical challenges as we once had. Although we have evolved into thinking creatures, our outmoded fear system continues to kick in when we perceive a social, academic or professional threat; it even springs into gear when we feel a need to defend our pride or ego. This fear energy often causes tension, distress and illness and can make us freeze under pressure.

It is easy to confuse emergency fear with *pressure* or *stress*. They are connected with fear, but they have separate qualities as well. Our emergency fear system activates when we face pressure, demands or threats. It can either inspire us to meet the threats or make us feel distressed if we feel they are too much to handle. Under pressure, people can perform better or worse than they do without pressure, but most perform worse.

There are two types of pressure: external and internal. External or *physical* pressures are things like your workload, a strict boss or demands to pay the bills or to score high marks in school. *Internal pressures* are self expectations or goals, or expectations that we feel other people have for us. Without a certain amount of pressure or challenge, life would be boring. We meet pressure through our fear reaction, and this reaction can cause good stress (eustress) or bad stress (distress); in other words, extra energy or debilitating tension. We all react differently to pressure. Our reactions depend on our genes, upbringing and experiences.

A Word About Stress

Stress is the outcome of our fear response. It stems from the extra fear energy, the hormones and focusing powers that are sent by our emergency fear system to help us deal with threats. We are hardwired to meet any type of threat with a physical response, just as we were thousands of years ago. When we are able to channel the fear energy productively, we experience what has been termed eustress, but when fear energy becomes too much for us to handle and is counterproductive, we experience distress.

For most people, stress means distress, because that is often the unfortunate outcome of our reaction to things. When people are distressed, they feel overly nervous, anxious, irritable, confused, tired and, often, unmotivated. Distress affects many of the body's systems—nervous, cardiovascular, endocrine and immune. It can even lower resistance to colds. There are two types of stress: *acute stress* is reaction to sudden demands, while *chronic stress* accumulates over time, often from a variety of pressures. Generally, the most stressful events are serious life changes, such as divorce or the death of a loved one.

Fear's Rowdy Cousin: Anger

We don't often think of anger as being related to fear, but it is. When we are fearful of certain things, we often get angry—when our son or daughter is misbehaving, when someone moves into our territory at work, or when we believe a teacher is unfair to us at school. This isn't *fear*, just annoyance, you say? But a deeper look may reveal that we get angry at our children because we are afraid of losing control of them, afraid of the coworker because she may knock us down in the office pecking order, and afraid of the teacher because he might fail us in a subject.

Whenever we want to take action against a threat, we get angry. Anger is fear's roughhouse cousin. It is the built-in enforcer that helps us meet our threats. Take the "d" out of danger and you have anger. It prepares us to fight, or at least to fake a fight, by releasing potent hormones like dopamine and testosterone from our emergency fear system. Like fear, anger can be productive or debilitating. It can force us out of the "freeze" mode to take action or to solve problems, but if it is unfocused, it can send us out of control.

We're all familiar with different types of anger. Anger can take the form of a violent burst of energy toward an attacker, a slow burn toward someone who has wronged us, or frustrated rage at a computer we can't control. It can seem like such a negative emotion that it suddenly makes us feel like a different person. In a sense, we *are* a different person, as our emergency fear system kicks in to make us stronger and more alert. People who always seem angry or on the verge of anger may have a hair-trigger chemistry or come from a competitive or embattled home environment. Angry people are often sick, with high blood pressure and a weakened immune system. If you keep pumping out the hormone cortisol, it can weaken your cardiovascular system. Angry people tend to overreact to things and to smoke, drink and overeat. Anger can wreck their lives by ruining their friendships and slashing their life spans.

A lot of anger is based on pride. People in business and sports who feel threatened often use anger as an achievement tool. Basketball star Michael Jordan would get angry when he felt opponents disrespected him, but he was able to channel this energy into his game. In researching the 50 top athletic performances of all time, I found that fear and anger were factors in most cases. Like humans, most animals get angry to protect their lives or their territory. If we didn't become angry from time to time, there would be no such thing as justice, but out-of-control anger can lead to great injustice.

Where Our Fears Come From

We have established that we have many fears and that some are actually good for us. But where do they come from? How on earth did some of us develop a fear of computers or a fear of saying no to our children? Why are we so frightened of public speaking or what others think of us? This is a complex subject and, although there has been much research, some of the findings remain unscientific, even fuzzy. After researching this subject since 1988 and interviewing many experts and phobics, I believe that our fears have four major roots, some of which can interact with one another. Let's take a look.

Our Primitive Genes

We all have worries and specific fears that were embedded in our ancestors millions of years ago, such as fear of the dark, fear of strangers (potential predators), fear of being alone (and thus losing the protection of others) and fear of death. These instinctual reactions to threats help to keep our species alive. They keep us cautious in the face of unknown circumstances. Without them, we'd always be walking in front of cars, putting our hands on hot stoves, hanging out in dark alleys and jumping into questionable relationships. Some experts call these *prepared fears*. They are visible in some people's fear of snakes and animals, which were threats to early humans' survival. Our predisposed fear of such creatures may be dormant, but it can be awakened by a single encounter. Once the fear is out in the open, it is difficult to suppress in some people, but not impossible.

Family Genetics

Many specific fears—such as fear of blood, fear of going to the dentist, or fear of heights—are passed along for generations through family genes. The genetic strain of some of these fears is stronger in some relatives than it is in others; one brother might fear heights while another happily goes skydiving or roller-coaster riding. (This is the case with my two sons.) Sometimes, specific fears skip a generation, for example, from grandmother to granddaughter.

Conditioning

Some experts call this *behaviorism*. You learned to be afraid of something because you saw (usually in childhood) how other people reacted to it. In other words, fear can be contagious. Or perhaps your parents told you to be fearful of something in order to protect you, although their worries might have been misguided. This phenomenon is a major root of racism: people who show fear or hatred toward other groups teach these feelings to their children and grandchildren. Of course, behavioral conditioning can also be good for us if it teaches us to avoid genuine dangers.

Trauma

People often learn to fear things that have hurt or shaken them in the past. The most striking example is post-traumatic stress disorder, in which soldiers and accident victims become fearful of certain situations linked to past traumas (they may even feel that they are reliving those traumas). A woman who was badly hurt in a car crash might recoil years later in a minor accident, or she might be too scared to drive. Tennis player Monica Seles became less aggressive and efficient after she was stabbed by a fan. Traumatic events may leave more than just psychological wounds: they may even change a person's brain chemistry. We often see the effects of trauma in animals; a pet may become fearful of going to the veterinarian's office after having a serious operation. Trauma is not *always* a bad thing; it can also discourage people from returning to dangerous activities when they are not skilled enough to handle them.

How many of the above four roots of fear contribute to the fears you have? It's difficult to say, since we are all unique and complex beings. It's possible that a combination of the roots is at play. For instance, I have what is classified as a blood (and blood injury) fear that borders on a phobia. If I give blood, I feel faint. I also feel anxious or sweaty when I see a gory movie, even though I know it is all fake. How did I get this way? For starters, my fear probably has a *primitive* base. Some experts believe that nature programmed us to pass out at the sight of a lot of blood so that in our panic we would not cause ourselves physical harm and more loss of blood (in my case, this is an exaggerated fear because I'm not physically threatened by a simple blood test). *Family genetics* may also come into play because several of my relatives also have a fear of medics and blood. In addition, I might have *learned* this behavior of avoiding medics because I saw that some of my relatives avoided them. I believe that a *traumatic event* was also a contributing factor: at age five, after living without my father for a year, we moved from England to Canada, where I developed blood poisoning in both of my legs and had some painful visits to the doctor.

In short, our twenty-first century fears come from a combination of things in our ancestral and our personal past. This combination, in itself, is changing our evolution of fear. In fact, fear is probably more complex now than it has ever been. In primitive times, our fears were more fierce but less numerous and more visible—we feared fire, predators, enemy tribes and a harsh environment. We have overcome many of these threats over time, thanks to our consciousness, cooperation with one another, planning and powers of adaptation.

As our brains evolved and our society became faster paced, our fears changed along with our needs. We are now in a transition stage between animals and a species of the future. We're sophisticated creatures, caught between the age of body and the age of brain, between cave and computer, with needs and fears tied to both. Many of our physical needs are now ensured by our government's safety nets, and yet we have more fears than ever: fear of technology, fear of keeping up with the neighbors, fear of downsizing and fear of saying no to our many responsibilities. This book covers a long list of more than 100 fears, but there could have been many more.

Many new fears stem from our ability to know what is happening around the globe. Our communications technologies alert us to such potential threats as recession, downsizing, weather disasters and crime trends. Some of these threats are legitimate, but many people exaggerate them and worry needlessly, especially if they watch a lot of TV news or tabloid reporting.

Because so many of our modern threats are social and professional in nature, we have adapted our fear defenses to help us "survive" in these areas. In our competitive, status-oriented society, it is vital that we be successful in our workplace or our school. Many of our needs and threats revolve around ego and self-esteem. A survey in the late 1990s revealed that more people were afraid of public speaking (and thus of making fools of themselves) than of death. That's what you call fearing for your ego!

A Word About Defense Mechanisms

These are psychological and/or emotional devices we put up to protect our pride or ego against perceived threats. These defenses and patterns of behavior are often developed unconsciously in childhood, and we are often unaware that we are using them. For example, if a father constantly tells a child she is inadequate, the child may feel threatened and anxious. To protect her psyche, she may develop a strong defense mechanism by always denying that she is inadequate. Once it is developed, this defense mechanism can become an automatic reaction, which can be repeated for the rest of her life in a variety of situations, not just those involving her father. When the child grows up, she may view constructive criticism from her spouse as a threat and react to it by putting up walls of denial. This mechanism can cause people to see too many things as threats, thus preventing them from growing and from learning the truth about themselves and the world.

Defense mechanisms can nevertheless be productive. They are evoked all the time by successful business people and athletes, whose mindsets are challenged and threatened as youngsters. My research shows that most of the people at the top of every profession come from unusually challenged backgrounds. They often develop a defensive mode of "I'll show you," and they use it in productive ways as they go through life.

Everyone Reacts Differently

We all react differently to pressure and to fearful situations, depending on our genes, our upbringing, our age, our experiences and even on our mood on a particular day or in a particular situation. Some people freeze while giving a speech while others are the life of the party.

"Our fear systems are all unique and they react depending on our nervous hardwiring, our self-esteem, our upbringing and our view of the world," says Karen Matthews, a professor of psychology at the University of Pittsburgh. "Some people are more sensitive than others and are so-called hot reactors, responding up to 30 times a day (to situations)."

Our hardwiring is crucial to the way we respond to situations. Some people are more highly strung or sensitive to dopamine and other aggressive hormones, while others have less access to endorphins and therefore tend to be less humorous. We are all born with a so-called worry gene; in some people it is shorter than it is with others and pumps out less of the soothing hormone serotonin. Furthermore, some people are born with a livelier left side of the brain, predisposing them to be generally more energetic and optimistic.

Environmental factors are also important. If you had a loving but not overprotective childhood, you may have a less fearful outlook on life. If you constantly get rejected, you may become fearful of criticism and taking chances, which may in turn result in low self-esteem, a common trait in anxious people. If you experienced a major trauma, you will likely be afraid of things associated with the trauma.

Gender sometimes makes a difference in peoples' reactions to threats. Through a combination of factors, men tend to be less fearful of physical situations and women tend to deal with social challenges better, although this is not always the case, especially in these times of changing gender roles. Age can also be a factor: as people accumulate more experiences that make them feel threatened, they may become more cautious. Adults often get more nervous during exams than children, but experiences in business and sports can give them confidence in such pressure situations.

Coping with Fear

Don't let the word "fear" scare you. There is good news because this book is more about solutions than problems. We can adapt to our fears, and we can even train some of them to work for us. In fact, we already have. Long ago, we overcame a fear that almost all other species have not been able to cope with—the fear of fire—and now we harness fire to our advantage by using it to heat our homes and fuel our rockets.

We can adapt to our new fears in similarly constructive ways. As a society, we are better aware of fears and phobias than we used to be, which puts us in a good position to deal with them effectively. We will probably never conquer all of our fears and worries. If we did, we would not survive as a species. The purpose of this book is to help you identify what fears you should act upon, which ones you should cope with and which ones you can use to your advantage.

We all cope with fear in different ways, depending on our personality, the type of fear and the circumstances. A remedy for one person may be poison for another. We can often deal with fear by simply relaxing, breathing deeply and putting things in perspective. That prevents our emergency fear system from kicking in beyond levels we can control, and it keeps our adrenaline output within reasonable bounds.

However, the world's most successful people often like to remain hyper and to use fear and its byproduct *eustress* as a performance tool—especially emergency fear. They learn not only to cope with their fears, but sometimes they redirect them over both the short and long term. For instance, basketball great Michael Jordan admitted at the peak of his career that he was afraid of looking inferior, so he sometimes got himself worked up and focused his hormonal energy and launched himself into "the zone."

There are even times when *distress* can be used productively. When we feel stressed out by situations at work or at home, we can focus this adrenaline and cortisol into whatever it is we are doing, or we can use it for the social good by volunteering for community organizations, churches or hospitals. (Of course, most people allow their emergency fear system to act as a sort of friendly fire to turn against them, but we can learn how to perform better under pressure through use of focusing techniques.)

In my own life, I have been able to get many of my fears and some specific fears and phobias under control through greater awareness and visualization, and by gradually facing my fears and gaining experience in pressure situations. For most of my life, I've been afraid of the water, but at age 49 I finally taught myself to swim. I've also learned to use some of my fears to my advantage. For example, when I was in my early 20s, I was so shy about my freelance writing that I was too scared to go into the office to pick up my weekly paycheck. But now I worry so much less about social embarrassment that I've become a professional speaker. I have been in "the zone" approximately 40 times in my journalism and amateur athletic careers. Much of my success has come from education—in researching fear since 1988, I have learned the techniques of psychologists, psychiatrists and average people who have learned to cope with their worries. In this book, I am passing them on to you.

As we continue to research, there is hope—even excitement— that the new facets of fear that we are discovering will help us deal with this powerful emotion more effectively. Let's take a look at ways of coping with worry, with specific fears and phobias, and with emergency fear.

Coping with Worry

Strategies:

- Identify if you are in a state of worry. Are your muscles tense? Is your mind racing? Are your teeth clenched? Are you feeling depressed?
- Schedule a time each day to do your worrying (no more than 20 minutes). Write down all that you are worrying about and what type of "threat" caused it. Identify the worries that really affect you and the ones you have some control over. Take action on those.
- Balance your worry. People who *always* worry never get anything done. People who *never* worry never get anything done. The trick is to worry about things we can have some influence over.
- If you determine that your worry is unhealthy and unproductive, try to defuse it by changing your thinking pattern. Or use deep breathing, meditation, music or humor.
- If worry is justified, redirect it into planning or action to meet the challenge. Don't let worry be an excuse for inaction, as it often is.
- Practice the serenity prayer: Grant me the serenity to accept the things I cannot change, the courage to change the things I can and the wisdom to know the difference.
- Focus on the solution, not the problem.
- If worries persist, make them 3-D by writing them down, putting them on a tape recorder and playing them back to yourself or sharing them with other people. This gives you a better perspective on worry and underscores that we all worry and we are all in this life together.
- Think and talk positively. Optimists are less likely than the

average person to have an accident or become ill. Avoid negative people; they can create a pity party.
- Bring balance and harmony to your life physically, profession-
ally, socially and spiritually to reduce pressure and stress.

References:

What You Can Change and What You Can't by Martin E.
Seligman, Pocket Books, 1993

Worry by Edward M. Hallowell, Ballantine, 1997

Dealing with Specific Fears and Phobias

There are no treatments that offer a 100 percent cure for specific
fears and phobias, but some produce encouraging results. At the
least, we can make our fears more rational and manageable. The
following are some ways that specific fears and phobias are treated
(you will see many references to them throughout this book).
Some of these methods can be used without professional assis-
tance, perhaps with help from family or friends. Others may be
more effective with the guidance of a therapist or a support group.

Strategies:
- Become more aware of your fears. Identify whether you are
afraid of something if it is affecting your life, and then be willing to admit it to yourself so you can do something about it.
- Face your fears. By exposing ourselves to what we fear, we
tend to become less afraid of it. Usually this is done over a
period of time, such as gradually getting used to fear of
heights by slowly stepping to the edge of a balcony. Therapists
call this behavior therapy.
- Use visualization techniques. Many people can simulate and
desensitize their fear by imagining themselves going through a
fearful situation step by step. If they are afraid of going to the
dentist, they picture driving to the dentist's office, sitting in the
waiting room and going through a dental procedure to a successful conclusion. There are even some virtual reality programs
available in which sufferers are hooked up to a sophisticated
computer experience for a realistic type of imagery.

- Make yourself less vulnerable by developing your resources. If you find you are shy, develop your people skills to boost your confidence. If you are self-conscious or arrogant, develop your spirituality through meditation, religion or volunteering.
- Get professional help. The most effective way to treat a phobia is to seek the help of a doctor, counselor or psychologist. Therapists may use one or more of the methods discussed in this section, or they may use group therapy or drugs such as the antidepressant Paxil, which helps to manage social phobias.
- Consider cognitive therapy and reprogramming. If your fears have developed from low self-esteem, you may have to assess your attitudes, needs and beliefs—and you may have to change them.

Unfortunately, less than 10 percent of people with phobias ever seek help for their problem; instead, they look the other way and hobble through their lives in denial, while avoiding the thing they are afraid of. Often, they are worried about their overreaction to their fears and are afraid that facing up to them will bring shame, feelings of inadequacy and other negative social consequences.

Thankfully, you do not have to be one of these people. As we proceed in this book to the various fears, you can use one or more of the above strategies to help you confront your fears.

References:

The Anxiety and Phobia Workbook by Edmund J. Bourne, New Harbinger, 1995

Facing Fears by Ada P. Kahn and Ronald M. Doctor, Checkmark, 2000

Phobias: Fighting the Fear by Helen Saul, HarperCollins, 2001.

The Phobia List, www.phobialist.com

Phobias Cured
4838 Delridge Way SW, Suite A
Seattle, WA 98106
(206) 721-8751
keith@phobiascured.com

Coping with Your Emergency Fear System

Strategies:

- Be aware that your emergency fear system has kicked in. With some people, it is subconscious and they are so intent on what they are doing, such as working on a job, that they don't notice they are tense or hyped up. You must also identify what caused your system to kick in: was it because of the natural pressures of a job or were you just defending your pride? Don't send your hormones on unnecessary journeys.
- You have two choices of how to deal with this fear energy: defuse it or lose it. You can calm down or you can redirect the energy into whatever you are doing at work, home or school.
- In most instances, you will simply need to defuse the fear energy and calm down. You can use traditional methods like slow, deep breathing, which adds oxygen and the soothing hormone serotonin to your system and also takes your mind off what was making you tense for a few moments, allowing you to get back into a rhythm. Humor, music and thoughts of loved ones can also relax you.
- Exercise. When you get too aroused, your body is asking for a physical response, so why not give it one through productive exercise, which also helps you become more healthy? If you don't have time for sports, 50 jumping jacks can do the trick. Also, rocking in a chair can alleviate stress buildup.
- Another way to calm down is to change your environment for a few minutes. At work, go outside and take a walk, or simply sit back in your chair and envision being on a beach somewhere. Your emotional chemistry can change by thought alone.
- There are situations in which you can *use* the extra energy and powers of fear, such as in physical jobs, sports and deadline work. Channel the fear energy directly into what you are doing, but trust your skills under this new pressure and don't allow the energy to distract you. Think of this technique as a two-stage process in which you go from fear to a dispassionate response.
- If you have problems channeling fear energy directly into your task, you may need a bridge between the fear and the dispassionate response, perhaps another emotion, such as anger, joy

or excitement. If the fear is making you too tense or hyper, think briefly of something that makes you angry or excited, then plug yourself into the dispassionate task. This changes your hormonal chemistry from too much adrenaline into more aggressive hormones such as dopamine and noradrenaline— and then your energy is mobilized and you can channel it into your work. But you must practice this formula until it becomes a type of flow from *fear* to *passion* to *dispassion*.

- The best way to keep your fear energy at a manageable level is to keep your pressures at manageable levels before you enter a situation. You do this by upgrading your skills, staying in good health and maintaining a positive frame of mind.
- If you are feeling too much distress, consider the possibility that pressures upon you may be too great at work or at home, or that you may be allowing your emergency fear system to be activated too often. You may be seeing too many things as threats. If so, try to put things into proper perspective.

Reference:

Intelligent Fear by Michael Clarkson, Key Porter, 2002

How This Book Is Organized

The following pages discuss more than 100 of the most common fears and phobias. Be aware that just because you have the symptoms does not necessarily mean that you have a full-blown phobia. You might just have a specific fear, which is not as serious. However, without treatment, it could develop into a phobia.

Here's how each section is organized, with fear of terrorism as an example.

fear of terrorism

Xenophobia (*fear of foreigners*) In this spot, each fear is given its phobic name, if it has one. If it does not, a phobic name closest to the one we are describing is used. For example, there is no phobic name for fear of terrorism, so the fear of foreigners (*xenophobia*) is used.

Quote: Each fear has a quote near the top. It could be a general quote about the fear or how to deal with it. "*People should be concerned, but I don't think that should keep you from seeing the world. You have to go on with life.*"—Barbara Ruth of Texas, visiting New York in 2003 during a heightened terrorism alert

Characteristics: This section examines the symptoms or feelings a person experiences in relation to a specific fear. For the fear of terrorism, here is a sample:

> In these times of terrorism alerts, many people report a general feeling of anxiety and lack of control; others feel angry about an unseen enemy and what that enemy might do. Some describe a feeling of insecurity and a loss of trust in others.

Background: This section examines why you feel afraid of a situation, and perhaps where the fear comes from. A sample from the fear of terrorism:

> Although North Americans had not experienced a strong fear of terrorism until September 11, 2001, and the subsequent war in Iraq, fear of an unknown attacker is a deep, primitive fear, closely tied to the fear of the unknown and fear of other races.

Strategies: This section contains strategies for coping with the fear. Examples:

- Don't become preoccupied with a threat that may never come. Remain active and keep up your normal routine. You should not allow fear of terrorism to wreck your way of life.
- Discussing your thoughts and feelings about terrorism from time to time is helpful, as long as you don't engage in inflammatory discussions that lead to more tension or to hatred.
- Keep up with news developments, but don't watch so much television news that the terrorism threat grows in your mind and becomes a constant preoccupation. Some people believe that becoming newshounds reduces their uncertainty about the world, but it usually creates more anxiety.

A mantra to tell yourself: "Life goes on." A mantra is a word or phrase that you can repeat to calm yourself or to gain confidence in a fearful situation. I have made a suggestion of a mantra for each fear, but you may want to come up with your own.

Quotable: In some chapters, there will be an additional quote on the subject.

References: The information about each fear is taken from a number of sources, such as author interviews with experts in the field, books, magazines and websites. One or two of them will be mentioned.
Why Terrorism Works by Alan M. Dershowitz, Yale University Press, 2002

See: fear of flying, fear of travel, fear of the unknown, fear of not having control, fear of death, fear for your children's safety, fear of other races, fear of strangers, fear of crowds

This is a section for cross-referencing the fear. If you have a fear of terrorism, it could be related to a fear of flying or a fear of other races of people.

Other boxes: There may be small boxes with various titles, such as "the facts are with you" (statistics showing that your chances of getting hurt in an airplane are extremely slim) and "author's two cents" (personal anecdotes).

The Awareness Quiz

Becoming aware of your fears is a big part of dealing with them. How many fears do you have? Do you really know? Have you really thought them through? It's human nature to feel uncomfortable about your fears. Many people don't even like thinking about them, and that is partly why these fears are never dealt with properly.

Take a moment to make a list of the things that make you feel uncomfortable, even fearful. With each thing, mark whether it makes you a little uncomfortable or afraid to the point of avoiding situations. Then decide if you need to do something about these fears (for example, if you have a fear of snakes and live in the city, it might not be a pressing concern). In addition, ask yourself if you are dealing with your fears as you mature and gain experience, or if you are getting more fearful about some things. If you aren't too afraid of what others think (or even if you are!), pass your answers around and encourage feedback. Indeed, encourage others to answer questions about their own fears. You might find that we all have worries and are looking for reassurance.

I've prepared the following quiz to help you assess your fears, worries and phobias. Don't fret; there's no rating system that would classify you as anywhere from emotionally healthy to nervous to certifiable. Simply examine your answers and put them into perspective. Are your fears affecting your life? In some instances, are you actually using your fears to your advantage?

In the space provided below, list some of the fears discussed in this book that affect you. Decide whether you are somewhat afraid of them or very afraid of them, if you are less afraid of them or more afraid of them than you used to be, and if you think you need to do something about these fears. You may want to comment on why you are afraid and what you could do about it, if anything. As an example, I'm including one of my own fears:

Situation: fear of strangers
Somewhat nervous: yes
Afraid to the point of avoidance: no
Less or more fearful than before: less fearful
Comments: As I've grown older, especially with my journalism experience of interviewing strangers, I've lost much of my fear.

Situation:

_____

Somewhat nervous:

_____

Afraid to the point of avoidance:

_____

Less or more fearful than before:

_____

Comments:

_____

_____

_____

Situation:

_____

Somewhat nervous:

_____

Afraid to the point of avoidance:

_____

Less or more fearful than before:

_____

Comments:

_____

_____

_____

PART 2

General
Fears

Fear of the Unknown

xenophobia (fear of foreigners)	*The future is called "perhaps" and the important thing is not to allow that to scare you.* —TENNESSEE WILLIAMS

Characteristics: Fear of the unknown can produce anxiety or insecurity in people, or cause them to avoid upcoming events or new relationships, jobs or projects. It can make people freeze, keeping them in old jobs they dislike or relationships that are unhealthy. And it can make them overreact to unfamiliar threats such as bioterrorism and the West Nile virus. On the other hand, fear of the unknown can keep people alert and inspire them to prepare for challenges, and to be careful when they are in unfamiliar surroundings.

Background: This is one of our most basic instincts, a first cousin to the fear of not being in control. It is a fear of the future. It was very useful in primitive times because people had less knowledge of what threats lay in other regions and so they had to be cautious and plan carefully for excursions. Fear of the unknown remains part of our basic genetic makeup. Today, of course, we are much more in tune with our world and what's to be expected. Our evolving brain is constantly analyzing, trying to predict the future and solve any problems it may bring. There are not as many things waiting in the dark, although many people remain puzzled, even fearful, of where we came from in this vast universe and what our place is in it. The need to understand such things is hardwired into us.

On a daily basis, fear of the unknown remains stressful and debilitating for many people, especially those who need to control things and have assurance about the outcome of their jobs and relationships. On the positive side, it can motivate them to prepare for legitimate challenges and add some spice and mystery to life.

Strategies:
- It sounds simple, but taking the time to research can eliminate many things you don't know about a project, an event, a health concern publicized in the media or a relationship. When you are prepared, doubt retreats and confidence grows. In short, expect the best, prepare for the worst.

- During a stressful job with many unknowns, you should prepare ahead of time, but once the job begins, try to stay in the present and focus on the process of what you are doing.
- Remember, if everything was known, we wouldn't continue probing. We might become so self-satisfied that we'd fizzle away as a species. If explorers and scientists had not surmounted their fear of the unknown, we'd still be all cooped up on one or two continents and terrified of fire.
- Many unknown fears and worries turn out to be exaggerated, such as the AIDS "epidemic" in North America. Think back to something you fretted over that never came to pass, or brought you much less discomfort than you anticipated—a trip to the dentist or a confrontation with a relative, for example.
- "Expect the unexpected" is a healthy mindset as long as you don't spend all day expecting to be successful 100 percent of the time and in control of every detail.
- Accept that there will be things in the future that you may feel deeply concerned and even helpless about. But remember that if there are no unknowns in your life, you likely aren't taking any chances. For example, you may be afraid to ask someone you've met on a date because of the "unknown" risk that they might reject you.
- If you fear the future too much, you may not be living enough in the present. If you constantly think about eternity, you will miss one of the precious moments that make up eternity—and that moment is now.

  A MANTRA TO TELL YOURSELF: *"Give it what it's worth."*

Reference:
Embracing Fear by Thom Rutledge, Harper San Francisco, 2002. He writes: "When we fear the unknown, two kinds of reassurance are available—when we reach out to someone we trust to have confidence in us...and the acceptance that there are no guarantees in new, unexplored territory."

See: This fear underlies many fears and phobias in this book, including the fear of not having control, fear of change and fear of taking chances.

Fear of Not Having Control

asthenophobia (fear of weakness)

Whenever I fear lack of control, I force myself to go into those situations—getting into a plane or driving in heavy traffic. It empowers me to know that I have hired these vehicles to get me from one place to another. —PSYCHOLOGY STUDENT LISA LINDEMAN

Characteristics: This is a worry that things and circumstances will be out of a person's sphere of influence. It causes some people to get involved in everything, trying like a movie director or drill sergeant to control people and the outcome of events. It causes others to get frustrated and give up control. People who feel powerless at work often become inefficient and distressed.

Background: It's quite normal to seek control over one's destinies, large and small, but some people try to control everything—often in good faith—and they succeed as long as others allow it. Seeking ultimate control may be rooted in self-centeredness, but it can also show that a person cares enough to make an effort. In other cases, people who believe they have no influence may blame the outcome of events on fate.

This fear manifests itself in a wide variety of areas—from people being afraid of flying or being a passenger in a car to parents' confrontation with relatives or teachers over their children. Often it stems from a lack of sufficient trust in others. People who seek too much control may come from an overprotected or underprotected environment. A parent may try to do too much for a child, and that is also an attempt to control everything.

Strategies:
- Step back and evaluate the amount of control you should have in relation to your abilities, the task and other people. For example, a teenager could seek primary control of the family dog if he has time to walk it and if others don't want that chore. But that should not give the teen the right to keep the dog in his room all the time.
- Some things are completely out of your control—tomorrow's weather, the way your father-in-law thinks and the way your

favorite professional sports team performs. Learn to accept these things. Having an overload of control and responsibility can make you anxious and give you an unrealistic perspective on things.

- The above having been said, you probably have more control over many things in your life than you believe, starting with your own health, which you can improve by eating, exercising and sleeping properly. If you feel powerless at work, perhaps you haven't tested your authority or are not willing to put in the effort or take the necessary risks. Perhaps you are afraid of being laughed at or being seen as incompetent. Take a position of power or leadership, perhaps in a group or committee. Use positive self-talk: "I have power. I have influence and I am going to exert it in a reasonable manner." If you rarely seek control in your life, perhaps you are afraid of responsibility.
- Learn to take satisfaction from cooperation and teamwork. Sharing and delegating and empowering others can be productive and can make you less anxious and less selfish.
- Let go once in a while. Showing responsibility and leadership is great, but once in a while, sit back, take a deep breath and remember that life will march on, even if you don't make all the decisions. Hard to imagine, isn't it?

A MANTRA TO TELL YOURSELF: *"Grant me the serenity to accept the things I cannot change, the courage to change the things I can and the wisdom to know the difference."*

Reference:

Stop Obsessing! How to Overcome Your Obsessions and Compulsions by Edna B. Foa and Reid Wilson, Bantam, 2001

See: Many or most of the specific fears and phobias in this book are related to the fear of not having control, including fear of the unknown, fear of change, fear of taking chances, fear of flying, fear of responsibility, fear of embarrassment and fear of panic attacks in public.

Fear of Change

tropophobia (fear of moving or making changes) *asthenophobia* (fear of weakness)	*Perhaps it is change without our consent that makes us cling to jobs we don't like, relationships that have grown stale or habits that don't make us happy, but are at least familiar.* — MANAGEMENT AUTHOR AND EDUCATOR JANE GREENE

Characteristics: This is the fear of trying new things or creating new habits. Because change often brings unrest, people may live in the same region all their lives or stay in the same job, surrounding themselves with safe or sentimental things, or they may refuse to consider new ways of thinking or behaving. Children may feel lonely or resentful after being forced to leave friends or group activities.

Background: If you don't think that humans have always been creatures of habit, check the anecdotes and observations in old books, including the Bible and other religious texts. The speed of social change has greatly accelerated, yet progress was relatively slow prior to that. As a group, we tend to latch onto familiar things in culture, religion and society like a security blanket. Throughout history, the majority of people have been cautious; it's the leaders and risk takers who drag us onto new ground.

In these often unsettling times, we have perhaps more need for familar things, structure and security than ever before, and change can be seen as a threat to those facets of our lives. Adults who fear taking chances may come from sheltered homes or may have been discouraged from branching out on their own or making their own decisions. Those who fear change tend to have repetitive patterns in their lives.

Strategies:

- Try to establish what your fear of change represents. It could really be fear of the unknown, fear of failure, fear of taking chances or fear of what others think. If you are afraid of taking risks in your career, it could actually be the uncertainty of the work environment that scares you, or fear of responsibility (more work and leadership), or fear of being judged or not measuring up.

- If it ain't broke, don't fix it. If you are truly satisfied with your life, your job and your family, don't look for ways to disrupt them. But spend some time examining this issue. Structure can be a good thing at work or in a task, but once in a while you might need variety to keep from getting bored.
- In today's world of uncertain jobs and an influx of new cultures, it's vital that we be flexible and ready to change our thinking patterns, and even our beliefs, if we are to succeed. And it *is* possible to change ourselves, even in midlife.
- Look upon a needed change as shedding a skin and coming out of it with new vitality and ideas. As author Lucinda Bassett says, "How many times have you heard someone say, 'Well, that's just the way I am...it's the mold you're fixed in.' There are many exciting things to try—new foods, dances, clothes, new countries to explore, friends to meet. You can be reborn at any time."
- Perhaps you should fear *never changing* because that could make you rigid, narrow-minded and dull.
- To change a bad habit, take small steps; research shows that people who try to lose weight or quit smoking too quickly often get discouraged when success doesn't happen overnight.
- Make sure that when you go through a change, you seek out opportunities to grow. In most people's lives, some type of change is inevitable, but growth is optional. You grow when you adapt to change and learn from the old ways.
- Keep doing what you're doing and you'll keep getting what you're getting. If you are okay with that, then there is not as much need for change.

A MANTRA TO TELL YOURSELF: *"What if I* don't *change?"*

Reference:

From Panic to Power by Lucinda Bassett, Quill, 2001

See: fear of the unknown, fear of not having control, fear of taking chances, fear of aging, fear of travel, fear of losing status, fear of your children leaving home, fear of becoming a parent, fear and stress in children, fear of disorder or untidiness, fear of ending a romantic relationship, fear of school, fear of downsizing, fear of retirement, fear of technology, fear of quitting

Fear of Taking Chances

ideophobia (fear of ideas)	*Ships in a harbor are safe, but that's not what ships are built for.* —WRITER JOHN SHEDD

Characteristics: This has similar symptoms to the fear of change—having a safe, conservative attitude and perhaps a reluctance to make decisions or try new things. It can hold people back in business, personal finances and relationships, and affect things like choosing a partner, a school or a profession.

Background: Although the human race has shown signs of creativity and risk taking, in many ways we are a conservative lot; change has come slowly over the course of thousands of years. "Taking a new step, uttering a new word, is what people fear most," said Dostoyevsky. It is natural for people to want to stay in a secure comfort zone, but without risk taking, there is little chance for growth.

If you are afraid of taking chances, you might be from a sheltered family or you may have had a controlling parent. But, of course, sometimes it's actually dangerous to take chances; if you agree to a business gamble with your family's security on the line, or if you risk large sums on the stock market or on horses, you may be acting foolishly.

Strategies:
- Before you take a chance, assess the risk of a situation. If you jump into every opportunity that comes along, you might become a reckless driver, an unfaithful spouse or an irresponsible employee.
- As in the fear of change and many other generalized fears, try to establish what exactly scares you about taking a chance. Is it fear of the unknown, fear of failure, fear of criticism or fear of what others think?
- Once in a while, try something fresh—a different strategy for a project, a meal you've never tried or even an alternative way to get to work or to school. If you have to, make a note on your calendar that you will try something new. Without risk, there

would be no inventions and no new friends. McDonald's Corp. founder Ray Kroc once said, "When there is no risk, there can be no pride in achievement and consequently no happiness."

- Don't believe that fate is entirely out of your control. Believe in opportunity and learn to recognize when it comes along. Many people can't or won't recognize opportunities, or they may complain of being powerless or not having enough luck or talent to venture into a new area. Don't keep saying that things *happen* to you. Consider *making* things happen.

- At work, be ready to take reasonable initiative. My wife, Jennifer, was advised not to take phone calls in her first six weeks as an account executive at the National Speakers Bureau, but when her boss stepped out of the office, she took the chance at a call and the risk led to the biggest sale by an account "rookie." This sparked Jennifer's confidence en route to a record first month of sales.

- If you lack confidence, especially in a new area, find a mentor who has expertise and confidence in that area. Pick that person's brain. It will flatter them and bolster you.

- Learn to become more resilient if your risk taking happens to fail once in a while. You'll feel more comfortable taking chances if you bounce back from the misses and you'll gain courage for the next "opportunity."

- Join the small percentage of people in the world who make the real changes because they're not afraid to go out on a limb or be vulnerable. Don't have inscribed on your epitaph: "Could have. Would have. Should have."

A MANTRA TO TELL YOURSELF: *"It's time for a little adventure."*

Reference:

Facing Fears by Ada P. Kahn and Ronald M. Doctor, Checkmark, 2000

See: fear of the unknown, fear of not having control, fear of failure, fear of criticism, fear of what others think, fear of change, sexual fears, fear of becoming a parent, fear of dating, fear of quitting

Fear of Responsibility

hypegiaphobia (fear of responsibility)   *As our culture increasingly glorifies the carefree pleasures of youth, many people grow despondent when the reality of adult responsibility pulls them farther away from their youthful hopes and expectations.* —FRANK PITTMAN, AUTHOR OF *GROW UP! HOW TAKING RESPONSIBILITY CAN MAKE YOU A HAPPY ADULT*

Characteristics: This is anxiousness or reluctance to assume responsibility or leadership in family life, work, school or relationships. It is often seen in young people as they are growing up. It can even prevent people from having children.

Background: There is an old saying that there are many more sheep than shepherds. Some people are afraid of the increased workload, commitment and complexities that responsibility brings. For many, it is natural to want to hold onto their carefree youth, but many people carry that attitude into midlife.

Many people never identify what it is about responsibility that frightens them. Sometimes, this fear is genetic, but often it has to do with the environment a person comes from, or an environment the person is presently living or working in.

Strategies:

- Assess how much responsibility you have in your life. How often do you make decisions? Do people look to you for leadership or just for a good time? Do you want more responsibility but are afraid of it or feel you can't handle it?
- Try to identify the aspect of responsibility that makes you uneasy—is it really fear of dealing with others and their issues, fear of added workload, or fear of criticism because of a decision you will make?
- Look around—other people have responsibility and, if they do not allow it to overburden them, they may enjoy it. Talk to them about it and try to apply their strategies to your situation.

- Learn to realize the satisfaction and growth that comes from something other than yourself and your own needs. "Responsibility is the thing people dread most of all," says author Frank Crane. "Yet it is the only thing in the world that develops us, gives us manhood or womanhood fiber."
- With responsibility, setting goals, and making decisions for yourself and others comes an adrenaline rush! You feel part of a team, and you feel a sense of accomplishment when you have input, whether it is for a work project, a Boy Scout troop or a Neighborhood Watch program.
- With a leadership role, you'll meet more people, find new opportunities and gather confidence. But you may want to take small steps at first; don't suddenly run for president. As you go along, explore responsibility but keep your workload in perspective.
- Develop people skills. Everybody has them, but perhaps they are dormant or unrealized. Maybe you even have leadership qualities. The world needs more good leaders. But, of course, not everyone is a leader. Perhaps you are an individual who works better alone.
- If you are a teenager, growing up isn't as bad as it seems. Life really isn't over at 20 or 30. You can still act like a kid during play.

A MANTRA TO TELL YOURSELF: *"Get in the game."*

QUOTABLE: *"A chief is a man who assumes responsibility. He does not say, 'My men were beaten.' He says, 'I was beaten.'"*
—*Antoine de Saint-Exupéry*

Reference:

Free Yourself from Fear by Valerie Austin, Thorsons, 1998

See: fear of the unknown, fear of failure, fear of criticism, fear of taking chances, fear of the opposite sex, fear of commitment, fear of becoming a parent

Fear of Confrontation or Conflict

testophobia (fear of being tested)   *You can stand up for yourself, expressing the way you truly feel. You are considerate of other people's feelings. You do not attack or blame, nor do you become meek and withdrawn.*
—CLINICAL PSYCHOLOGIST ALLEN ELKIN

Characteristics: People are often reluctant to confront someone or to bring a situation to a head. Some people will either avoid a problem or intervene without careful preparation, just to get it over with. Most people get nervous prior to conflict, but some freeze and cannot express themselves properly.

Background: Most of us deal poorly with confrontation and conflict because we don't allow ourselves to experience them fully. We are uncomfortable with the emotions and issues, and so we remove ourselves as fast as possible without resolving the situations or expanding our abilities to deal with them. Confrontation and conflict resolution are usually distressing, especially when they involve serious issues. Emotions can rise and there may be the threat of becoming physical. At work, some conflicts will resolve themselves and produce healthy competition or change. Others hurt cooperation.

Many people avoid conflict for fear of losing friends, others because they are very sensitive to emotional situations. Women are generally less likely to confront than men. People from large families tend to learn about confrontation early in life. Resolving things productively can be liberating, can build confidence and can also prevent problems from festering. How you handle adversity at work can have more impact on your career than how you handle the good times. Those who overcome conflict and adversity rise to the top of their organization.

Strategies:

- In approaching conflict, you must be brave but also clear-minded and cautious. Be certain that the issue you want to confront someone about is legitimate. Write it down and look at it the next day to see if it holds up.

- Prepare yourself with the facts before you confront or try to resolve a conflict. This will give structure and power to your meeting. In addition, prepare yourself emotionally by imagining in advance what might happen. In your mind, take yourself through all of the steps. You should even imagine a negative response, and see yourself reacting well. Try to imagine the emotions that may arise. This is called visualization or imagery.
- Try to confront the person face-to-face; the phone or a letter or e-mail should be secondary options because these have less impact.
- If you are squeamish, force yourself to show up. You'll find that once you are face-to-face with the person, the words will come. If they don't, take deep breaths. Remain calm, but be mentally tough and stand up for yourself.
- When confrontational or emotional issues come up at work, talk them through and allow each person time to express thoughts and feelings. Have a group session to air grievances.
- Remember that confrontation can be healthy. Although constant arguing can be harmful to a marriage, research shows that couples who never argue are 35 percent more likely to divorce, in part because they won't deal with their frustrations and therefore let them build up.

A MANTRA TO TELL YOURSELF: *"Take the bull by the horns."*

References:

The 100 Simple Secrets of Great Relationships by David Niven, Harper San Francisco, 2003

What Every Supervisor Should Know by David Engler and Lester R. Bittle, McGraw-Hill, 1992

See: fear of competition, fear of not being loved, fear of taking chances, fear of oneself, fear of showing emotions, fear of asking for a raise or promotion, fear of the boss, fear of firing an employee, fear of choking in sports, fears for your marriage/partnership

Fear of Not Being Loved

anuptaphobia (fear of staying single)	*The one thing we can never get enough of is love. And the one thing we never give enough of is love.* —HENRY MILLER

Characteristics: People may avoid contact with others for fear of rejection or not being accepted, or they may seek to fill an emotional hole with constant work or substance abuse. This fear can result in possessiveness, depression or cynicism. It can also lead people to put up defensive walls to protect themselves. But a person who makes an effort to be loved may inspire the feelings and affections of others.

Background: Our need to be loved—socially, spiritually and physically—is as strong as our needs for food, drink and oxygen. It keeps us together as a species and prevents us from becoming hermits. But love is a very complex emotion and spiritual resource. It takes many forms—sexual attraction, love of family and self, love of work and spiritual love. Love can be composed of trust, respect, acceptance, strong affection, tenderness and devotion. Some people may seek affection in one area of their life (their job) to compensate for lack of it in another (at home). If people's needs for affection and attention are too great, they may have come from a loveless home. But this fear can also be genetic and run in families.

Strategies:

- Examine your motives for seeking people's attention and love. They may be very natural and healthy, but they may be misplaced or out of proportion. Consider the words of business consultant and author Brian Tracy: "Much of what we do in life we do either to get love or to compensate for the lack of love."
- Don't try too hard to get people's attention or affection. If you throw yourself at them, people may recoil. "In our desperate rush to become intimate, we may tell too much too soon," says relationship psychologist Harriet Lerner. "Sharing vulnerability is one way we feel close to each other, but sharing indiscriminately or prematurely has the opposite effect."

- If you don't get the reaction you require from a person, don't take it personally; they may react the same way to others. Some people may not be able to love you because they don't know how to love themselves. Learn to give love yourself. As the old song goes, "You got to give love to get love."
- If people close to you don't give you enough affection, open up the communication lines and talk with them about it. Tell them that their affection is important to you, a way of showing that they care about you. If you continue to get a lack of love at home, seek gratification through volunteering or through work, or perhaps seek deeper spirituality through meditation, by becoming a mentor to others or by joining a volunteer organization or a church. By giving your love to others, you receive it in return.
- Learn to balance your life and your needs. Love is important, but so are career, school, play and peace of mind.
- If you come from a loveless home, don't overcompensate by expecting too much attention from your spouse, children, friends or coworkers. Deep emotional issues may require the attention of a therapist.
- Learn to love yourself and not rely so much on others. It's not the end of the world if everybody doesn't like you. If everybody loved you, you would have far too much responsibility and pressure. Take the advice of actress Drew Barrymore: "I want people to love me, but it's not going to hurt me if they don't."

A MANTRA TO TELL YOURSELF: *"Love myself first."*

References:

Centering and the Art of Intimacy by Gary Hendricks, Fireside, 1993

The Dance of Connection by Harriet Lerner, HarperCollins, 2001

See: fear of intimacy or love, fear of rejection, fear of criticism, fears for your marriage/partnership, sexual fears, fear of being alone

Fear of Intimacy or Love

philophobia (fear of being in love)

aphenphosmphobia (fear of being touched)

What we want most in life is love. What we're most afraid of is love. Sad but true.
—PSYCHOLOGIST PAMELA L. CHUBBUCK

Characteristics: This is an inability or refusal to love or to share yourself, particularly your deepest thoughts and feelings, with others. It may prevent close relationships, social or romantic. Some people fear being kissed or touched or having their work or interests closely examined. If you find it easier to have relationships with nature or pets or to watch television, you may have this fear.

Background: Many people are reluctant to love or to be intimate for a number of reasons. Love is a very complex emotion (see fear of not being loved). Although humans are social beings, we may feel that we are unlovable to others, defective or unworthy, perhaps from our childhood experiences or from a feeling of being abandoned or rejected. This fear may also be genetic, and it can skip a generation or two in a family tree. Sufferers may not be aware that they are afraid of being loved or touched. This fear is beneficial when it keeps people from falling in love or jumping into relationships too easily.

Strategies:

- Be aware that, generally, love is good for your health. It activates the parasympathetic nervous system, which reduces stress and activates soothing hormones such as endorphins and serotonin. It is also good for your social life and spiritual well-being.

- Try to understand your own needs better. Establish a good relationship with yourself by being emotionally honest and intimate with yourself before you try to become intimate with others. Explore your inner feelings, especially those you have about yourself. You may have many false beliefs and attitudes about yourself that were drummed into you as a child. They may be painful or subconscious, so you may have to force yourself to write them down, say them aloud and root them out.

- If this fear is severely affecting your life and relationships, consider seeing a therapist or counselor. You might have serious issues from your childhood. Counselor and author Robert Burney writes about such cases, "We were traumatized as children and the defenses we adapted to protect us caused us to traumatize ourselves as adults. We have experienced getting our hearts broken, our hopes and dreams shattered...[and] feel[ing] rejected over and over again."

- It's possible that you feel safe when you're in a comfort zone in which you don't reach out to others. But are you happy? Is this situation healthy? Do you have enough confidantes?

- Show your emotions once in a while. Laugh, cry or rejoice with others. Rather than revealing weakness, this vulnerability can actually make you appear stronger to others. If you feel a sense of shame about intimacy, reduce it by listing the good things you have to offer to others.

- You are worthy of having close relationships with others. Seek them out and don't shrink at the first sign of criticism or rejection. Yes, getting burned can be a painful experience. If it happens, join the club, because all of us have been emotionally rejected at one time or another. Learn something from it, especially about yourself, then move on with your life.

- Consider that besides a fear of intimacy, you may also fear relationships with others because they often require commitment and hard work.

A MANTRA TO TELL YOURSELF: *"Open up a little."*

Reference:

Codependence: The Dance of Wounded Souls by Robert Burney, Joy to You and Me Enterprises, 1995

See: fear of not being loved, fear of showing emotions, fear of invasion of territory or privacy, fear of the opposite sex, fear of commitment, sexual fears, fear of failure, fear of what others think, fear of criticism

Superstition or Fear of the Supernatural

wiccaphobia (fear of witchcraft)	*Virtually all superstition is created by primitive limbic reasoning. Most cultures—most individuals—are a mixture of primitive reasoning and sophisticated reasoning.*
phasmophobia (fear of ghosts)	

—RUSH W. DOZIER, AUTHOR OF *FEAR ITSELF*

Characteristics: Some people believe that rituals or symbols will bring good luck or stave off evil. They will knock on wood, avoid black cats, visit psychics or move to condos without a 13th floor. Some people believe in jinxes; they think that by talking about the possible outcome of an event, they will alter it.

Background: Our ancestors explained the mysteries of life and the universe through myth. Many ancient beliefs have been passed down through ritual and tradition, in part because of our enduring need to understand the world and our place in it. As well, there are many things we still do not understand and thus fear. For those things, we often put up defenses that we imagine will protect us from the unknown, such as good-luck charms. People who believe in the paranormal tend to be more willing than skeptics to see patterns or relationships between events; there is some evidence that they also have higher levels of the hormone dopamine in the brain. Many religions and cultures have superstitious components. Some people still fear a hex or curse placed upon them.

Strategies:

- In the big picture, we must understand that many superstitions are harmless, even funny, but they are less so if you waste a lot of time and effort humoring them. They can even be hazardous if you trip while constantly trying to avoid cracks in the pavement, which some people consider bad luck.
- Think superstitions through: what unseen power will stave off disaster or failure if you suddenly wave a rabbit's foot in front of it? And how powerful would that dark force be if it backed away from such a trinket?

- We are all seeking patterns and structure in our lives. Establishing a rigid schedule prior to a high-pressure event can give you structure and confidence. For example, superstitious baseball star Wade Boggs would eat chicken before every game to ensure his success. But what happens to your psyche if something occurs to change that routine—if chicken is not available?
- If you think you are jinxed, you are. If you think you aren't, you aren't. Your mindset can become a self-fulfilling prophecy as you either "give in" to unseen forces ("I can't win, so what's the use of trying?") or try harder because you believe you have some control over your fate.
- If you are constantly worried about fate, superstition or the supernatural, examine the amount of control you have, or don't have, in your life. It's possible that, in feeling you are powerless, forces beyond your control are dominating you. If you fear bad luck, you could miss opportunities and be gullible.
- It is hard to disprove the supernatural. But for many years, magician James (The Amazing) Randi has offered $1 million to anyone showing evidence of the paranormal or supernatural. No one has been able to collect. He says, "Those who allow themselves to be taken in by psychics and supernaturalists are not stupid; they are naïve, trusting and perhaps careless." And perhaps they have been conditioned by their superstitious parents.
- Have fun with superstition; make a game of it at a party.

A MANTRA TO TELL YOURSELF: *"You only have bad luck if you think you do."*
QUOTABLE: *"Fear is the main source of superstition."*
—*Bertrand Russell*

References:

The Encyclopedia of Superstition, edited by Christina Hole, Metro, 2002

The James Randi Educational Foundation, www.randi.org

See: fear of the unknown, fear of not having control, fear of religion, fear of destiny, fear of the dark, fear and stress in children

Fear of Religion

theophobia (fear of gods or religion)

peccatophobia (fear of sinning)

Religion is a great force, but you must get a man through his own religion, not yours. —GEORGE BERNARD SHAW

Characteristics: Distrust, fear or loathing of "other people's" religion is common throughout the world. A person may feel tense in the presence of someone from a particular faith. In extreme instances, religions and cultures may come into conflict. Lesser symptoms are a person feeling discomfort from being lectured, talked down to or converted. There may also be a fear of becoming regimented.

Background: We all have an "us vs. them" gene from primitive times that makes us distrustful, even fearful, of people who are different from us, and that fear can be directed toward other cultures and religions. This instinct once kept us vigilant against potentially harmful tribes from other regions. As we've become civilized, we've tamed this instinct significantly and become more tolerant, although it is still strong in many parts of the world. In moderate forms, it prevents strangers from walking all over us. People who fear the heavy influence of outside forces such as a god are more likely to develop anxieties than other people.

Fear of religion is actually often fear of people from other *regions* because, throughout the world, religion tends to be geographic—predominantly Christian in the West, Hindu and Buddhist in the East, Muslim in the Middle East, and so on.

There are 22 religions in the world with more than 150,000 adherents, from Christianity (2 billion) to Islam (1.3 billion) to Scientology (600,000).

Strategies:

- Educate yourself. It wasn't until the horrific events of September 11, 2001, that many North Americans became aware that some extreme elements in the Muslim community were targeting Western culture. In fact, until then, there was little understanding of Islam in the West. Imagine how others might view your beliefs if they knew nothing of your background.

- Be tolerant of others who have beliefs that don't correspond with your own. A tolerant society may be a more advanced society.
- Visit a temple or church from a religion you know little about. Many religions won't try to convert you to their way of thinking. If a religious person does try to convert you through fear of damnation, you might want to consider if you want to join a religion that uses such fear tactics.
- Don't dismiss the value of religion. Many, if not most, religions have a strong upside in charity work, compassion, a sense of values and community involvement. They give people structure and peace of mind in an often stressful world. As well, they can keep some cruel people in line.
- Don't feel inferior or left out if you are one of the 850 million atheists in the world; you may believe in evolution, you may be a humanist, or you may be spiritual without adhering to a traditional religion. In North America, there is freedom of religion, and perhaps there should also be freedom *from* religion.
- Keep an open mind. Beliefs *can* change. Try to remain open-minded about the "facts" of religion and where humans came from, even to the point of considering a change of belief. And don't be swayed by popular opinion. Remember that, until fairly recently, most of the people on earth *believed* that it was flat. More recently, many people *believed* that women were second-class citizens. As we became enlightened and gathered the facts, we realized that neither of these beliefs was well-founded.

A MANTRA TO TELL YOURSELF: *"My beliefs are important."*

Reference:

The World's Religions: Our Great Wisdom Traditions by Huston Smith, Harper San Francisco, 1992

See: fear of the unknown, superstition or fear of the supernatural, fear of death, fear of other races, fear of strangers, fear of terrorism, fear of destiny

Fear of Destiny

Zeusophobia (fear of fate)

The word "fate" is the refuge of every self-confessed failure. —ANDREW SOUTAR

Characteristics: This fear includes feelings of cynicism and powerlessness as well as a sense that everything is meant to be, and thus has been preplanned, perhaps as part of God's will. It can also involve the belief that others get more breaks than you do. Many people who fear destiny are attracted to astrology, psychics and religion. Some people get the feeling that something terrible is going to happen to them even if they have no reason to think so.

Background: This fear is as old as history and is related to early humans' inability to explain or conceptualize their place in the universe. They felt they had little control over their future, which they thought must be influenced by the stars, the weather or the gods. Even today, many people feel that they have little control over their lives, and some hold destiny or fate responsible for their condition. As Andrew Soutar said, it's an easy excuse for failure.

Throughout history, most people have been followers; only a small percentage have been true leaders who make key decisions. Some followers, through either lack of talent, effort, opportunity or healthy thinking, believe their future is largely out of their hands. People who believe in the heavy influence of outside forces in their lives are more likely to develop anxieties.

Strategies:
- You probably have more influence over your "destiny" than you think. You might believe that promotions at work are given out not through anything you can do, but through office politics. Even if this belief is partly right, you can still improve your chances by good performance. Don't fall into what psychologist Martin Seligman calls "learned helplessness," in which people believe they will not make a difference, so they do not try.
- Work hard at the things you have some control over and increase your skills in those areas. Once you assert some control, you will develop confidence and more control.

- Don't give up too easily, and don't use excuses or blame invisible outside forces for your failures. That's an easy way to absolve yourself of personal responsibility.
- Don't believe too much in luck. Remember, bad breaks happen to everybody. It's how you react to them that separates winners from those who don't get ahead. Remember the words of self-help guru Dale Carnegie: "When fate hands you a lemon, make lemonade."
- Make a self-fulfilling prophecy work for you. Believe that destiny is on your side or that there are ways for you to force your will on the future. The night before the final round of the 1999 Ryder Cup, U.S. captain Ben Crenshaw told his players that destiny was with them. They went out and played their best golf and came from behind to defeat the Europeans.
- Consider that if everything is predestined, then we are just going through the motions. Just get up in the morning and go to work, take few risks, don't allow your voice to be heard and don't seek new acquaintances or experiences. If you accept that, then perhaps destiny *is* out of your hands.

A MANTRA TO TELL YOURSELF: *"I have a say in my destiny."*

Listen up:

"Que sera, sera. Whatever will be, will be." A catchy old tune. But don't be so quick to swallow the lyrics. Maybe you've been conditioned by other such mindsets and aren't aware of it. Do your part, and then whatever will be, will be.

Reference:

The Anxiety and Phobia Workbook by Edmund J. Bourne, New Harbinger, 1995

See: fear of not having control, superstition or fear of the supernatural, fear of religion, fear of death

Physical Fears

Fear of Flying

aviaphobia (fear of flying)

My husband was my motivation to fly. I made up my mind I wasn't going to let my fears of flying, my nervousness about driving, control me anymore. —New York fitness expert Mandy Laderer, who had avoided flying for 15 years

Characteristics: Sufferers experience apprehension, tension and a variety of other symptoms of anxiety. They may avoid flying for fear of crashing, being the victim of terrorism, feeling turbulence or allowing someone else to control their destiny. Some may also fear embarrassment if they start to sweat or become tense or nauseous in front of other passengers. They may drink alcohol during the flight.

Background: This fear is costly to the airline industry and to corporations, whose executives must fly to get from city to city quickly. Even before the tragedy of 9/11, a poll showed that 44 percent of Americans reported some fear of flying and 52 percent had lost confidence in airline safety. Now those numbers are higher. Overachievers and perfectionists tend to be the most nervous passengers because of their need for control; they tend to have had parents who demanded perfection. Twice as many women as men suffer from this condition. Most fearful fliers never seek help.

Strategies:
- Always remember that the facts are with you. Plane crashes are extremely rare; in the United States, the chances of dying in a plane crash are 500,000 to one for frequent flyers. Flying is the safest mode of travel, far safer than driving. (When plane crashes do occur, they are always reported in the media and often have fatalities.) You think rationally in other areas of your life—you can do that here.
- Admit your anxieties and talk to others about them. You will find that many people have at least some anxiety about flying. If you are honest enough to identify yourself as a nervous flier, tell the flight attendants. They have dealt with many others like you and will reassure you.

- Don't try to suppress all of your worries in one flight. Slowly desensitize yourself and your fears will decrease as you gradually see how safe it is.
- Feel confident about the pilot and crew. They are professionals. When you're driving on the road, most people are amateurs at the wheel.
- Prior to and during the flight, use relaxation exercises and visualize going through all the steps to a successful conclusion.
- If possible, fly with someone you trust.
- Get a massage before you fly; some airports have massage services. Avoid caffeine or alcohol before or during a flight.
- If you control your emotions, your catastrophic thinking will ease. In the words of psychologist R. Reid Wilson: "People who come to me for therapy come to realize it's not about the plane, it's they who are the anxiety-producing machines." Use deep breathing and meditation strategies. Take a relaxation tape or CD with you.
- Pay close attention to safety demonstrations and read the pamphlet in front of your seat. Notice that the attendants describe safety precautions "in the *unlikely* event of an accident." Stay occupied during the flight by reading or working (I get some of my best thinking done on planes, perhaps because of the high altitude), or get up and talk to other passengers.
- Don't become preoccupied with what happened on September 11, 2001. Airport and airplane security have improved since then.
- Check to see if your city has a fear-of-flying class organized by AAir Born.

A MANTRA TO TELL YOURSELF: *"I'm in good hands."*

References:

Flying Without Fear by Dr. Duane Brown, New Harbinger, 1996
The Fear of Flying Clinic, www.fofc.com

Many airlines offer programs. See also the U.S. Federal Aviation Administration website at www.faa.gov

See: fear of not having control, fear of travel, fear of death, fear of the unknown, fear of heights, fear of terrorism, fear of panic attacks in public, fear of destiny, fear of driving

Fear of Terrorism

xenophobia (fear of foreigners)	*People should be concerned, but I don't think that should keep you from seeing the world. You have to go on with life.*

—BARBARA RUTH OF TEXAS, VISITING NEW YORK IN 2003 DURING A HEIGHTENED TERRORISM ALERT

Characteristics: In these times of terrorism alerts, many people report a general feeling of anxiety and lack of control; others feel angry about an unseen enemy and what that enemy might do. Some describe a feeling of insecurity and a loss of trust in others. These sentiments may keep people from traveling. Since the 9/11 attacks, many people have reduced their flying and bought emergency supplies for home. At the same time, the 9/11 attacks have increased feelings of patriotism and sparked more teamwork, spirituality and blood giving. Some people say the awareness of terrorism actually makes them feel more alive and more appreciative of what they have to lose.

Background: Although North Americans had not experienced a strong fear of terrorism until 9/11 and the subsequent war in Iraq, fear of an unknown attacker is a deep, primitive fear, closely tied to the fear of the unknown and fear of other races. Fear of terrorism has been a fact of life in the Middle East and other regions for a long time. Although people in those areas remain alert, many report becoming desensitized to the threats and going on with their daily lives. Historically, most Americans eventually return to their normal routine after national crises. Immediately after 9/11, many residents of New York turned to psychiatric and antidepression medication, but a few weeks later, prescription levels returned to normal.

Strategies:
- Don't become preoccupied with a threat that may never come. Remain active and keep up your normal routine. You should not allow fear of terrorism to wreck your way of life.
- Discussing your thoughts and feelings about terrorism from time to time is helpful, as long as you don't engage in inflammatory discussions that lead to more tension or to hatred.
- Keep up with news developments, but don't watch so much

television that the terrorism threat becomes a constant preoccupation. Some people believe that becoming newshounds
reduces their uncertainty, but it usually creates more anxiety.

- Come up with a safety plan in your home and neighborhood and
  rehearse it with family. It will give you some sense of control.
- Don't scapegoat or judge an entire race of people, religion or
  culture because some of its members are terrorists—some
  members of *your* race and culture may be terrorists as well.
- It takes time to get over traumas like 9/11 and the Iraq war, and
  it can be difficult to go on if one feels under threat. If you remain
  anxious after an extended period, see a counselor.
- Without becoming paranoid, report suspicious activity or vehicles in your neighborhood to police. Join a Neighborhood
  Watch group and share your ideas with others.
- Reassess your priorities. Do those little hassles at work or your
  grumpy neighbor seem so relevant in light of these bigger issues?
- Be sure to talk to your children about terrorism. Assure them
  that, although everything in the world is not always good or fair,
  their world remains stable and they have your unconditional
  love. Encourage your kids to go about their normal routines.
- Here's what you might need as a safety kit for a potential
  emergency: bottled water, a three- to five-day supply of non-
  perishable food, a first-aid kit, a battery-powered radio, a
  flashlight, duct tape, a utility knife, a small fire extinguisher,
  toilet paper, soap, clothes and bedding.

A MANTRA TO TELL YOURSELF: *"Life goes on."*

References:

A *Faceless Enemy* by Glenn E. Schweitzer, Perseus, 2002

Why Terrorism Works by Alan M. Dershowitz, Yale University
Press, 2002

American Red Cross, www.redcross.org

U.S. Federal Emergency Management Agency, www.fema.gov

See: fear of flying, fear of travel, fear of the unknown, fear of not
having control, fear of death, fear for the safety of your children,
fear of other races, fear of strangers, fear of crowds

Fear of Being Mugged

harpaxophobia (fear of robbers or being robbed)	*I have three words of advice for victims— breathe, breathe, breathe.* —EMERGENCY EXPERT DEBBIE GARDNER

Characteristics: Apprehension or caution about going out, especially alone and in certain areas, affects many people. They may fear being robbed, beaten up or humiliated, and they may carry their good clothes in a bag to be inconspicuous. This condition particularly affects the elderly and people who feel helpless; it can even keep them housebound. Some people get anxious just watching violent movies.

Background: Since our distant past, people (especially the weak) have always been wary of enemies and predators. We are all programmed with an emergency fear system to help us against physical threats. At its peak, this system creates what is known as the fight-or-flight response, giving us enhanced strength, speed and concentration. In primitive times, the hair would stand up on a frightened person's body, making them appear bigger and more powerful to an enemy (this phenomenon still exists to a small extent, which is why the hair stands up on the back of your neck when you're frightened). But since we are generally not used to such physical arousal these days, many people freeze when confronted with a mugger. Men tend to have this fear less than women because they are conditioned through sports and roughhousing to be more confident physically.

Strategies:
- Be sensible about where you go, especially at night, but don't let your fear become so exaggerated or dominant that it affects your life and schedule.
- Don't walk with valuables, flashy jewelry or laptop computers at night. But do carry identification. If you have a headset on, you might not be able to hear things around you. Keep your hands out of your pockets and free.
- Take a self-defense course. Such courses are especially valuable for women, who are generally not as strong as men and not used to the feelings of confrontation and arousal from contact

sports. Many self-defense courses are noncompetitive and feature such components as relaxation and meditation. They will give you confidence on the street.

- Walk confidently with your head up, as though you know where you're going. If you walk a lot at night, carry a whistle or a shrill alarm.
- If you think you are being followed, cross the road or go to a place with a lot of people.
- If you are attacked, the first thing you must do is control yourself. Assess the situation and keep your mind active. If you feel yourself freezing, hyperventilating or panicking, force yourself to breathe deeply from your stomach.
- Don't try to be a hero. Get away if you can. Most people are not trained in defending themselves, whereas the assailant has the advantage of surprise and is probably street-tough. Run fast, pumping your knees high.
- If the thug has a weapon, give him what he wants. Your possessions simply aren't worth it. They can be replaced, but your spleen cannot.
- Screaming or shouting often works by scaring the attacker and releasing you from the freeze mode. If the incident lasts for a while, you might want to change tactics from running to fighting to talking your way out of it.
- If you have no alternative but to fight, inflict pain on the attacker—kick his groin, gouge his eyes or stomp on his foot. Use your head to pop him under his jaw, or use your fingernails or teeth. Fight dirty.
- If you have had a traumatic mugging, put it into perspective: you are just a normal person who experienced an abnormal situation. It doesn't mean it will happen again.

A MANTRA TO TELL YOURSELF: *"Breathe!"*

Reference:

Survive Institute, www.surviveinstitute.com

See: fear of death, fear of illness or pain, fear of strangers, fear of getting involved in an emergency, fear of travel, fear of dogs and animals, fear of the dark, fear of being alone, fear of confrontation or conflict

Fear of Getting Involved in an Emergency

dystychiphobia (fear of accidents)

Heroes are a window into the soul of a culture. —PSYCHOLOGIST FRANK FARLEY

Characteristics: If you are afraid of stopping to help someone involved in a mugging, a fire or a car crash, you're not alone. Most people flinch or at least hesitate in such emergencies. Some people leave the scene or freeze in their tracks. Others will not travel in certain areas or at certain times of the day because of this fear. Some people avoid emergencies for fear of fainting or because they don't like the sight of blood.

Background: Sadly, research suggests that most people don't help during an emergency on the street for fear of getting hurt, of later having to go to court or of a lawsuit. Research also shows that in emergencies, it is most often men who come forward to help, perhaps because of social conditioning and because men are more used to feelings of arousal through physical action and sports. As our society gets more insular and less personal, chances are that fewer people will help during emergencies. And yet when teamwork is involved, such as during the tragedies of war and terrorism, people have shown courage and empathy and many heroes have been born.

Strategies:
- Take a first-aid course to give you confidence. If you have such training, calmly tell people so at the scene of an emergency.
- Assess the situation and make sure someone notifies authorities immediately.
- Look at the victim. If you were in such a pickle, would you want people to walk away from you?
- If you start to panic, freeze or lose confidence, go up to a victim and touch him or her. Often this will defuse your fears. Or think of a loved one to motivate you, or even use humor. And remember to breathe deeply.
- Focus on what needs to be done and put your anxiousness and

fear energy into that. If you have trouble focusing, briefly get angry at yourself or others. This activates aggressive hormones such as dopamine and testosterone in your nervous system. Before he rescued three unconscious people from a burning car in Fredonia, New York, Robert Nobel got angry with his friends who refused to get involved because they were worried about a lawsuit if the rescue backfired. His anger sent him into a zone in which his powers were increased.

- If you have panicked in the past, don't consider yourself a coward—even tough people falter from time to time and choke in pressure situations.
- If you decide to take action, remember that your power and certain aspects of your focus will improve as your fight-or-flight system kicks in. As heart rate rises, strength and desire are boosted, but complex motor skills decrease. If you are really pumped, you may experience altered perceptions such as tunnel vision or tunnel hearing, in which you don't notice important things on the periphery.
- If you need to perform a task that requires fine motor skills (such as using car keys), make a fist and release it quickly several times. This ensures that blood will stay in your hands; otherwise the fight-or-flight system will send it to the big muscles of your arms and legs to prepare you to fight or run away.

A MANTRA TO TELL YOURSELF: *"Somebody needs me."*

References:

The American Red Cross First Aid and Safety Handbook by Kathleen Handal and Elizabeth Dole, Little, Brown, 1992

Intelligent Fear by Michael Clarkson, Key Porter, 2002

Carnegie Hero Fund Commission, www.carnegiehero.org

See: fear of blood (and blood injury), fear of not having control, fear of illness or pain, fear of making mistakes, fear of taking responsibility, fear of confrontation or conflict, fear of being mugged, fear of death

Fear of Blood (and Blood Injury)

hemophobia (fear of blood)

Children cry oftener from seeing their blood than from the pain occasioned by falls or blows. —BENJAMIN RUSH, AN 18TH-CENTURY AMERICAN PHYSICIAN

Characteristics: At just the thought of seeing blood, a person may feel faint, anxious or nauseous and experience rapid breathing. Sufferers of all ages are particularly susceptible to this fear in hospitals, in doctors' or dentists' offices, while getting injections or giving blood, or at the scene of car crashes and accidents. Some people feel faint just from medical odors. Some women avoid becoming pregnant because they fear medical situations and blood. Ironically, few people who suffer from this fear actually feel threatened with injury or blood loss.

Background: Up to 5 percent of the population has this fear. Women are more susceptible than men. People feel faint at the sight of blood because they get a sudden drop in heart rate and blood pressure; this is called a vasovagal reaction. There are two unproven theories as to why nature makes some people pass out: so the victim will not do anything that may cause further blood loss, or so a person seems lifeless to an attacking predator. This fear tends to be genetic and runs in families, although it can be sparked by a traumatic event. It often starts in childhood.

Strategies:

- This can be a serious fear if you let it prevent you or your loved ones from getting regular medical treatment and checkups. That creates a much bigger problem for you, and something you should genuinely be afraid of.
- If you have this fear, admit it aloud. Denial only drives it deeper into your subconscious and prevents you from coping with it. People won't laugh at you; they have their own phobias to worry about.
- Talk to your doctor or dentist about your fear; they have many other patients who suffer from it, and they are experienced in helping you. They certainly won't laugh at you.

- Talk about it with people you trust, particularly if they have this fear. You can even start your own little support group: Fainters Anonymous (FA).
- Come to realize that, while loss of your own blood would be a problem, the sight of someone else's blood causes you no physical harm.
- Toughen up. Desensitize yourself by watching gory television shows and movies, if only for a few seconds or minutes at a time.
- The next time someone is losing blood in your presence, reach out to help, even if you only put on a Band-Aid. When you focus on that process, you won't notice the blood as much. When I was a police reporter, I rarely noticed the trauma at accident sites because I was so focused on getting the story or the photographs. Distracting yourself from a gory site can also work.
- If you do feel faint, sit down and put your head between your legs. This has helped me many times and I have never fainted.

A MANTRA TO TELL YOURSELF: *"It can't hurt me."*

Author's Two Cents:

I have coped better with my blood phobia since I volunteered to be a "victim" in a staged automobile wreck for a television news show. It was a little traumatic, but I was glad I forced myself to do it. When I saw myself in the rearview mirror, made up with artificial blood, I managed a ghoulish smile.

Reference:

Facing Fears: The Sourcebook for Phobias, Fears, and Anxieties by Ada P. Kahn and Ronald M. Doctor, Checkmark, 2000

See: fear of doctors or dentists, fear of getting involved in an emergency, fear of embarrassment, fear of death, fear of panic attacks in public

Fear of Death

thanatophobia (fear of death)	*Fear not death, for the sooner we die, the longer shall we be immortal.* —BENJAMIN FRANKLIN

Characteristics: When surveys are conducted of people's greatest fears, death is always near or at the top of the list. People feel anxious in situations that may result in death, illness or physical harm; they can get uneasy simply by thinking or talking about those situations. Some people avoid hospitals, travel, funerals, the elderly and risk-taking ventures. Others, especially the ill or elderly, can become preoccupied with death.

Background: Everyone has some fear of mortality, and a healthy dose of this keeps us alert to danger. Fortunately, the major defense systems of humans are set up to ward off death. In Western society, life expectancy has risen in recent times, although there is still a high rate of deaths attributed to heart and anxiety problems. In some ways, dying has become more mysterious because seriously ill people are kept in hospitals. Death is the ultimate unknown, and fear of it is particularly intense in teenagers.

We may also fear leaving behind loved ones who rely on us. Many people are uncomfortable talking about death or making a will, and this discomfort can make death more foreboding. At the same time, death is highlighted in the media and the arts. Many people who have faced death lose some of their fear of it. Singer Gordon Lightfoot said in 2003, after recovering from a serious illness: "In the past I had a fear of death. I feel much better about accepting death now."

Strategies:
- The best antidote for the fear of death is to live. We will all die one day; it's how we live that is important. Soak in the details of daily life—the robin's warble, the crimson sunset, the thrill of holding a child. Say, "I will enjoy life." Don't deny death; it should be included in your overall view of life. Say aloud, "One day I will die. It is inevitable, but there is much to experience, enjoy and accomplish in the meantime."

- If you can't imagine a world without you, join the club. Being alive is all that we know. But you can live beyond your flesh by leaving part of you behind in your family and friends, in your work and deeds, and in your kindness.
- Deepen your spirituality with family, friends or religion. Delve into who you are and what you want to achieve, for yourself and others.
- You will die once; don't die a hundred times by constantly thinking about it. Prepare for that day, however, with a will and instructions about your funeral. Review these with your family.
- If someone you know is dying, rather than wallowing in pity, do something for them and share time with them. Help them focus on everyday life.
- If you are terminally ill, remain positive, but briefly visualize the eventual process of dying. "Write down what you would do if you only had six months to live," writes Judy Tatelbaum in *The Courage to Grieve*. "This exercise allows us to contemplate what is important."
- If children have an intense fear of death, it could be that they fear being left alone. Reassure them that they will be safe and that no harmful forces are lurking around the corner.
- Lighten up. Remember what comedian W.C. Fields wanted on his headstone: "All things considered, I'd rather be in Philadelphia." As author/speaker Allen Klein says, "Joking about death, or anything else that oppresses us, makes it less frightening."

A MANTRA TO TELL YOURSELF: *"I'm alive."*

References:

Lessons from the Dying by Rodney Smith, Wisdom Publications, 1998

Video: *Overcoming the Fear of Death* by Deepak Chopra

See: fear of the unknown, fear of illness or pain, fear of being mugged, fear of travel, fear of religion, fears for your children, fear of aging, fear of retirement, fear of delivering bad news, fear of flying, fear of terrorism, fear of heights, fear of water and swimming, fear of doctors or dentists, serious worries

Fear of Illness or Pain

algophobia (fear of painful situations such as visits to doctors and dentists)

There are major differences between being concerned about health and suffering from hypochondria. —DAVID S. GOLDMAN, CLINICAL ASSISTANT PROFESSOR OF PSYCHIATRY AT NEW YORK UNIVERSITY SCHOOL OF MEDICINE

hypochondria (intense and unwarranted fear of illness or a preoccupation with health issues)

Characteristics: This condition involves worry or anxiety over symptoms of illness and pain or the potential that they might occur. Many people avoid physicians, hospitals, funerals and the elderly (or, conversely, they visit the doctor more than they should). A person might be preoccupied with illness and talk about it all the time or watch television shows about emergencies or health issues. Many elderly people fear illness because they believe they would be a burden to others. Hypochondriacs may be preoccupied with bodily functions.

Background: Everyone worries about their health from time. That's good if it motivates us to eat well and exercise often. Exaggerated concern about a variety of illnesses (hypochondria) affects men and women in equal numbers. About 25 percent of all patients seen in health clinics and doctors' offices have this condition. It usually begins between the ages of 20 and 30. Hypochondria costs the U.S. health care system about $30 billion annually. Hypochondriacs have medical costs up to 14 times greater than the average person. Poet Alfred Lord Tennyson was thought to be a hypochondriac.

Strategies:
- You can alleviate many of your fears through education and prevention. Have regular checkups and talk to your doctor about your concerns. If you get anxious about your health, you might get short-term relief through deep breathing, meditation and other relaxation techniques.
- Establish whether you have normal health concerns or hypochondria, which has three symptoms: a morbid fear of

disease; preoccupation or obsession with bodily symptoms and functions; and a firm conviction of having a disease, despite medical assurance and test results to the contrary.

- Hypochondria can be difficult to treat, but results have improved in recent times because of new medications, behavioral techniques, greater awareness of the problem, group therapy and changes in doctor-patient relationships. A diagnostic assessment may be required, including reviewing the medical history of the patient and conducting physical and mental examinations. If you know someone who is a hypochondriac, be empathetic and understand that their symptoms seem real to them.
- If you are worried about upcoming surgery, ask a lot of questions and develop a rapport with your doctor, nurses and surgeon. Visit the hospital ahead of time and get a walk-through of the procedure.
- If you have a serious illness, understand that medical science and procedures have never been more effective. Seek out family and friends for emotional support and perhaps for physical needs (such as getting a ride to a clinic).
- If you are afraid that illness or pain will affect your career, learn new ways to do your work, or find other work to do.
- If someone close to you has an illness, allow yourself to feel concern and pain, but don't allow the person to feel guilty about your concern.
- Avoid television shows about illness, and don't allow your fears to become exaggerated through media hype.

A MANTRA TO TELL YOURSELF: *"Deal with reality."*

References:

Hypochondria: Woeful Imaginings by S. Baur, University of California Press, 1998

Phantom Illness by C. Cantor, Houghton Mifflin, 1996

See: fear of death, fear of the unknown, fear of not having control, fear of aging, fear of doctors or dentists, fear of retirement, fear of blood (and blood injury), fear of embarrassment, serious worries

Fear of Doctors or Dentists

iatrophobia (fear of going to the doctor)

dentophobia (fear of dentists)

Showing up is 80 percent of life.
—WOODY ALLEN

Characteristics: Who doesn't have at least some anxiety over visits to physicians, clinics, dentists or hospitals? Sufferers may worry about needles, viruses, pain, blood, medical procedures or bad news. People may avoid their physician even for routine checkups. Others worry their fear will cause them to blush, to feel embarrassed or even to faint. People who have had a painful experience with a physician or dentist may be reluctant to return.

Background: Anxiety about doctors and dentists has been common throughout history. It can be uncomfortable to have another person poking at you with instruments or diagnosing a little wart or withdrawing your blood. Most people are at least somewhat afraid of pain and of hearing bad news. Much of this fear is left over from times when visits to physicians were more painful because medical science was crude. It is when we avoid doctors and dentists that this fear becomes a phobia. In addition, some people fear that physicians are not qualified to treat them or may cheat them. Research suggests that men are half as likely as women to use health services for prevention purposes, but twice as likely to use emergency services. About twice as many people fear dentists as doctors. Blood phobias tend to run in families. This fear is also produced in people who have had a traumatic experience earlier in life.

Strategies:

- Understand that your anxiety is probably more of a problem than whatever you are going to the physician about. Most of the time, your ailment will be minor and can be handled with medication or relatively painless procedures. Medical procedures have come a long way; in particular, visits to dental offices are far less of a big deal than they used to be. With modern drills and anesthetics, it's rare that dentists hit a nerve.
- It should be repeated over and over that the best medicine is

preventive; get regular checkups and put the upcoming dates on your calendar. Encourage other members of your family to do the same.

- If you are apprehensive about making an appointment, sit down alone and make a firm decision that you will go, then book the appointment that day. Coming to grips with the decision will relieve much of the pressure and fear. Avoid making appointments during a stressful time at work or at home.
- Consult friends and family to find a physician who is not only competent, but understands patients' anxieties. Develop a relationship with a physician you trust.
- Prior to a visit, visualize yourself driving to the physician's office, sitting down in the office and going through the procedure with a successful outcome.
- Talk to others in the waiting room. Laugh at this fear and share it with others and with the doctor. Make cynical remarks about the outdated magazines in the waiting room.
- During a procedure, you may want to have a mild sedative or use "guided imagery," imagining a pleasant experience like sunning on a beach.
- If you are afraid of needles, try to relax, perhaps by progressively tensing muscles in your feet, legs, buttocks, abdomen, arms and shoulders as you wait for the injection, then releasing the muscles.
- Be wary of physicians who readily write prescriptions for you without much examination or consultation.

A MANTRA TO TELL YOURSELF: *"It's good for me."*

References:

Dr. Keith Livingston (phobia expert), (206) 721-8751

Dr. Eric Spielder (Philadelphia dentist), Dr.Spielder@aol.com

See: fear of blood (and blood injury), fear of not having control, fear of the unknown, fear of illness or pain, fear of death, fear of embarrassment, fear of delivering bad news, fear of panic attacks in public

Fear of Aging

gerascophobia (fear of aging)	*How old would you be if you didn't know how old you was?* —SATCHEL PAIGE, WHO PLAYED MAJOR LEAGUE BASEBALL AT AGE 55
gerontophobia (fear and hatred of the old)	

Characteristics: For a variety of reasons, a person may worry about reaching 20, 30, 50 or 65. This fear may be linked with concerns about friends and family, health, appearance, retirement or death. The elderly may worry more after their friends die or become ill, or they may worry about getting Alzheimer's, diabetes or heart attacks (anginophobia), having surgery or becoming a burden to others. Some women fear menopause. Other common concerns of aging are loneliness, poverty, falling and being injured while alone, loss of responsibility for one's life, being attacked, memory loss and sexual inadequacy.

Background: This is a primitive fear that remains strong today, but it is being reduced—people are living longer and are able to enjoy their golden years. Genetically, the human species is not programmed to live as long as we do—for most of our history, the average life expectancy was just 18 years! It is a fact that, after age 30, things start going downhill physically, but the good news is that we are born with 10 times more physical capacity than we actually need.

Intense fear of aging can lead to anxiety and hasten the aging process through the release of aggressive hormones. This fear is good when it forces us to take care of ourselves or, when we are younger, to take on responsibility. In some societies, the elderly are more respected than they are in others. Some studies show that memory loss among the elderly is not widespread.

Strategies:

- As you grow older, discover what millions of people have found—that each age has its benefits. People tend to be most energetic and physically fit in their youth, but they mature in their 40s and they can live very active lives in their 50s and beyond, when they often feel more free after seeing their children leave home. Age brings experience and wisdom.

- Don't get caught up in our society's obsession with youth. Don't listen to the often negative portrayals of various age groups, particularly the elderly, in the media. People are able to work longer and live more vital lives into their 70s and 80s than ever before. And when you turn 30, your social life need not be kaput.

- The most significant predictors of healthy old age are low blood pressure, low serum glucose levels, a good diet, not being overweight and not smoking while young. After age 50, the best diet is low fat with plenty of fruits, vegetables and protein, along with increased calcium and vitamins D and B_{12}. Another predictor of good health is a positive attitude and a zest for life. "No one grows old by living, only by losing interest in living," said novelist Marie Beynon Ray.

- Be sure to get regular physical checkups and exercise in every stage of life. "An ounce of prevention is worth a pound of cure" still rings true. To avoid undue strain, try swimming and cross-country skiing instead of running and tennis.

- If you have problems with memory loss, leave yourself written reminders and lists of things that have to be done.

- If you have physical problems and drive, don't be embarrassed to get a handicap sticker. And welcome the chance to get retested or to refresh yourself with a safe-driving course.

- Remain optimistic as long as you have something to do—like being a friend, a volunteer, a grandparent, a gardener or a reader of books. But understand that others around you may be more pessimistic.

- Enjoy your freedom of speech. As you get older, you can humor people less and feel more comfortable speaking the truth.

  A MANTRA TO TELL YOURSELF: *"I'm getting wiser."*

Reference:

Centenarians: The Bonus Years by Lynn Adler, Health, 1995

See: fear of retirement, fear of death, fear of the unknown, fear of not having control, fear of change, fear of being alone, fear of not being loved, fear of illness or pain, fear of falling, fear of driving, fear of losing status

Sexual Fears

erotophobia (fear of sex) hypoactive sexual desire (having little desire for sex) primeisodophobia (fear of losing one's virginity)	*Don't worry about what others are doing. As long as you are both satisfied and happy, you are normal ... our sex drive continually evolves as our life changes. The dynamics of our life and our relationship all affect the ebb and flow of our sexual desire and arousal.* —SEX AND MARRIAGE COUNSELOR RAJAN BHONSLE

Characteristics: Sexual anxieties are common. Some men worry about lack of arousal or poor performance, while some women worry about being frigid or not receiving intimacy, and some even worry that their vaginas are too tight. Some people worry that they have too much sex drive. Many parents worry that their children will get involved in sexual situations too early or with the wrong partner. Some young women mistakenly fear menstruation; they may believe that release of their blood is unnatural (it isn't) or feel shame about it.

Background: Almost everyone has some anxiety about the sensitive subject of sex, and most people experience arousal problems at least occasionally. For others, problems are more serious and could even be linked to deviancy. About 25 percent of Americans sometimes experience little or no sexual desire.

Modern humans have always had fears, guilt and self-consciousness about sex (we are the only animal to have sex in private). Although sex talk and awareness has become more common in the past 20 years, we still don't like to talk about sexual problems. And North American society can be quite judgmental, if not downright Victorian. In the big picture, it's good to be cautious about sexual issues. If we had no sexual fears at all, casual intercourse, unplanned pregnancy and sexually transmitted diseases would be rampant.

Strategies:
- Keep in shape. Get a physical checkup; sexual dysfunction can be the early warning of potential medical problems, or a sign that you need to adjust the medication you are taking.

- Educate yourself. Although our society still has much to learn about sex, there is more good information now than ever before. Some fears, particularly about homosexuality and masturbation, are conditioned through culture and religion and are not necessarily based on facts.
- Be responsible in your sexual decisions—especially with regard to when, at what age and with whom to have sex. Pay attention to the consequences your acts may have on others. Always practice safe sex.
- If you are having problems, examine your relationships and emotional well-being. Emotional factors—such as relationship problems, lack of trust, past trauma and guilt—can affect your sexual life.
- In a society flooded with sexual images, don't compare yourself to models or sell yourself short.
- Mix things up once in a while and ask the other person what they want in bed. Visualize what you want to happen and perhaps talk it over with your partner.
- Focus on what your partner is doing to you. If you always close your eyes, you might lose some of the experience and intimacy. Talk about the experience afterwards; find out what worked and what didn't.
- Try to understand the opposite sex. Men and women tend to have different needs in sex, men for action and women for intimacy. If you find that to be the case, try to reverse roles once in a while.
- If problems persist, see your doctor or perhaps a sex therapist. Some drugs can help.

A MANTRA TO TELL YOURSELF: *"Safe and healthy."*

References:

Resurrecting Sex by David Schnarch, HarperCollins, 2002

Sexual Marriage, www.sexualmarriage.com

Talk Sex with Sue Johanson, www.talksexwithsue.com

See: fear of not being loved, fear of intimacy or love, fear of homosexuality, fear of the opposite sex, fear of dating, fear of embarrassment, fear for your children's safety, fear of religion, fears for your marriage/partnership, serious worries, fear of what friends think, fear of harassment

Fear of Enclosed Spaces

claustrophobia (includes fear of being in closets, elevators and crowds)

It is a curious fact that many people who are afraid of small, enclosed spaces are also frightened by being in large open spaces. —PSYCHOLOGIST STANLEY RACHMAN

stenophobia (fear of narrow places, escalators, tunnels)

Characteristics: If you feel anxious or have a fast heartbeat in a crowded space, you may suffer from this specific fear or phobia. Some people panic or feel like they are going to suffocate, and this is sometimes related to their stepped-up breathing patterns. Sufferers tend to avoid elevators and small offices for fear of getting trapped or becoming embarrassed about their reaction. This fear is common in patients who undergo an MRI scan in a narrow chamber. Some people imagine themselves being buried in sand.

Background: Claustrophobia—almost everyone is familiar with this term. It is perhaps the most common of the *exaggerated* fears, affecting about one in 10 people. About 2 percent of people have a severe case. A 2002 survey revealed the No. 1 fear of men was being buried alive and the No. 2 fear of women was being tied up. Psychologists believe that claustrophobia may be innate, and further developed through a bad experience. One in three cases begins in childhood. It's related to the primitive fear of lurking predators who trapped their prey in a confined area. Claustrophobics often have social phobias. Some experts believe this fear can be traced back to fear of Stone Age humans' fear of being suffocated in a cave.

Strategies:

- Prepare for potential stressful situations in hotels or office buildings by checking in advance the size of the rooms and the availability of stairs.
- Slowly desensitize yourself by going into confined spaces. Start with ones that are not too small, such as large closets, then gradually seek out smaller ones, such as crawl spaces. Have someone there with you.

- Don't allow this kind of fear to trap you. You cannot suffocate in an elevator, and the galvanized steel cables will not snap. Although your fear feels very real, it is unreasonable.
- If you feel enclosed in a theater or an arena, sit in the aisle. However, if you are more afraid of what people think of you squatting in the aisle, then get back in your seat (some fears are worse than others!).
- On escalators, proceed slowly but surely while holding the railing. You may want to have someone go in front of you. Remember, there are very few accidents involving escalators or elevators. Safety standards are high. Your chances of an accidental fall will increase, however, if you feel overly nervous.
- In all situations of feeling enclosed, keep a sense of perspective about your exaggerated fear; try to use deep-breathing techniques and humor. Hey, you could make the Guinness Book of World Records as the first person to die from claustrophobia!
- Bring your fear out into the open and write or talk about it. Edgar Allen Poe dealt with his claustrophobia by writing horror stories such as "The Black Cat" and "The Premature Burial." If you voice your worries into a tape recorder, hearing your own voice talk about them can help you put things in perspective.

A MANTRA TO TELL YOURSELF: *"Snug in a womb."*

Reference:

Facing Fears by Ada P. Kahn and Ronald M. Doctor, Checkmark, 2000

See: fear of panic attacks in public, fear of embarrassment, fear of crowds, fear of not having control, fear of driving, fear of the dark, fear of crowds, fear of dogs and animals

Fear of Heights

acrophobia (fear of high places) catapedaphobia (fear of jumping from high or low places)	*Don't get me started on intuitive. You know what's intuitive? Fear of heights. Everything else we call intuitive, such as walking or using a pencil, took years of practice.* —DONALD NORMAN, RISKS DIGEST

Characteristics: Sufferers of this condition may feel discomfort, intense fear, vertigo (dizziness) or panic while standing atop high buildings, elevated highways or hills, or while skiing or on amusement rides. Some people may feel drawn to jump. Those who fear heights may have nightmares about falling, but they may not be afraid of flying or living in glassed-in apartment buildings. Babies may begin to respect heights after they start to crawl.

Background: This is a common fear, especially in mild forms. If we didn't have it, we'd be hurtling off rooftops and escarpments. It is probably a leftover from the days when primates started walking on two legs and left the plains for the Great Rift Valley and needed an inner protective device to keep them from going off cliffs. Most animals do not fear heights.

People with problems of coordination, balance or the inner ear may have this fear. It is sometimes related to the fear of falling (basophobia), the fear of looking up (anablepophobia) and the fear of high objects (batophobia). People with the latter fear may avoid ladders and ask others to get things from high shelves.

Strategies:

- Exposure therapy often works; people can be gradually exposed to heights while in a relatively relaxed state. For example, they can look out of a window from the third floor until they feel relaxed, then repeat the experience on higher floors (but perhaps not all in the same day).
- Give yourself control. In a program called LearningMethods, sufferers are taken to a hill where they slowly walk toward the edge, always giving themselves the chance to go back but reminding themselves that they control their decision. They are

told to let their feelings of anxiety come out and to stay near the edge for some time. Gradually, they relax.

- If you have little need to be in tall buildings or on top of hills, you may want to ignore this fear. But, of course, you can try to control it to give yourself satisfaction or to open up your world. Looking down from on high can even be exciting!
- There is no shame in going to a therapist. Wendy Black had an embarrassing fear of climbing a slide at the playground with her children. "I was freezing and couldn't move my feet," she said. "It affected my self-esteem." With help from psychologist Martin Antony of St. Joseph's Hospital in Hamilton, Ontario, Black began climbing small ladders until she was able to join her kids on the slide. Eventually, she was even able to go up Toronto's CN Tower, the world's tallest free-standing structure.
- Lean on your friends. Hironobu Yasuda of Japan was afraid to go up the Eiffel Tower, but was encouraged by his friends to try skydiving. "I couldn't have jumped out of a plane without my wonderful friends," he said. "There was a whole new world and the beautiful sky; I had never seen such a beautiful world!"
- Safety in childhood can reduce such fears. The Navajo Indians, who were carried on their mother's back in a cradle in infancy, were often hired as fearless construction workers on high-rises.
- If your children have no fear of heights, they may be prone to injury and falls. They may have *hypophobia* (lack of fear) and an underactive nervous system.

A MANTRA TO TELL YOURSELF: *"Slow, but safe."*

Reference:

The Anxiety and Phobia Workbook by Edmund J. Bourne, New Harbinger, 1995

See: fear of falling, fear of death, fear of not having control, fear of illness or pain, fear of embarrassment, fear of flying

Fear of Falling

basophobia (fear of falling)

climacophobia (fear of falling down stairs)

A major problem confining older people to their homes isn't falling itself, but fear of falling. —JONATHAN HOWLAND, PROFESSOR OF SOCIAL AND BEHAVIORAL SCIENCES AT BOSTON UNIVERSITY

Characteristics: This is cautiousness or lack of confidence with walking, running or bicycling, especially among children, the elderly or the injured. People may avoid long walks, escalators, crowds or winter weather and become housebound. Some athletes may be cautious because of this condition. Elderly people often fear that constant falling will motivate others to institutionalize them.

Background: This fear may be partly physical and partly psychological, involving a potential loss of control or embarrassment. Even for a healthy person, tripping or falling is embarrassing. Falling can be caused by an illness, problems of balance, the inner ear or coordination, or overcompensating to deal with potential dizzy spells. The good news is that this fear makes us more cautious during the times we are physically vulnerable. At least one-third of people over 65 fall every year.

Strategies:
- If you feel you are cautious because of a physical problem, check with your physician. You may be afraid because of a condition you aren't consciously aware of, such as an issue with medication or an equilibrium problem. If you are undergoing therapy, check with your therapist to see if you need a brace, a walker, a cane or a wheelchair. Don't be embarrassed to get a handicap sticker for your vehicle.
- Develop confidence as you go along. You might have more control than you think; human balance is a wonderful resource if you trust it.
- If you have a history of falling but are in relatively good health, check out martial arts centers; they can teach you methods to break your fall that limit injury.

- If you are recovering from a sports injury, the best thing to do is get right back in the saddle to regain your confidence. Everyone falls occasionally; it's all about how you react to it.
- Note that when children fall on the playground while with their friends, they often bounce up laughing, even if they are bleeding. But when their parents are around, they often stay down crying. This fact can teach us not to tumble too easily into self-pity.
- A regular exercise routine, especially in a group, can raise your physical and mental confidence.
- Walk with a buddy. It will give you more confidence and a support system in case you do fall.
- For the elderly, try to keep active, especially after periods of immobilization. By moving around less, you will lose conditioning in muscles and balance, and that may increase your risk of falling. If you are a senior, you should install handrails on stairs, review all medications, increase lighting in your home, get routine checkups and wear sturdy shoes.

A MANTRA TO TELL YOURSELF: *"Slow, but sure."*

References:

The Complete Idiot's Guide to Conquering Fear and Anxiety by Sharon Heller, Alpha, 1999

Professor Jonathan Howland, jhowl@bu.edu

Subtle Fact:

A study revealed that people aged 63 to 90 who wear bifocals are twice as likely to fall as those wearing single-vision glasses. The bifocals decrease their ability to discern potential dangers on the ground when walking or climbing stairs.

See: fear of heights, fear of embarrassment, fear of illness or pain, fear of not having control, fear of aging, fear of flying

Fear of Travel

hodophobia (fear of road travel)	*The world is a book, and those who do not travel read only one page.* —St. Augustine

Characteristics: This is an uneasiness about leaving your area. Some people rarely stray from one place. Others are fearful of traveling in a car or on public transit or in a boat, or of crashing or being the victim of a terrorist attack. Some people don't like going on vacations because they are afraid of people or crowds.

Background: Most people have always had some anxiety about travel, which takes them away from the safety, friendly faces and routine of their home. Having a safety or comfort zone is natural. However, travel is educational and those who do little of it risk being narrow-minded and may stereotype people they've never met. They end up relying on rumors and media reports for their notions about life outside their little world. Following the tragedy of September 11, 2001, tourism suffered and flying became less popular.

Strategies:

- Try to identify what is behind your fear of travel—is it a physical or health fear, apprehension about strangers, fear of change or a general lack of confidence? Once you have identified it, you can work on improving those specific areas in your life.
- Research your trips well through travel agencies, the Internet, chambers of commerce, magazines and videos. Keep a list of important phone numbers, hotels and addresses in a small book. Leave your itinerary with others. Travel only with essentials, especially for air flight. And carry medical information and two forms of identification.
- Don't let finalizing all the details drive you crazy. There will always be one little thing you'll miss. As long as the big plans are taken care of, the small details don't matter so much.
- Don't stick to a rigid schedule; if you miss one stop, your strict plans could all fall apart. Leave some room for spontaneity.
- If you don't like crowds or heavy traffic, go on vacation after Labor Day, when you'll find less congestion and fewer tourists.

- Be wary of media reports about the dangers of big cities; the media tend to focus on the sensational. When I started extensive travel in the mid-1990s, I was surprised to find that most U.S. cities are safe as long as one avoids certain neighborhoods. At the same time, don't go out of your way to look like a target; when in a strange place, don't display jewelry or wealth or bring attention to yourself.
- Travel gives you a great chance to broaden your view of the world while seeing other cultures. People who never travel can be closed-minded and have distorted views. Allow yourself to try something new that you've seen in your travels, such as a way of dancing or a new dish.
- To gain some control in a new city, rent a car. Toronto writer Craig Daniels has anxiety about traveling, but partly overcomes it by driving, even in cities like Los Angeles and New York.
- Despite the fear of terrorism, most travel is safe and airports are more secure now than they were prior to 9/11. Accept that long lineups and security checks are there for your safety. Rather than whine about them, relax by taking deep breaths.

A MANTRA TO TELL YOURSELF: *"I'm competent enough to travel."*

References:

Frommer's Fly Safe, Fly Smart by Sasha Sagan, John Wiley and Sons, 2002

Traveler Beware by Kevin Coffey, Corporate Travel Safety, 1999

www.travel.com

The Facts Are With You:

Despite worries over terrorism, more than 600,000 people board planes each day in the United States.

See: fear of the unknown, fear of flying, fear of driving, fear of strangers, fear of people, fear of terrorism, fear of change, fear of weather, fear of panic attacks in public

Fear of Driving

amaxophobia (fear of riding in a car)

dystychiphobia (fear of accidents)

Being a friendly driver is contagious.
—LEON JAMES AND DIANE NAHL, IN THEIR BOOK *ROAD RAGE AND AGGRESSIVE DRIVING*

Characteristics: Driving or riding in a vehicle makes some people nervous or angry. Others get tense and grip the steering wheel so tightly, it's referred to as the "white knuckle" response. People may fear losing control of the vehicle, getting hurt in a crash, getting annoyed by traffic jams, or being on the receiving end of road rage from other drivers. Some fear criticism from backseat drivers.

Background: Hurtling along in a 2,000-pound vehicle can make anybody hesitant. There may be more emotions on the roads than ever before because of the increase in the number of vehicles and drivers, a variety of driving styles, more cell-phone use by drivers and the high levels of stress in our society. Driving is not exactly natural to humans—it's about as far away from the cave as you can get! Some people, feeling their territory has been invaded by another driver, act out behind the wheel because they feel anonymous in the confines of their vehicle. Others fear driving because they have physical or coordination problems. Because of the risk of accidents, a healthy respect for driving is good for everyone.

Strategies:
- Driving is safe if you have the proper mental, emotional and physical perspective. Before you start your ignition, put your mind in neutral and remind yourself that you just want to get from point A to point B safely and in a reasonable time.
- But don't be *too* relaxed. You want an arousal level just slightly above neutral for driving, to keep you alert to potential problems. If you are apathetic, your reaction time will decrease.
- Treat your car as your home away from home. You spend a lot of time in it. Make it quality time.
- If you worry about traffic jams, buy a quality sound system for your vehicle and listen to your favorite music. Careful, though, about fast music: research shows that drivers who listen to heavy metal have a higher rate of accidents. You might also consider

carpooling or taking public transit (I take a bus to work).
- Travel with someone you enjoy, or take an interest in your surroundings (but not too much) as you drive.
- Humor is a good outlet for reducing negative driving emotions. Laugh at other drivers who would otherwise annoy you.
- If another driver cuts you off or impedes you, don't take it personally: he or she doesn't even know you! Give other drivers the benefit of the doubt—they may be coming home from a funeral, on the way to an emergency or just having a bad day.
- If you become angry at another driver, don't try to punish him. Resist the urge to strike back. If you were outside your vehicle, you probably wouldn't even consider acting aggressively.
- After an accident, don't get emotional. Get all the details, such as everyone's name, license number and insurance. In certain jurisdictions, you may not have to report a minor accident to police.
- Keep your driving skills sharp, perhaps with a defensive driving course to keep you prepared for hazardous weather. Older drivers may want to be retested because reaction times can decrease with age. Be sure everyone in the car, including children, is wearing a seat belt.
- Keep your vehicle in top shape and remember to rotate your tires.

A MANTRA TO TELL YOURSELF: *"Shift into neutral."*

The Facts Are With You:
For every 100 million miles driven in North America, there is less than one fatality.

References:
Road Rage and Aggressive Driving by Leon James and Diane Nahl, Prometheus, 2000

LearningMethods, www.learningmethods.com

See: fear of not having control, fear of illness or pain, fear of invasion of territory or privacy, fear of death, fear of aging, fear of enclosed spaces, fear of travel, fear of oneself

Fear of Dogs and Animals

cynophobia (fear of dogs) zoophobia (fear of animals)	*Some are mad if they behold a cat.* —WILLIAM SHAKESPEARE, *THE MERCHANT OF VENICE*

Characteristics: Some people avoid certain places (such as relatives' homes) or refuse to have pets because of this fear. The most common fears are of dogs, cats, horses and (ugh!) rats. In extreme cases, some people won't leave their homes for fear of encountering a dog on the street. Others are allergic to animals. Some people fear that birds will attack them (ornithophobia). Others fear that rats and mice carry dirt and disease (suriphobia).

Background: As humans, it is natural for us to be at least cautious about other species. At one time, we were at the mercy of aggressive animals and harbored intense fear of them. Today, a certain amount of fearful respect for them remains.

Fear of animals is often developed in childhood through bad experiences or lack of contact. A United Kingdom study showed that 59 percent of people feared lizards and 51 percent feared rats. French emperor Napoleon Bonaparte was afraid of cats. Fear of animals tends to run in families.

Strategies:

- Gradually expose yourself to the animals that frighten you. Start by looking at pictures of them, then view them in pet stores or humane shelters, then go to the home of someone you know who has access to them. Consider buying yourself a pet that isn't too threatening.
- Try to understand your fear. Ask relatives if you had a bad experience with animals as a child, then tell yourself it's time to deal with it.
- If an aggressive dog lives in your area, politely report it to the owner; if that doesn't work, go to the humane society or the police.

- If an uncontrolled dog approaches you, ignore it, stand still and look off in the distance. Some animals will sense if you are afraid. If that doesn't work, point at it and shout. If it tries to bite, pick up something to use as a shield or weapon. If a dog is leashed, don't assume it's safe. Allow it to come close slowly and sniff you.
- Get bites immediately checked at a clinic or hospital. Get witnesses and the name and address of the owner.
- Remember that some of society's fears about animals are unfounded: bats don't deliberately try to entangle themselves in your hair, bee stings are rare, and horses are not waiting to kick you. And most domestic animals like humans.
- No matter how much he squeals, don't let a monkey take over the wheel of your car (from David Letterman's Top 10 list).
- Cats are usually docile, but don't allow a strange feline to come to you unless it approaches you in a friendly manner. Be aware of your allergies if you visit a home with a cat.

A MANTRA TO TELL YOURSELF: *"Most dogs have more bark than bite"* OR *"Caution without panic."*

Reference:

Understanding Dogs by Clinton R. Sanders, Temple University Press, 1999

See: fear of snakes and spiders, fear of illness or pain, fear of embarrassment, fear and stress in children, fear of not having control, fear of enclosed spaces

Fear of Snakes and Spiders

arachnophobia (fear of spiders) *ophidiophobia* (fear of snakes)	*We fear serpents with a destructive hatred purely and simply because we are taught so from childhood.* —NATURALIST W. H. HUDSON

Characteristics: With their unusual appearance and movements, it's hardly surprising many people are squeamish about spiders and snakes. People's anxiety, rapid breathing or nausea can be set off by just seeing a picture or thinking about the creatures. Some people are afraid they might bite. Others even fumigate their homes and are reluctant to eat outdoors or vacation in certain areas. Sufferers may think they will faint, but they rarely do.

Background: Humans have harbored a fear or distaste for spiders and snakes since prehistoric times, when they were out in the open and exposed to poisonous creatures. Today, most people with fear of snakes have had no direct contact with them, leading experts to believe this fear is innate. It can be activated for some people just from thinking about snakes or hearing stories about them.

Fear of snakes is often latent; children under two don't seem afraid, but the fear emerges at ages three or four. It can also be acquired through teaching; in the Bible, the devil appeared as a serpent. Fear of spiders is often caused by an incident in childhood. Some people's fear of snakes and spiders is actually a disgust they have for the creatures' appearance.

Strategies:
- Gradually expose yourself to spiders and snakes. First, look at pictures of them or simply think about them, but when doing so, do not see them as a threat to you. When you are ready to confront them, slowly approach a snake or spider. Maintain some distance while you relax in their presence. Give it as long as you want, and don't force yourself to conquer your fear all in one day.
- Educate yourself: most snakes and spiders are not poisonous. Unless provoked, most will not attack humans. Think of how ugly, huge and threatening *you* appear to *them*.

- Learn more about the characteristics and habits of snakes and spiders and their value to nature. They did not evolve just to give you the heebie-jeebies.
- If this fear inhibits your lifestyle, see a doctor or psychologist.
- In areas inhabited by rattlesnakes, wear long, loose pants and calf-high leather boots. Rattlesnakes are usually not aggressive toward people unless startled or cornered.
- To discourage snakes from moving into your yard or home:
  - Eliminate cool, damp areas; remove brush, tall grass and rock piles; and keep shrubbery away from foundations.
  - Control insect and rodent populations to dry up their food supply.
  - To keep them out of basements and crawl spaces, seal all openings with mortar, caulking compound or hardware cloth.

The Facts Are With You:

Of the 34,000 species of spiders, only 12 are poisonous.

References:

Snake: The Essential Visual Guide to the World of Snakes by Chris Mattison, DK Publishing, 1999

Phobias Cured
4838 Delridge Way SW, Suite A
Seattle, WA 98106
(206) 721-8751, keith@phobiascured.com

Dr. Brenda Wiederhold
Virtual Reality Medical Center
San Diego, CA 92121
1-866-822-VRMC, bwiederhold@vrphobia.com

See: fear of dogs and animals, fear of illness or pain, fear of death, fear of embarrassment, superstition or fear of the supernatural

Fear of Water and Swimming

hydrophobia (fear of swimming)	*People wish to learn to swim and at the same time to keep one foot on the*
ablutophobia (fear of bathing)	*ground.* —MARCEL PROUST

Characteristics: Many people are apprehensive about swimming in deep water, bathing or boating. Some people are embarrassed about their body shape and don't want to be seen in a bathing suit. Others feel a fatal attraction to rushing water, as Marilyn Monroe did while filming the movie *Niagara*.

Background: In our evolution, we've become land creatures more than sea creatures. Some experts believe that the fear of water can be linked to our ancestors the monkeys, who were poor swimmers. Some people fear water after they are traumatized by being involved in or seeing a near-drowning. People afraid of deep water often fear loss of breathing and physical control; in some cases, they fear water creatures or seasickness. Frederick the Great, King of Prussia, was so fearful of water that he rarely washed. Actress Natalie Wood, who was afraid of the water, drowned.

Despite the many people who fear water, it is worth noting that humans can easily get used to water; babies can learn to swim at age three. Many people who seek help for this fear respond well to treatment, and they often even manage to overcome traumatic experiences involving water.

Strategies:
- With regard to swimming, understand that the water is buoyant and ready to keep you up, no matter what your weight is. It is almost impossible to sink if you relax. Proceed slowly. Get used to the water by first dangling your feet from the side while breathing deeply and trying to relax. Consider using a flotation device.
- Take swimming lessons. When you have mastered a technique, it will give you confidence and allow you to get out of a situation if you panic. Or go in the water with a buddy.
- Tips for learning to swim: try a stroke easiest for you, perhaps the breast stroke, where you don't have to put your face in the

water; don't anticipate the worst; keep your mind on your technique, not the possibility of sinking and your proximity to the wall; don't panic; remember that you have more time to react than you think; don't take this book in the water.

- Remember that water is our friend—without it, we wouldn't be here. We can float in water and see and hold our breath under water. Our ears even close instantaneously when we jump in. The human body is made up mostly of fluids, and we came from water in our mother's womb.
- For babies afraid of getting their hair washed, be careful to keep water out of their eyes and ears. Wash with water from a glass rather than from faucets, which can scare some babies. Try to distract the child with a game or music.
- For seasickness, pills and acupressure wristbands show results.
- If you worry about how you look in a bathing suit, remember that others are worried about how they look to *you*.
- If you have a home swimming pool, always have a latched gate to protect children and keep appropriate safety devices on hand. Most child drownings occur in swimming pools.

A MANTRA TO TELL YOURSELF: *"I won't sink."*

Author's Two Cents:

I have been apprehensive about swimming all my life, and I used to think I was a *sinker*. That sensation of water going up my nose was awful. At age 49, I finally taught myself to swim in a condo pool; two years later, I helped to save my wife from drowning by channeling the energy of my fear into my swimming stroke in order to reach her.

Reference:

Researcher Sheri Stein, Sheristein@hotmail.com

See: fear of death, fear of not having control, fear of embarrassment, fear of falling, fear of panic attacks in public, fear of your appearance

Fear of Loud Noises

acousticophobia or ligyrophobia (fear of sounds)

When I tried to lead a session in science, some of the students raised their voices. I had to raise my volume and soon it was a shouting match and I couldn't stand the noise. I hit the panic button. Now I have to avoid those situations. —AN ALBERTA HIGH SCHOOL TEACHER

Characteristics: Some people fear machines, sonic booms, popping balloons, emergency sirens, thunderstorms and even vacuum cleaners because of their noise. They might avoid car races, airports, factories and the outdoors. Others fear music (musicophobia), partly for its noise, or rock music for its brashness and rebelliousness. Victims of car crashes may remember only the noise and may subsequently fear loud noises.

Background: This is one of the basic genetic fears. It serves a useful purpose because an unexpected noise could mean an emergency situation. All animals react sharply to loud noises. Soldiers or accident victims may respond to sounds that remind them of trauma. Children may fear vacuum cleaners, saws and emergency sirens. This fear could also be the result of sensitive hearing. Many people recoil at the sound of their car horn going off (especially accidentally) in a parking lot. Others fear the embarrassment of their reaction because they see that others are just laughing at the noise.

Strategies:
- If you live in a high-noise area, try to anticipate loud noises from train whistles, ship horns and sirens.
- Desensitize yourself to noises by going to airports, factories, truck stops or fireworks displays. Make a tape recording of the noises that frighten you and replay them at various levels. Consider using earplugs in factories and at rock concerts.
- Most noises in Western society are controlled; if you hear an unusually loud noise, there may be a reason to become alert. Perhaps something has exploded or is collapsing. Check the immediate area.

- Telephones can sound alarming because of the possibility that bad news might wait at the other end. Soften the phone's ringing sound.
- Noises can not only be frightening, they can also be serious distractions when you are trying to concentrate on something. Learn to respect the sounds and noises you hear and try to tune out those that distract you unnecessarily. You will want to be in tune with your child's cry, even though at times it may be unnecessary and annoying. Baseball players are famous for tuning out the screams of enemy spectators while focusing on hitting a 90-mile-per-hour fastball. Golf is often a game of distractions, but Tiger Woods' father taught him to ignore them by deliberately shouting when he was about to swing.
- If you have new neighbors, tell them politely if loud music or noise bothers you. As a last resort, call the police.
- If you always jump at noises, examine your hearing or your anxiety levels and the pressures on you in daily life.
- Move into a condo with thick walls.
- If you have a pet with sensitive hearing, expose it to low-volume noises while giving praise or food, then gradually increase the noise level. Provide a safe place for the pet to retreat to when it hears a frightening noise.

A MANTRA TO TELL YOURSELF: *"Noises won't hurt me."*

Reference:

Facing Fears by Ada P. Kahn and Ronald M. Doctor, Checkmark, 2000

See: fear of the unknown, fear of disorder or untidiness, fear of death, fear of illness or pain, fear of weather, fear of crowds

Fear of Weather

astrapophobia (fear of thunderstorms)

chionophobia (fear of snow)

Not even God can hit a 1-iron. —GOLFER LEE TREVINO AFTER BEING STRUCK BY LIGHTNING

Characteristics: This is the preoccupation with weather and weather forecasts, not so much because of health concerns but with regard to driving, property damage, travel and outdoor activities. Some people feel a loss of control in storms, yet others can be exhilarated by them. Many seniors retire to the south to escape northern winters.

Background: Primitive people were so frightened of severe weather that they thought it was evil or sent by the gods to punish them. Many cultures made a god of the sun, which heavily influences the weather. Even today, fear of weather is somewhat healthy because weather can be unpredictable. In some cultures today, the end of the world is supposed to come with a snowbound winter. Eight million Americans suffer from inordinate fear of storms and other weather events.

Strategies:
- Put things in perspective; these days, although weather can change quickly, severe surprise weather is rare. It can usually be predicted and announced over the media. Listen to a radio or television station that has periodic and reliable weather reports.
- Convince yourself that you can tolerate the weather, because, in most cases, you can. Fear of weather can be like fear of terrorism; in both cases, people's fears are often disproportionate to the actual threat. How many people in your area are injured by weather? You're more apt to get a stress-related illness from worry.
- Use common sense in exposing yourself to the elements. Prepare for the sun with sun block, and for rain and snow with a jacket. In cold weather, dress in layers and wear a hat. If you use a cane, buy one with an ice pick for a tip.

- Keep your vehicle in top condition, and make sure it has the right equipment. While driving, use caution without dallying. Some people take defensive driving courses, which are good preparation for heavy weather conditions. In winter, keep road salt and a shovel in the back of your vehicle.
- Tips for getting caught in a thunderstorm: if you can hear thunder, you are close enough to the storm to be struck by lightning. Find shelter in a building or car and keep the windows closed. Go to a low-lying place away from trees, poles and metal objects. Squat low to the ground, but do not lie flat. If caught in the woods, take shelter under shorter trees. If boating or swimming, get to shore immediately.
- If you are inside during a thunderstorm, unplug appliances and turn off the air conditioner. Telephone lines and metal pipes can conduct electricity. Avoid using running water. Draw blinds and shades over windows to prevent glass from shattering due to objects blown by the wind.
- Buy a nature CD with sounds of storms and winds and play it frequently. Go to a local science center that has simulations of weather patterns and get to understand them.

A MANTRA TO TELL YOURSELF: *"I can't control the weather, but I can control my reaction to it."*

Reference:

The Weather Network, www.theweathernetwork.com

See: fear of not having control, fear of death, fear of illness or pain, fear of the unknown, fear of loud noises, fear of falling, fear of travel, fear of driving

4

Fears of the Ego

Fear of Embarrassment

erythrophobia (fear of blushing)

tremophobia (fear of trembling)

We are terrified of being terrified.
—FRIEDRICH NIETZSCHE

Characteristics: People with this condition worry about becoming self-conscious, blushing, stuttering, trembling, freezing under pressure, passing wind in a group of people or being stared at or singled out, perhaps after making a mistake. Serious sufferers may avoid meetings, crowds, criticism or compliments, leadership roles, emotional circumstances or potentially embarrassing situations.

Background: Even the most confident people get embarrassed occasionally. We all like to feel we are in control. Everybody tries to protect their ego, pride or reputation to some extent, but that isn't always possible. Some people get embarrassed easily because they are too sensitive or lack confidence. Blushing is a recent development in human evolution, linked to the development of our brains, self-consciousness and pride. Animals never blush. "Man is the only animal that blushes," said Mark Twain. "Or needs to." Fear of blushing is more common in women than men, yet research shows that those who fear blushing actually do not blush more than people who don't worry about it.

Strategies:

- Try to establish how easily you get embarrassed. Do you get flushed easily in social situations? Do you hesitate to have your photograph taken, to ask for directions when you're lost, to speak your piece in a group or to show your emotions? Do you feel that people are always watching you? This is called the spotlight effect, but research has shown that most people are not watching others to judge them.
- Don't fear making errors or being human; others don't care as much as you do if you have goofed up. If you make a big deal out of your mistakes, you'll make more of them and bring on more embarrassment.

- Accept that you will get embarrassed from time to time, and that it may even be good for you. Laugh it off.
- Learn to raise your panic or discomfort threshold by ridiculing yourself while alone. Say aloud to yourself, "You dummy, how can you be like that?" See how you react, and learn not to take barbs personally.
- Practice embarrassment by bringing attention to yourself in a crowd or by admitting a weakness. On the golf course, deliberately dribble the ball off the tee and smile it off. In each case, watch not only your reaction, but the reaction of others. You will quickly learn that people don't pay that much attention to you, and that you will survive your embarrassment.
- Keep your expectations about yourself reasonable, and don't keep activating your nervous system by defending your weaknesses. We all have our weak spots. Be humble without being self-deprecating. This attitude can take a lot of the pressure off and reduce the situations in which you may feel embarrassed.
- If you get embarrassed easily, you might have to consider the state of your confidence and self-esteem. Talk to someone about it. Consider seeing a therapist.
- If you get embarrassed while you are alone about something that happened when you were with people, chances are that you did something you shouldn't have. For example, if someone said in passing that you might have cheated or "fudged" in the board game Scrabble and you still feel embarrassed when thinking about this later on, chances are you really did cheat.

A MANTRA TO TELL YOURSELF: *"Who cares?"*

Reference:

Beyond Shyness: How to Conquer Social Anxieties by Jonathan Berent, Simon and Schuster, 1993

See: fear of not having control, fear of making mistakes, fear of what others think, fear of getting a compliment, fear of showing emotions, fear of public speaking, fear of singing or dancing

Fear of Failure

atychiphobia (fear of failure)

atelophobia (fear of imperfection)

Failure is just another opportunity to more intelligently begin again.
—HENRY FORD

Characteristics: This widespread fear involves an insecurity or nervousness about a task or a relationship through fear of failing at it. It can lead to worry, indecisiveness, tension, poor productivity and problems in relationships, especially during a pressure situation.

Background: Fear of failure can improve effort and productivity, yet it can also be the parent of many orphans: fear of rejection, fear of loss of control, fear of making mistakes and fear of loss of self-esteem and status. Perfectionists are particularly susceptible. This fear may be learned in the early years, particularly if a person is hounded into doing well or is constantly ridiculed. It can also breed if a person doesn't get recognition for successes or comfort for failures. Some people with obsessive-compulsive disorder have a fear of not doing everything right. However, studies show that failure can actually breed success if it is accepted and viewed in a positive way. Getting something right the first time can actually inhibit creativity!

Strategies:
- If you fear failure at a certain task, it may be simply that you don't have the required physical, mental or emotional resources to meet the challenges and pressures of that task. Upgrade yourself and you'll increase your confidence and expertise.
- Examine whether you are afraid of failing or whether you are really afraid of something else. For instance, your intense anxiety about an upcoming test or job interview may actually be rooted in fear of what your parents or a close friend will think if you don't succeed.
- If you are afraid of failing in *many* areas, examine your ego or confidence issues: are you concerned too much about what others will think if you fail?

- Put your fear into the preparation for a task, not in the task itself. Then focus on the task, your skills and the solution, not on the fear. For example, if you are afraid of an upcoming mathematics test at school, study hard, but when the big day comes, trust yourself and focus on the answers, not on the possibility that you might fail.
- Don't be so hard on yourself. Do you expect to be perfect? Mistakes are not terrible. Everybody makes them. Get on with life. Laugh at yourself without demeaning yourself.
- If you often procrastinate, examine the possibility that, rather than simply being lazy, you might be afraid of failing.
- Don't let failure sap your motivation. Winston Churchill said that success "is going from failure to failure without loss of enthusiasm."
- Up to 70 percent of successful people express feelings of failure, sometimes believing they are fakes or imposters, but this feeling increases their drive to succeed and to prove that they are legitimate.
- If you fail at something important, like an exam or a work project, do something pleasurable to distract yourself from the trouble. Studies show that if you think about failures and problems in a negative way, you come up with fewer solutions.
- In the big picture, if you work hard enough and have enough patience, it is difficult to fail in North America.
- So what if you flunk from time to time? You should only regret failing if you don't get something out of it.

A MANTRA TO TELL YOURSELF: *"Most of the time, I'll succeed."*

Reference:

Overcoming Social Anxiety and Shyness by Gillian Butler, New York University, 1999

See: fear of making mistakes, fear of criticism, fear of rejection, fear of what others think, fear of embarrassment, fear of not having control, fear of taking chances, fear of success or happiness, fear of competition, fear of choking in sports, fear of exams

Fear of Making Mistakes

atelophobia (fear of imperfection)	*Inside of a ring or out, ain't nothing wrong with going down. It's staying down that's wrong.* —MUHAMMAD ALI

Characteristics: This condition involves being hesitant about a job at work, school or home, or about issues in one's personal life, for fear of making a goof of oneself. It can create self-doubt and a reluctance to take chances, and it can prevent people from setting and achieving goals. It can also cause shaking, which would be especially bad for people who work with their hands or fingers.

Background: Fear of making mistakes is the short-term manifestation of the deeper problem of fear of failure. Fear of making mistakes can have its roots in insecurity and low self-esteem. Because society tends to be judgmental, we fear that mistakes will bring us criticism or negative evaluation. Fear of accidents may lead people to hesitate, which can actually make them more susceptible to accidents. On the plus side, fear of making mistakes can motivate us to organize our work and to make a better effort. This fear is often rampant in perfectionists.

Strategies:

- Don't enter a project expecting a guarantee that you will not make mistakes. That is an unrealistic attitude, perhaps even an arrogant one. If you think that way, you'll likely put too much pressure on yourself and make more mistakes.
- If you are involved with an important or high-pressure project, stop worrying and use your talents and training to focus on the task. This mindset will result in fewer errors.
- If you make a serious error, don't use the "I'm not perfect" excuse. If you do, it makes you even less perfect.
- Guess what? The last thing another person wants to see is someone who is perfect. People who are "too perfect" tend to be dull, and the rest of us find them intimidating. Perfection won't bring you many friends.
- Unsuccessful people are those who, fearing mistakes, don't go for the gold. It's okay to make blunders; in 2001, Barry Bonds

hit a record 73 homers but he struck out 93 times! ("Never let the fear of striking out get in your way," said another home-run slugger, Babe Ruth).

- Learn from your mistakes or you may repeat them. Give yourself credit when you bounce back.

- Try to establish whether or not you are a perfectionist by listing the number of times you become anxious over control issues, and why. If you establish that you are a perfectionist, you may want to back off a little. Perfectionism is the fear of being human. Being good is good enough for now. Says clinical psychologist Monica A. Frank, "As you overcome your fear of making mistakes, you will be able to take risks, which allows a person to be successful in career and personal relationships."

What to Tell Children about Mistakes:

- Tell your children it's okay to make mistakes.
- Admit your own mistakes and show how you can learn from them.
- Talk about mistakes made by famous media figures.
- Help your children to learn positive self-talk and to label the mistake—not themselves—as the problem.
- Develop a strategy for dealing with the next mistake.

References:

Behavioral Consultants P.C.
13230 Tesson Ferry Rd.
St. Louis, MO 63128
(314) 843-0080
Monica Frank, Monica@behavioralconsults.com

Education consultant Michele Borba, Michele@moralintelligence.com

See: fear of failure, fear of taking chances, fear of criticism, fear of not having control, fear of the unknown

Fear of Success or Happiness

cherophobia (fear of happiness)	*God would never let me be a success. He'd kill me first.* —GEORGE COSTANZA ON *SEINFELD*, AFTER HEARING THAT HIS PROJECT HAD BEEN UNEXPECTEDLY BOUGHT BY NBC TV
successophobia (fear of success)	
euphobia (fear of hearing good news)	

Characteristics: This condition is akin to fear of failure, but not as common and certainly more subtle and harder to detect in a person. Some people don't realize there is such a thing as fear of success; in a way, it sounds ridiculous. Who wouldn't want to succeed? Yet some people hold back in their job, at school or in social settings for fear of becoming more successful or happy. Others fear having pleasurable feelings (a condition known as hedonophobia).

Background: Some people fear success because they think it might set them up for failure at a higher level. Some are afraid of the trappings of success because they have seen how it has changed others. People may also fear that if they are successful, fate will come crashing down on them shortly thereafter, perhaps because they harbor a feeling that they don't deserve success. Others may feel guilty for achieving happiness when they feel that others don't get the opportunity that they have had. It's a frightening thought sometimes, but nature doesn't want us to be happy as much as it wants us simply to survive. Talk about being complicated beings with a complex background and history!

Strategies:

- If you feel some guilt over success or happiness, try to establish where it comes from and how to change it. Is there an inner voice in your head that keeps telling you that you are not good enough? Ask it for some evidence. Who's to say that you're not worthy of success or contentment? You? If you feel this way, you should heed the words of ex-South African president Nelson Mandela: "We ask ourselves—who am I to be brilliant, gorgeous, talented and fabulous? Actually, who are you not to be?"

- Don't easily dismiss the possibility that your failure may be related to worry about succeeding. It wasn't until golfer Ian Leggatt realized he might be suffering from the fear of success that he finally won his first PGA Tour event at age 36 in 2002.
- Put things into perspective. With the right amount of time and effort, there's no reason you can't reach success.
- Don't intentionally set yourself up for a setback, or give a mediocre performance in a job, just to avoid the agony that you feel may be ahead once you succeed.
- There is no "cosmic" fate that will hit you with failure as soon as you succeed. But if you think there is, you could create a self-fulfilling prophecy.
- Life is short enough as it is; allow it to be sweet when the chance arises. Go for the gold. Other people might want the opportunity you have, but never get it. However, don't feel guilty for others who don't have the opportunity you have; just make the most of your chance.
- If you worry that success will bring more attention to you, develop your people skills so that you will be better prepared to handle it.
- Let's turn this scenario around. It's funny, but when things are going badly, we don't suddenly expect the best to happen, do we? (Maybe we should.)
- The actual definition of happiness may scare people. Happiness is a long-term achievement involving work, sacrifice and love. If you think of it as a short-term feeling, you might be more prone to fearing it will slip through your fingers.

Reference:

Toward a Psychology of Being by Abraham Maslow, John Wiley and Sons, 1998. Maslow makes this point: "We fear our highest possibility, as well as our lowest one. We are generally afraid to become that which we can glimpse in our most perfect moments."

See: fear of failure, fear of taking chances, fear of criticism, fear of embarrassment, fear of what others think, fear of asking for a raise or promotion, fear of getting a compliment

Fear of Criticism

enissophobia (fear of criticism)

criticophobia (fear of critics)

Find the grain of truth in criticism—chew it and swallow it. —DON SUTTON

Characteristics: Fear of critical remarks from others affects us all from time to time. Some people allow stinging criticism to stay in their system for days or weeks, like a virus. Fear of evaluation or criticism leads some people to take fewer chances in everything from their job to their landscaping at home to their choice of clothes. Many people get defensive when they believe they are going to be criticized.

Background: By nature, we all have defense mechanisms set up to protect our psyche from harm. In some people, these mechanisms act like armor that tries to repel everything that comes its way. Because many people are negative and reluctant to balance criticism with praise, we have learned to brace ourselves for the worst. But sometimes, this fear is caused by fear of the truth and all that truth represents, including change. We can make criticism work for us if we accept it as a helpful tool for self-improvement. It's human nature to be more critical of others than we are of ourselves; for example, we may hold a higher standard for a neighbor to be friendly with us than we have for ourselves to be friendly with him.

Strategies:

- Learn to distinguish between destructive and constructive criticism. The first thing to say to your critic is "Thank you." Then step back and analyze the remark. Accepting criticism can build character, encourage growth and keep the ego in check.
- Don't take everything personally. Most criticism is not aimed at you as a person. Look on all criticism as helpful in one way or another. It can tell you what you need to improve, or it can tell you about the source of the criticism. Some critics are people who can't deliver the goods themselves. They may be unhappy and looking to release their frustration on someone else. But if their criticism is about an important subject, get a second opinion.

- Don't adopt a defensive attitude; you'll only *invite* criticism that way.
- If you strike back at a critic out of reflex, examine your attitude and defense mechanisms. Are you defending yourself for the sake of it? Will the truth suffer just to protect your pride or reputation? On the other hand, if you accept all criticism without dialogue, perhaps you are trying to please others too much.
- Get used to hearing critical phrases like: "I didn't like the way you did that," or "I thought your idea was not productive." When no one is around, criticize yourself out loud. "Boy, you goofed on that one!" Or ask people you feel comfortable with what they'd like to see changed. Your ego is like your immune system: it needs exposure to criticism to get stronger and more resilient.
- The fear or anger you feel when you are criticized becomes hormonal energy. It feels negative, but you can channel it into your work or other parts of your life.
- Understand that the more successful you become, the more you'll be criticized. Criticism is a sign that you and your ideas have a stage.
- If you are criticizing others, ask for their input first; this will minimize their defensiveness. (Much of the time when we are being criticized, we are thinking of our rebuttals even before the critic is finished.)
- Try to make your criticism constructive, emphasizing what the recipient is doing, or can do, rather than what he did.

A MANTRA TO TELL YOURSELF: *"What I am afraid of?"* OR *"Can I use this?"*

References:

Elbert Hubbard's Scrap Book by Elbert Hubbard, Firebird Press, 1999. He writes, "To avoid criticism, do nothing, say nothing, be nothing."

The Power of Positive Criticism by Hendrie Weisinger, Anacom, 2000

See: fear of rejection, fear of what others think, fear of embarrassment, fear of failure, fear of showing emotions, fear of taking chances, fear of not being loved, fear of singing or dancing

Fear of Rejection

athazagoraphobia
(fear of being
ignored)

What doesn't kill you makes you stronger.
—Friedrich Nietzsche

Characteristics: Fear of rejection is deeper and often more painful than fear of criticism—it can be viewed as the fear of being left out of something. This can lead to a self-degradation, shyness and even avoidance of social situations. A person may hold back for fear of not getting approval. When you feel rejected by someone close to you, it can really wound your soul.

Background: It's human nature to want to be accepted and liked. Extreme cases could come from childhood rejection or abandonment. People who are very sensitive and people with low self-esteem often suffer from harsh fear of rejection.

Strategies:
* Keep things in perspective. Criticism of your work might be meant as a simple critique with constructive components, not as all-out rejection of you or your work.
* Keep plugging along. A young Elvis Presley was told he couldn't sing by his high school teacher and by the club manager at his first performance, who told him to go back to truck driving. Good thing he didn't!
* Don't let rejection from someone else define you as a person; you're worth more than that. At the same time, do accept your occasional failures as part of who you are—an imperfect being trying to get better.
* If you want to get some experience with rejection and thus develop a thicker skin, get into a job or volunteer position in which you have to make cold calls. People may be gruff with you and even hang up the telephone, but you will learn not to take it personally.
* If you avoid a situation for fear of rejection, you may have regrets later.

- If rejection results in self-pity, you may have self-esteem issues to examine and deal with.
- Gaining approval and acceptance for your skills or your personality is often a journey and a risk. Some people will like you, others won't. Learn about yourself from both.
- Psychotherapist Harry Frith-Smith was not close to his father and developed a type of emotional hole as a result. He attempts to close this hole by playing pickup basketball and poker, by singing in a jazz band and by helping others with their own emotional holes.
- Remember that if someone wholeheartedly rejects you, the issues may be about them, not about you. Or it may be about both of you.

A MANTRA TO TELL YOURSELF: *"Sticks and stones will break my bones, but names will never hurt me "*

Author's Two Cents:

Before my first book was published in 1999, I had received approximately 2,500 consecutive rejections over 32 years. The first 100 were the toughest to take, so I used them to wallpaper my office.

Reference:

Friedrich Nietzsche, The Man and His Philosophy by R. J. Hollingdale, Cambridge University Press, 1999

See: fear of criticism, fear of what others think, fear of failure, fear of taking chances, fear of dating, fear of not being loved

Fear of Getting a Compliment

doxophobia (fear of receiving praise) | *I can live for two months on a good compliment.* —MARK TWAIN

Characteristics: Some people worry about getting into situations in which they could receive a compliment. Although this condition may be subconscious, it may prevent them from trying hard for fear of getting a compliment and subsequently becoming self-conscious about it. It may also cause them to avoid award ceremonies at work for fear of embarrassment or blushing.

Background: If this sounds a lot like the fear of success, it is. Many people receive a compliment and don't know how to respond. We live in a fairly judgmental society and so we are perhaps more used to getting barbs than bouquets. We've also been conditioned to be modest. Some people fear that receiving a compliment at work might lead to higher expectations for them in the future. Nonetheless, a compliment can give a person a warm, motivating feeling when it's accepted properly. If it is not accepted with grace, the giver might not come back with a future compliment, and thus the circle of self-doubt would continue.

Strategies:
- Get used to the sound of your name being exalted. Compliment yourself aloud when no one's around: "You did a good job with that." Give yourself a pat on the back and don't feel sheepish about it. Smile and show emotion. Then rehearse a possible scenario whereby you respond to the compliment with a thank you and keep the conversation going for a while.
- When a person gives you a compliment, accept it without conditions and without downplaying it. If you say you don't deserve it, you may come across as falsely modest. Receiving praise is a bit like receiving a gift—you should accept it with good grace. If it sounds sincere, you may also want to return a compliment, perhaps by saying: "Coming from you, that's a real compliment."

- If others are entitled to your compliment in some way, name them, and explain why. If the praise comes from your superior at work, thank him or her for putting you in a position to succeed in the first place.
- Receiving and giving compliments are ways to develop greater rapport with people. Give compliments to others. Be sincere and specific, but if they don't respond, don't get irritated or act coldly. Perhaps they have inferiority—or even superiority—issues.
- Be prepared to face the fact that you might lack confidence or even have an inferiority complex. Talk to someone you trust about it. Why shouldn't you be worthy of praise? On the other hand, you might have a superior attitude. Perhaps you feel you should receive more praise than you get, or you may feel that the person giving you praise is not worthy of you.
- If you still feel uneasy getting praise, tell that little nagging voice in your head to please keep quiet. Then give it a compliment: "Thanks, anyway, for keeping me in mind."

Reference:

Beyond Shyness by Jonathan Berent, Fireside, 1993

See: fear of embarrassment, fear of criticism, fear of success or happiness, fear of showing emotions, fear of invasion of territory or privacy

Fear of What Others Think

allodoxaphobia (fear of others' opinions)

scopophobia (fear of being looked at)

ego defense (author's definition of how we protect our ego)

In this case, the truth will set you free.
—PSYCHOLOGIST KENNETH SAVITSKY, COMMENTING ON RESEARCH SHOWING THAT FAR FEWER PEOPLE NOTICE OUR MISTAKES OR JUDGE US HARSHLY THAN WE BELIEVE

Characteristics: It is common to feel insecure about how others view you or your work or to feel inadequate in others' eyes. This condition can result in poor performance and can even prevent people from seeking jobs or realizing their dreams. Some people are afraid of being stared at. Some people who worry intensely about what others think can develop a phobia of being imperfect. But this fear can also spur a person to greater heights.

Background: As social creatures, it's natural for us to seek the approval and acceptance of others. A desire to impress someone can be a sign of a healthy relationship, but becomes destructive when it is exaggerated. Those who want to impress others too much often come from homes in which they were not loved enough. This fear can be a good motivator; research shows that people try harder when others are watching—even joggers, who speed up when they believe people are observing them.

Protecting our ego has become important to us in a competitive society. Defending our ego or pride sets off the same fear defense system that is activated by physical threats. Our nervous system has problems differentiating the two; in each case, powerful hormones and energies are released to help us deal with threats. Many high achievers perform incredible feats because they are overcompensating for lack of attention as children. On a smaller scale, fear of what others think motivates us to take care of ourselves and acquire social graces; if we didn't care, many of us would stay in our pajamas all day or pick our noses without guilt.

Strategies:
- Recognize that it is important what *some* people think of you, such as your boss or the people you care about, but it is unimportant what most others think, particularly about trivial issues.

- This is worth repeating: be aware that your nervous system has a hard time distinguishing between a physical threat and a threat to your ego. If you worry too much about others' opinions, you can become anxious and driven by adrenaline.
- If you are trying too hard to please others, examine your motives and attitudes, perhaps even your values. If you want revenge on those who doubt you, you might be able to use this emotional drive productively. "I wanted revenge," actor Anthony Hopkins once said. "I wanted to dance on the graves of a few people who made me unhappy. It's a pretty infantile way to go through life—I'll show them—but I've done it, and I've got more than I ever dreamed of."
- If you do make mistakes, understand that most people probably don't care that much. As psychologist Kenneth Savitsky points out, "You can't completely eliminate the embarrassment you feel when you commit a faux pas, but it helps to know how much you're exaggerating this impact."
- In the end, ask yourself, "Am I going to live my life according to other people's expectations or my own?"
- Make sure you pay attention to your own needs.
- As with many other fears in this section, it's a good idea to practice embarrassing scenarios. You will get used to not caring what others think about inconsequential situations.
- There will always be people who don't like you. If you try to please everyone, you might end up pleasing fewer people, perhaps even no one.
- If you want to impress someone with a job, prepare for it well, and don't make your expectations too high or you might become overly nervous.

A MANTRA TO TELL YOURSELF: *"People's opinions of me are not that important."*

References:

Pressure Golf by Michael Clarkson, Raincoast, 2003

Six Pillars of Self-Esteem by Nathaniel Branden, Bantam, 1994

See: fear of criticism, fear of failure, fear of making mistakes, fear of rejection, fear of not being loved, fear of people, fear of public speaking, fear of embarrassment, fear of showing emotions, fear of what friends think

Fear of Invasion of Territory or Privacy

aphenphosmphobia
(fear of being
touched)

Good fences make good neighbors.
—ROBERT FROST

Characteristics: This condition relates to defending one's territory at work, at home or in public. People with this fear may protect their privacy or personal space, if only through body language. Its effects are often seen in traffic; drivers, believing they are anonymous, are more likely to act out against other drivers who have cut them off. Some people get fidgety standing in a line when they feel someone is gaining an advantage over them. Many nonsmokers get irritated if smokers bother them with secondhand smoke.

Background: Defending territory is a strong and deep-seated animal instinct with roots in our Stone Age past. In our civilized society, many people subdue this instinct until a part of their lives they hold dear is threatened. For example, I know a quiet, mild-mannered man who sometimes acts out in his car because he believes other drivers have entered his personal space. A man whose golf is important to him may get angry if someone in another foursome breaks etiquette and hits the ball near him. Fear of being touched may relate to sexual fears. In many situations, it is difficult to establish where one person's rights begin and another's end.

Strategies:
- Examine the boundaries you establish in your life. Are you too protective in some areas and not enough in others? Are you defending your ego too much? Are you too touchy about criticism?
- Set your borders firmly and fairly, then stand up for the rights you have established.
- Don't protect your rights and territory at the expense of others or at the expense of truth.

- Allow people inside your private space once in a while, if only to learn to become less defensive about it. By *intentionally* letting people go ahead of you in a shop or while driving on the highway, even if they don't have the right of way, you might raise your threshold for tolerance. You should also raise your tolerance levels for others who may be from different backgrounds and who may not share your beliefs about territorial boundaries.
- If someone "trespasses" on your realm at work, don't take it personally; try to find a polite way to let them know. Shift your mindset to neutral and evaluate the situation as objectively as possible.
- If you find yourself overreacting to others in traffic or perhaps in an amateur sports competition, it could mean that you don't have enough control in other areas of your life. While playing a pickup game of basketball at the YMCA, a man started a fight over a foul call. He later apologized, explaining that he felt he was letting someone control him in a personal relationship.
- After all the above has been said, psychologists add that it's okay and even healthy to keep a private space for yourself, even if you are happily married. It could be a quiet time each day or a hobby or a trip that you sometimes take by yourself.

Reference:

Diagonally-Parked in a Parallel Universe: Working Through Social Anxiety by Signe A. Dayhoff, Effectiveness-Plus, 2000

See: fear of other races, fear of strangers, fear of not having control, fear of intimacy or love, sexual fears, fear of driving, fear of solicitors and telemarketers

Fear of Losing Status

kakorrhaphiophobia (fear of defeat)	*I don't want* that *dress.* —A SOCIALITE TO A DRESSMAKER, COMMENTING ON A WARDROBE DESIGNED FOR ANOTHER WOMAN WHOM SHE FELT WAS BENEATH HER

Characteristics: This condition involves anxiety about one's status. For a variety of reasons, people may be reluctant to give up their level of power or achievement or their level of financial, academic, social or career status. When people feel that they are losing status, they may become angry, withdrawn or depressed; conversely, they may become highly motivated and focused. Some people may become rude or disrespectful toward others they believe are not in their class.

Background: Wherever pecking orders or class systems (even subtle ones) are in place, this fear will be important, if sometimes subconscious and unspoken. The baby boomer generation may suffer from this fear more than its predecessors did. In a society in which competition is a driving force, pride is often at stake. Whenever a standard has been set, people find it difficult to drop below it. It's natural for people to hang onto what they have; few people willingly accept a lower quality of housing or food, and few people want to give up travel and vacations. This fear has its benefits, though, and keeps people on their toes, striving to reach another level, or at least to stay on the level they've reached.

Strategies:
- Consider the areas in which you might be reluctant to give up your status, and think about whether or not that's healthy for you and those around you. You might not want to give up your position at work because this would lead to a loss of power or salary, yet you might be willing to relinquish authority in a relationship if you are smothering the other person.
- Make a list of your priorities and keep them in perspective. There's not necessarily anything wrong with congratulating yourself if you've worked hard to give your family the best and encouraged them to remain humble and appreciative about it.

A certain amount of pride can be healthy, but do you keep a lot of status symbols—shiny cars, walls filled with plaques, bumper stickers saying "My child is an honor student"— merely to impress people?

- Don't overwork yourself just to keep up with the Joneses. Your desire for status may be unhealthy if it makes you distressed, tired and run down, or if it makes you neglect your friends and family.
- Talk to people who have gone through the process of gaining wealth and status, and who have accepted a leveling or even a decline in these as they got older. You can learn from them.
- Don't be afraid to swallow humble pie once in a while. It can make you grow as a person. To keep your head from swelling, take a volunteer job, perhaps in a soup kitchen. You are no better than anyone else; you may have had a different upbringing and support system, more resilient genes, and a different set of opportunities and talents that allowed you to be more productive than others.
- Examine your issues of ego and self-consciousness. What is your reaction when your neighbor parks his new SUV near your five-year-old sedan? Does materialism play too large a role in defining who you are?
- At work, if your competitors drive themselves too hard to get the upper hand, that's their problem; don't allow it to become yours.

A MANTRA TO TELL YOURSELF: *"Remember priorities."*

Reference:

No Contest: The Case Against Competition by Alfie Kohn, Houghton Mifflin, 1986

See: fear of invasion of territory or privacy, fear of competition, financial fears, fear of what others think, fear of what friends think

Fear of Oneself

autophobia (fear of being alone)

phonophobia (fear of one's own voice)

I have more trouble with myself than any other man. —EVANGELIST DWIGHT L. MOODY

Characteristics: People may avoid situations from fear of how they might react. For example, many people avoid relatives because of potential confrontations; others avoid singing or dancing for fear of blushing. On a deeper level, some people are afraid to confront the truth about themselves and may be in denial about such things as their own rudeness, depression, alcoholism or anger. U.S. General George S. Patton once said, "I don't fear failure. I only fear the slowing up of the engine inside of me which is pounding, saying 'Keep going, someone must be on top, why not you?'" Many people with this fear do not like to be alone because it gives them too much time to think about themselves.

Background: We rarely think about being afraid of ourselves because confronting this feeling may be embarrassing or mean we have to change. That's why denial is so popular. Nevertheless, it may be worth overcoming this fear because there may be important issues that need addressing. Many people don't like themselves enough, and most are not as self-aware as they should be. In the words of psychotherapist Nathaniel Branden, "Most human beings are sleepwalking through their own existence."

Strategies:
- Get to know what makes you tick, explore why you act or react in a certain way and figure out whether that is good or bad. Write down your attitudes, motives, beliefs, needs, reactions—and then evaluate them. Be prepared to explore your inner feelings and perhaps your past.
- Explore your weaknesses. Are you afraid of a situation because you might panic, be lazy, or become angry or too frank? You might avoid leadership because you worry that you don't have the confidence to confront colleagues. As the philosopher Aristotle puts it, "I count him braver who overcomes his desires than him who conquers his enemies, for the hardest victory is over self."

- It is okay to be imperfect and even to fib once in a while. No one is so self-assured that they don't misrepresent themselves at times. Each of us is a work in progress. Be kind to yourself and you will learn to respect yourself more. A.J. Mahari, who has been treated for a personality disorder, says: "One of the most beneficial gifts you can give yourself is the ability to sit with yourself being who you are and accepting that, all your mistakes, shortcomings and weaknesses included."

- Assess whether you avoid competitive situations at work, home or school because of the fear of your own potential reaction.

- By exploring your fear, you'll develop greater understanding of yourself and the possible routes to self-growth. Most often, we change only when change is forced upon us. What if we *volunteered* to change?

- Before you try to improve, learn to love or at least to understand rather than fear yourself. Get to know your strengths as well as your weaknesses.

- If you fear in advance how you might react to a situation, it may be a sign that a defense mechanism is helping to hide one of your faults. I sometimes avoid pickup basketball games with younger players because I worry that the ugly side of my ego will come out. When I catch myself thinking this way, I make myself join the game and work on building a healthier ego.

- If you are angry with yourself, assess the situation, but after it is over, heed the advice of author Alexander Chase: "To understand is to forgive, even oneself."

- Deepen your spirituality by putting less emphasis on yourself and your needs and more on others'. Volunteer your time.

A MANTRA TO TELL YOURSELF: *"Knowing me can only help me."*

References:

The Road Less Traveled by M. Scott Peck, Simon & Schuster, 1998

The Six Pillars of Self-Esteem by Nathaniel Branden, Bantam, 1994

See: fear of embarrassment, fear of competition, fear of showing emotions, fear of being alone

Fear of Showing Emotions

angrophobia (fear of anger)	*People who never get carried away should be.* —MALCOLM FORBES, ART COLLECTOR, PUBLISHER
counterphobia (fear of fearful situations)	

Characteristics: This condition often involves a reluctance to cry, laugh or show anger, embarrassment or other emotions. People may become expressionless or rigid in reacting to situations, or they may avoid potentially emotional situations. Some people fear laughter (geliophobia).

Background: It is hard to define exactly what emotions are, but one definition is that emotions appear when needs are not being met or have recently been met. We often hide our emotions for fear of looking weak or out of control, or for fear that others will be able to read us. Some people see emotions as inferior to reason and thought. Many men fear that by crying, they'll appear effeminate. Members of older generations and of certain cultures (including Western cultures) discourage the showing of emotions and encourage always being in control. A person who had problems showing emotions as a child will likely have the same trouble as an adult because his or her emotional suppression will become automatic.

Strategies:

- Gauge how you react to certain people and situations, and why. Are your needs being met, or do you sometimes need to hug someone and still hold back? Do you withhold a belly laugh when one is called for?
- Try to let go once in a while and experience the buzz of emotions, including their highs and lows, their cleansing effects, and the freedom they give you from your hangups. On the other hand, if you cry at the drop of a hat, you may be out of control, in which case you'll want to raise your emotional threshold in certain areas.
- Don't believe that crying is always a sign of weakness, because the reverse is often true. Crying shows that you are not afraid to show how you feel, or that perhaps you are but you go

ahead and do it anyway. That takes courage and humility, both of which build character.

- You may be afraid to let your emotions come out because you fear the truth. Often we don't want to reveal our true feelings to others. We may be afraid to show that we are sentimental, that we care deeply for someone, or even that we despise someone.
- Remember that the most attractive men and women in entertainment, such as actors Mel Gibson and Julia Roberts, have a vulnerable quality to them that endears them to their fans.
- Try to be less focused on yourself, especially in your concern for how others view you. As clinical psychologist Gillian Butler says, "The less self-conscious you are, the easier it is to be yourself, and to join in spontaneously with what is going on around you."

Author's Two Cents:

A stiff upper lip helped my British ancestors get through two wars and the Depression, but it gave some of us emotional problems. I was finally able to cry in front of my kids when they were in their early teens—when Canadian sprinter Ben Johnson was caught cheating at the Olympics. My sons put their arms around me. I felt not ashamed, but liberated. Later, when my first grandchild was born, I was not only pleased when my son cried, I joined him.

References:

Facing Fear, Finding Courage by Sarah Quigley, Conari, 1996

Managing Your Mind: The Mental Fitness Guide by Gillian Butler and Tony Hope, Oxford, 1997

See: fear of singing or dancing, fear of not having control, fear of intimacy or love, fear of embarrassment, fear of criticism, fear of what others think, fear of confrontation or conflict

Fear of Having a Photo Taken

camera shy *eisoptrophobia* (fear of seeing oneself in a mirror)	*When you smile for the camera, smile not just with your lips but with your eyes. Tap your source of joy from within by thinking happy thoughts, remembering loved ones or happy moments.* —PORTRAIT AND FASHION PHOTOGRAPHER DOMINIQUE JAMES

Characteristics: This condition involves fear of cameras. It's common for people to act unnatural or to pull a face in front of a camera. Some people avoid group pictures or even throw their hands over their face or leave the room.

Background: Many people are simply self-conscious. Others have a difficult time suddenly "turning on" before a camera. Camera-shy people may worry about their appearance or try to look the way they think other people think they should look. On a deeper level, they may have image or self-esteem issues. The recent popularity of video cameras has made many people loosen up about having their pictures taken.

Strategies:

- Take a look at some of your photos. Are you satisfied with them? Do you look the way you think you should look?
- When you make a fuss for a photographer, you bring more attention to yourself than if you just relaxed and let her shoot. The only person who is conscious of your being self-conscious is you, and this self-consciousness can give you a reputation for not wanting your picture taken.
- At picture time, take a few seconds to compose yourself and relax your facial muscles. Put your chin down to eliminate your neck. To hide a double chin, extend your neck slightly forward toward the camera.
- Remember that an amateur photographer is not focusing so much on you as he is on the mechanics of getting the picture done.

- If you don't perk up, the picture will turn out badly and you'll be documented for history as grumpy. Remember that people will pay more attention if you *don't* smile. Laugh for the camera while thinking about this silly fear or pretending that the birdie is someone who makes you chuckle. Or look at the lens like it is a mirror. In fact, practice by smiling at yourself in a mirror.
- Imagine the best-case scenario: you may wind up in a studio in the mall as a picture of the month, along with those angels and perfect weddings.
- Act naturally. The camera is just another eye looking at you. People tend to make too much of it.
- Buy yourself a camera and shoot other people. When you realize what it's like from the other side, getting your picture taken won't be so painful a process.
- If you don't like pictures of yourself in a group, cut your head out.
- Photos are great! They're a record that you lived.

References:

Overcoming Anxiety by Reneau Z. Peurifoy, Owl, 1997

Kodak PhotoNet Online, www.photonet.com

www.takegreatpictures.com

See: fear of embarrassment, fear of what others think, fear of your appearance, fear of criticism, fear of getting a compliment

Fear of Choking in Sports

anginophobia (fear of choking)

author's definition of choking: When emotions have a negative effect on an athlete's performance.

It's okay to have butterflies in your stomach, just get them flying in formation.
—ANONYMOUS

Characteristics: From time to time, most athletes fear failing in clutch situations. Some remain underachievers because they seize up under pressure, often losing their self-confidence and feeling anxious and tense. Some athletes fear crowds. Others thrive on pressure and use their fear hormones to improve their performance.

Background: When an athlete feels intense pressure, the fight-or-flight response causes her muscles to become tense with an overload of adrenaline and her fingers to shake as blood is diverted to the large muscles. Fine motor skills can break down, along with focus, but emotional drive and skills involving strength can improve. There may be more choking these days in elite amateur sports because of the pressure of gaining professional status or a university sports scholarship. A survey of 1,000 Americans showed that 44 percent feared embarrassing themselves in a sport. At the same time, there are more sports psychologists and teachers than ever before to help athletes with these kinds of emotional issues.

Strategies:
- If you're playing for fun, don't get too psyched up and don't put your ego on the line; that attitude just ruins everyone's game. What is there to prove?
- If you prepare your skills in advance, emotions can enhance your performance in competitive sports, especially if you train with pressure or simulated pressure. Pretend that a game is on the line and that your effort will make the difference.
- If you feel that your emotions will affect your performance, use visualization before the event. Picture everything. Imagine that mistakes or problems come up along the way, but visualize yourself dealing with them and attaining victory. Some athletes even imagine the sounds and smells of an event; when the action starts, they feel they've already been there.
- Stay in the present and focus on the task rather than on the

potential results, allowing your hormones to sharpen your skills.

- Some star athletes have used their insecurity and "I'll show you" attitude to produce record performances. They channel their insecurity and fears into their preparation, then focus tightly on their skills during the event.
- Try to stay in an optimal or manageable level of arousal during the performance. Optimal levels of arousal for various sports are as follows (5 being the highest): 5, football blocking and tackling, 220-yard and 440-yard runs, weightlifting; 4, long jump, sprints, swimming, wrestling; 3, most basketball, soccer and gymnastic skills, boxing, high jump; 2, baseball pitching and hitting, football quarterbacking, tennis; 1, archery, bowling, golf short game, basketball free throws.
- Serious athletes can raise their optimal levels of arousal over the course of a career, especially if they train under pressure.
- If you get too worked up during the action, use deep breathing or positive self-talk to keep oxygen in your system and relax you. In special instances, you can divert the "fear hormones" by briefly getting angry and putting them directly into your skills. Other strategies include looking at your task as a challenge or using a mantra, such as "Just do it!"
- Find a cue, such as a mantra or thought, that brings you back to an optimal level of arousal. Olympic gold medal diver Greg Louganis thought of his mother when he was nervous.
- If you make a mistake, forget it for the time being or it could lead to further frustration. Pretend to flush it down a toilet.
- If you choke from time to time, admit it. It doesn't mean you're a choker. The world's best athletes choke under pressure once in a while.

A MANTRA TO TELL YOURSELF: *"Focus!"*

References:

Competitive Fire by Michael Clarkson, Human Kinetics, 1999

Mental Training for Peak Performance by Steven Ungerleider, Rodale Press, 1996

See: fear of failure, fear of not having control, fear of what others think, fear of competition, fear of illness or pain, fear of confrontation or conflict, fear of crowds, fear of making mistakes, fear of success or happiness

PART

5

Fears at Home

Fear and Stress in Children

In many ways, children resemble phobic adults, with simplistic, generalized reasoning and an unsophisticated linking of cause and effect. —RUSH W. DOZIER, IN HIS BOOK *FEAR ITSELF*

Characteristics: Children get nervous about many things—other people, the dark, being alone, monsters, going to school, and not living up to parents' or their friends' expectations. Youngsters are dependent on others for survival. Some may feel "separation anxiety" when they are away from their parents, and it may keep them from joining activities. Research on children aged 5 to 12 shows that 20 percent fear ghosts and the supernatural, 15 percent fear being alone, in the dark or in strange places, 14 percent fear people or animals, and 13 percent fear being hurt, ill or in pain. About 25 percent of children between 6 and 12 have nightmares.

Background: Children have more fears than adults because they haven't had enough experience to rationalize or adapt to many of their fears. It can be scary when you are doing things for the first time. Today's kids have lots of demands. Both parents may be working, leaving a void in the nurturing process. Young girls may fear they are not as attractive as teenagers in fashion ads. As they get older, children become more afraid of social harm and getting their feelings hurt. Inhibited children may be highly reactive and have an increased heart rate. Most children outgrow most of their fears.

Strategies:
- Don't smother your children and make all the decisions for them and do all their worrying. Kids should be allowed to face their fears gradually through experience and education.
- Reassure your children about life by telling them you love them, but more importantly, show them you love them by your actions.
- If children have specific fears, encourage them to gradually face the fear, but don't do it all at once with a sink-or-swim approach.
- Be aware of what is available at your child's school. Many middle schools in the U.S. are putting stress management skills on their curriculum. Some Girl Scout groups have a badge for taking a stress reduction course.

- If children get nightmares, monitor their television and movie watching. Even some cartoons are scary. Don't belittle your children's fears. They are real to them.
- Children fear failure just like adults do, and they feel inadequate when they fail. Once they start a project or join a club or group, encourage them to see it through. Tell them it's okay to fail once in a while.
- If a child develops an inferiority complex, encourage him to keep his expectations in perspective and accept his limitations. Help children to respect and love themselves.
- Many children pick up distress and mindsets from their parents. Show affection and respect toward your spouse when your children are around, and avoid serious confrontations in front of them. Their feelings and fears about the world are often conditioned by the level of conflict in the family.
- A family pet is a great way to relieve stress and keep children active, but make sure it doesn't run the house.
- Make sure your kids have quiet time and fun and don't push them too much into organized activities. Research shows that from 1981 to 1997, children's leisure time dropped from 40 percent to 25 percent. "The baby boomers want to give their kids everything and have their kids be in everything: soccer, swimming or piano," says child psychologist Sharon Post. "The kids may feel there just isn't a lot of joy in accomplishment. There's more pressure."

A MANTRA TO TELL YOURSELF: *"Help them face their fears."*

References:

Cool Cats, Calm Kids: Relaxation and Stress Management for Young People by Mary L. Williams and Dianne O'Quinn Burke, Impact, 1996

Keys to Parenting Your Anxious Child by Katharina Manassis, Barron's, 1996

See: fear of change, fear of not being loved, fear of making mistakes, fear of being alone, fear of the dark and all of the fears at school

Fear for Your Children's Safety

*Healthy children will not fear life if their elders have integrity
enough to not fear death.* —PSYCHOLOGIST ERIK ERIKSON

Characteristics: This is the worry about the health and safety of
one's children. It can affect every aspect of life, from concern
about their day care or school to worry about the safety of the
playground or about them getting the flu bug. This fear can make
some parents overprotective, even paranoid. Some parents don't
even allow their children to take healthy risks or to develop relationships, and may keep them out of activities and organizations.
One survey showed that parents worry more about their kids driving safely than about drug and alcohol abuse or pregnancy.

Background: Most parents fear for their children, and this fear
may last their whole lives. Since parents are children's primary
caregivers, this is nature's way of ensuring our survival as a
species. Throughout the animal kingdom, parents are usually overprotective; that's why visitors in forests fear bears when the cubs
are nearby. In fearing for our kids, though, sometimes we fear for
ourselves. We worry about how we would react if something happened to them. And we fear that if our children come to harm, we
might get the blame.

Strategies:

- Teach your kids to be street-smart, to be friendly but cautious
  and intelligent about their choices of friends and activities.
- Don't make your kids grow up in a bubble. Your children will
  never be as safe as you think they should be, and sometimes we
  show a double standard by not allowing them to take the
  chances we would take. If you overprotect, they may not learn
  to be self-sufficient when they need to be, and they will likely
  become fearful adults. However, remember that inhibited children may need more reassurance for challenging situations,
  such as leaving the house or joining an organization.
- For parents who constantly worry when their children go to
  school or a playground to be with friends, understand that it is
  usually safe. In fact, the chances of your child being abused by

someone are very small. Be wary of sensational media reports of crimes against children. In recent years, the mainstream media have sometimes made it appear that there are rashes of child abductions when, in fact, they have simply chosen to focus on that subject for a while.

- If they are not allowed to take some chances, children will be set up for a boring life and perhaps develop an inflexible mindset. Do you want them to be unfulfilled?

- Don't leave young children alone. Have them walk to school with an older child or take them yourself. If they are home alone, tell them not to answer the door and to tell callers that their parents are unable to come to the phone. Monitor your children's Internet use and caution them not to meet strangers after exchanging e-mails.

- Teach children how to use 911 and leave phone numbers of relatives and friends near the phone. As they get older, teach them solid fundamentals about things like sex, driving and drug abuse.

- When selecting a good day-care program, make sure that it has: a good child-to-adult ratio, experienced staff, proper and updated physical facilities, a low staff turnover rate, and high-quality interactions between staff with children.

- If your children take too many risks and do not take legitimate safety concerns seriously, such as following rules and regulations on schoolyard apparatus, they may have an underactive nervous system and not realize the dangers involved.

A MANTRA TO TELL YOURSELF: *"Street-smart, but friendly."*

References:

Protecting the Gift: Keeping Children and Teenagers Safe (and Parents Sane) by Gavin de Becker, Dell, 2000

Two Jobs, No Life by Peter Marshall, Key Porter, 2001

www.thefamilycorner.com

See: fear of the unknown, fear of not having control, fear of responsibility, fear of terrorism, fear and stress in children, fear of becoming a parent, fear of bullies, sexual fears, fear of children leaving home, fear of driving

Fear of Children Leaving Home

empty-nest syndrome: a feeling that can envelop parents when their children grow up and leave home

There is nothing more thrilling in this world, I think, than having a child that is yours, and yet is mysteriously a stranger.
—AGATHA CHRISTIE

Characteristics: When children leave for university or move out of the family home, many parents feel some anxiety; some even become depressed. But the children's departure can also bring a sense of relief and fulfillment after years of responsibility and hard work.

Background: A parent's desire to protect his or her children never wears off. Nature has programmed this into us. When someone has lived with you for two decades or more (children tend to stay home longer these days), it is natural to feel sadness when they leave and to miss them deeply. Some people also feel as though they are suddenly living in a vacuum. This feeling strikes more women than men, but that may be changing as parenting roles evolve.

Strategies:

- Don't let the empty nest sneak up on you. Prepare yourself for the time your children will leave home by starting something new, perhaps a hobby or a paid or volunteer job. Renew old friendships. Begin to look on the empty nest as a transition period to a new time in your life.
- Congratulate yourself. Feel proud that you have helped your child graduate into the big world. Hold a party or buy a gift for yourself or your child.
- When your children start living away from home, don't show up at their place every day or even every few days; if you do, they won't learn self-sufficiency. But try to be close enough at hand that they can still seek you for comfort or advice.
- If you feel an emotional or physical void, try something you've never done, something exciting, like skydiving or coaching a Little League baseball team.

- Spend time with other people whose children have recently moved out of the family home.
- Don't sit at home fretting about your children leaving, and don't exaggerate the way life was with them. It's hard to focus on life if you are always weeping sentimental tears.
- If you are married, this is a time to rediscover one another and get a second wind in your relationship. You now have time to devote to each other, which you didn't have with a full house. But don't smother one another because your children are suddenly gone.
- However it turns out, don't despair—the birds will fly home again, perhaps with their own children. That will bring you a whole new set of wonders and challenges to deal with and enjoy.

A MANTRA TO TELL YOURSELF: *"Hold them close, then let them go."*

References:

How to Survive and Thrive in an Empty Nest by Jeanette and Robert Lauer, New Harbinger, 1999

www.thefamilycorner.com

See: fear for your children's safety, fear of not having control, fear of change, fear of the unknown, fear of being alone, fear of not being loved

Fear of Becoming a Parent

lockiophobia (fear of childbirth)

fear of storks!

There are at least two advantages to having a baby—homeless people will not sift through your trash anymore and your tolerance will develop for loud, piercing shrills. —FROM WWW.THEFAMILYCORNER.COM

Characteristics: Some people are apprehensive about having children, for a variety of reasons—health issues, financial constraints or the drastic change of lifestyle. Others fear they will be too anxious or overreact as parents or do too much for their kids. This fear can make people avoid friends or relatives who have children.

Background: Who wouldn't have some concerns about bringing another human being into the world and raising him or her? What a responsibility! This fear can make people consider whether they are fit to be parents, but it might also make qualified parents more anxious than they should be. Being a parent takes, patience, strength, knowledge, compassion and financial responsibility, but all of these qualities can be strengthened by actually going through parenthood. There is really no manual for how to be a parent, but by tapping into their common sense and strengths, people can learn to become effective full-time caregivers. Some people don't respect parenthood enough and have children without properly caring for them.

Strategies:

- Talk openly with your partner if you want to have a child. Discuss whether you are responsible and financially and emotionally stable enough. Don't feel pressure to have kids just because most people in your family or circle of friends did. Not everyone has to be a parent; the human species will carry on.
- If you are unsure whether you can be an excellent parent, ask your doctor or midwife to refer you to a social worker for information. Talk to family members and friends who have children.
- Prepare yourself for a roller-coaster ride. It takes hard work and patience and a willingness to learn as you go along. But you will grow and earn a greater understanding of life.

- All babies are different—even those from the same parents—and they don't come with a user manual. Raise them as such (although you will want to keep the same standards for all your children, which is another issue).
- If you are pregnant, channel your anxiety into constructive behavior: start prenatal care early; eat well and learn about nutrition; avoid drugs and stop smoking or cut down; get regular exercise; read a book about raising children; prepare your home for the newborn; go to childbirth education classes; sing to your baby.
- Remember that serious problems during pregnancy and with a newborn are rare. Before the baby arrives, discuss with your partner the sharing of responsibilities.
- Have patience, tolerance and desire. We are born with parenting skills; they may be latent, but they can be developed.
- In the early days of parenthood, make time for yourself and occasionally leave the child with someone you trust. It will relieve some of the pressure of being together all of the time. Expect some strains between you and your partner as you make the transition into parenthood; a new mother may be occupied with the child and the father may feel ignored.
- If you are thinking about becoming a parent after the age of 30, be aware that many experts believe that when parents are more established in their careers, children are less of a threat. Older men tend to be better fathers, and both parents are generally calmer, more patient and better able to go with the flow.

A MANTRA TO TELL YOURSELF: *"Am I up to the job?"*

References:

The Eight Seasons of Parenthood by Barbara Unell and Jerry Wyckoff, Random House, 2000

The ABCs of Pregnancy, www.abcbirth.com

Child and Youth Health, www.cyh.com

See: fear of the unknown, fear of responsibility, fear of commitment, fear of change, fear of intimacy or love, fear of invasion of territory or privacy, fear of illness or pain, fear for your children's safety

Fears for Your Marriage/Partnership

A great marriage is not when the perfect couple comes together. It is when an imperfect couple learns to enjoy their differences.
—HUMORIST/AUTHOR DAVE MEURER

Characteristics: Worry about whether one's marriage or partnership will last is quite common. There can be numerous negative consequences, such as people becoming too close to their children, being possessive or distrustful of their partner, or feeling distress and withdrawal. One person may try too hard to compensate for the other. Some women overlook physical abuse to maintain a relationship. But healthy worry can create more effort, compromise, intimacy and ultimately a stronger relationship.

Background: There will always be changes, swings and even fears in partnerships. If kept manageable, this is a good fear and motivates people to work on their bond. When a marriage is not healthy, at least one person's needs are not being met and at least one person is not putting in enough effort. Most arguments are about money and children. About half of today's marriages end in divorce, and often there is more than one reason for it. In recent times, the number of marriages has steadily decreased in North America.

Strategies:
- Be on the lookout for signs of trouble: Is communication breaking down? Is one person or both people losing interest? Are disagreements and distrust becoming more frequent?
- Become close friends. You're together every day. Talk, talk, talk—about things big and small and sometimes inconsequential. Find out what the other person wants and needs. Have fun and socialize with others; double-date.
- Don't put too much pressure on the other person to change or to compromise. Respect your partner and give him or her the freedom to think for themselves, and give them *time* to themselves. Even in the closest friendships, we are still individuals.
- Keep responsibilities close to 50-50, although that may not be possible in some areas.
- Men, be aware that, because of their social conditioning and perhaps genetic programming, women generally do more than you

in parenting and keeping relationships working. Pitch in and take off some of the load in this new age when most women are also working outside the home.

- One definition of love is when two people's needs come together (or is that knees?). But love often comes after marriage and takes work, commitment, sacrifice and genuine caring. As psychologist/author Stephen Covey says, "Love the feeling is a fruit of love the verb."
- Draw on one another's strengths, but don't judge weaknesses too harshly. Be prepared to discover that the thing that annoys you about your partner may be a flaw that you also have.
- Tend to the little things that show you care—for example, leaving a note behind when you go on a trip or doing an unscheduled chore without taking credit.
- If you have children, allow them to bring you together, not to pull you apart. That means working together, often with some compromise, on your parenting approach.
- Work on keeping your sex life healthy. That is not easy if both of you are busy, but you must make time for pleasure.
- If you have serious problems, see a counselor or discuss them with people you trust.
- After fights, kiss and make up. Don't break up without having put in a solid effort.

A MANTRA TO TELL YOURSELF: *"What's right for us?"*

References:

Making Love Last Forever by Gary Smalley, Word Publications, 1997

The Five Love Languages: How to Express Heartfelt Commitment to Your Mate by Gary Chapman, Northfield, 1992

www.dearpeggy.com (advice on how to deal with an affair)

www.sexualmarriage.com (for sexual issues)

www.marriagebuilders.com (for general issues)

See: fear of not being loved, fear of sex, fear of intimacy or love, fear of rejection, fear of becoming a parent, fear of the opposite sex, fear of being alone, fear of commitment

Fear of Family Get-Togethers

syngenesophobia (fear of relatives) soceraphobia (fear of parents-in-law)	*[At a party] think about sharing friendship and happiness, and how you fit into all of it, rather than trying to do what you think everyone else wants you to do.* —ANXIETY RESEARCHER CATHLEEN HENNING

Characteristics: Some people are reluctant to attend family gatherings, especially when certain people are expected to be there. Others may feel anxious and shy at a party, or become confrontational with others, especially if there is baggage in the relationship. This fear can keep relationships in the family from growing.

Background: You can choose your friends, but you can't choose your relatives, so the old saying goes. Families are thrown together, for better or for worse, and there will always be discomfort and personality clashes in some cases, especially if one person views another as controlling or rude or sees them as competition. Some people don't want to get too close to relatives because of the work entailed in a relationship. But the family is a natural phenomenon, and we can learn a lot about ourselves from our family.

Strategies:
- Approach a get-together with the idea that you are going to give something or learn something. The more selfish or self-conscious you are, the less likely you are to have a good time.
- Make a family tree. Family is important and deep-rooted in human evolution; don't let yours dissolve easily. We all have some responsibility for maintaining harmony in the extended family, if only to give the children a chance to have relationships. But don't force family structure on those who don't buy into it.
- If you are a guest, take something special for the hosts, such as an unexpected box of sweets or a house gift.
- Think back to parties you dreaded; they rarely turned out as badly as you had anticipated. You might have even had a laugh or a memory to cherish.

- Lower your expectations with relatives, especially if you see them rarely. Remember that we are often more critical of other people than we are of ourselves, particularly if they have a fault similar to one of ours. To ease the pressure on get-togethers or holidays, try to keep in touch with relatives throughout the year. Schedule periodic family reunions.
- If you have a serious problem with a relative, get it out into the open when you are alone with them, if only for your peace of mind. If you share it in front of others, it could damage your relationship further.
- Try not to drag your problems along with you on family vacations. Organize a variety of settings and activities so everyone can let their family issues go for a day or two.
- If you host a party, use common sense: have a variety of activities and food; if possible, have indoor and outdoor areas; make rules for smoking; provide accommodation or cabs for drinkers. Then relax—it's up to the guests to enjoy themselves. You'll never please everybody.
- Consider the fact that maybe you are too shy and need to work on your people skills. Hey, maybe it's not them, it's you!

A MANTRA TO TELL YOURSELF: *"Make an effort."*

References:

How to Entertain People You Hate: Tips on How to Have a Good Time with Bad Company by Ari Alexandra Boulanger, CCC Publications, 2003

Why Bother? Why Not? A Hollywood Insider Shows You How to Entertain Like a Star by Laurin Sydney, Cliff Street, 2000

See: fear of what others think, fear of criticism, fear of people, fear of singing or dancing, fear of not having control, fear of responsibility, fear of confrontation or conflict, fear of not being loved, fear of intimacy or love, fear of oneself

Fear of a Break-in

| *scelerophobia* (fear of burglars) | *I feel depressed. I'm scared. I can't sleep all night. I go into my bedroom and I know somebody has been there.* |
| | —ZEZA, VICTIM OF A BREAK-IN |

Characteristics: It's common for homeowners and residents to worry about someone breaking into their home and stealing their valuables or harming them. This fear can cause some anxious people to rarely leave their home, particularly if they have already been a victim. Some people, fearing a home invasion, are reluctant to answer their door. Others feel traumatized for years after an incident.

Background: A break-in is an invasion of physical and personal privacy. In the United States, there is one burglary every 15 seconds. Although there is no foolproof way to protect our homes, 90 percent of break-ins can be prevented through common sense and a little thought. This fear motivates us to protect our loved ones and possessions.

Strategies:

- Your fence should be see-through (with no thick hedges in front) so that burglars who get inside can be seen from the street. Clear shrubs and "hiding places" away from doors and windows.
- Make sure you keep porch, garage and rear lights on all night.
- If you live in a high-crime area or near a highway, consider motion-detector lights. Burglars hit 40 percent more often within three blocks of major "getaway" thoroughfares.
- Lock all doors and windows, even when you're home. An unlocked second-floor window can be entered. Keep ladders locked away.
- Don't hide a key near a door; that's one of the first things burglars look for. And don't leave notes on the door when you're away.
- Install deadbolt locks on entrances. Glass panels on sliding doors can be easily smashed, so use Plexiglas.

- Keep money and valuables locked up or hidden well. Make a list of your valuables, even take photos of them. If they don't have serial numbers, put your driver's license number on them, making them easier to track if they're stolen.
- Make everyone in your house streetwise and wary of suspicious characters in the neighborhood.
- Inform your neighbors when you will be away and ask them to watch the premises. And don't advertise your absence. Have someone pick up your newspapers and mail, and don't leave a message on your answering machine referring to your absence.
- Once you have done all of the above, relax. Remember that when you have done everything in your control, there is no point worrying.

A MANTRA TO TELL YOURSELF: *"Safety first."*

Reference:

Keep Safe! 101 Ways to Enhance Your Safety and Protect Your Family by Donna Koren Wells and Bruce C. Morris, Hunter House, 2000

See: fear of the unknown, fear of invasion of territory or privacy, fear of being mugged, fear of being alone, fear of the dark, worry at night and sleeplessness

Fear of Delivering Bad News

An important part of leadership is the ability to deliver bad news. Unfortunately, it's as unnatural as the embouchure for the oboe (trust me), so we usually flub it on our first time out.
—BUSINESS CONSULTANT BOB LEWIS

Characteristics: Delivering bad or sensitive news can cause anxiety for a lot of people, especially if it is about an illness, downsizing, or the fact that the person didn't get a job or is being let go. Some people pass the buck to others to deliver the news.

Background: We are rarely comfortable with the feeling of fear, whether it is our own fear or that of others. And we know that delivering bad news to others usually evokes a negative emotional response. Telling someone about an emergency or the death of a relative is a job that police never get used to. Many medical schools still don't train students in how to tell patients and relatives about serious illnesses. Most people are uncomfortable talking about death, and many emergency services personnel use gallows humor to deal with it. In general, we deal poorly with emotional issues.

Strategies:
- Try to pick the right environment to tell someone bad news, and try to make it a private, face-to-face meeting.
- Plan carefully what you are going to say and how you will say it. Make sure you are calm; use deep breathing or meditation, perhaps even visualization as you rehearse what you are going to say. Unlike good news, bad news should not be delivered spontaneously.
- If you're having trouble making the decision to do it, remind yourself that this is a great chance to show responsibility and leadership. Draw on your inner strength. Seek the advice of others, who may know something about the person you don't know. If you always pass the buck about telling bad news, work on your people skills. You might have to toughen up mentally.

- If the news is deeply sensitive, touch the person first. It helps you connect with them, and vice versa. Have them sit down (some people can faint). Speak softly, slowly and confidently; the person may pick up on your anxiousness. You may have to repeat the bad news because some people immediately freeze upon hearing it.
- Be frank and to the point, and try to avoid sugarcoating the news. Begin with, "I have some unpleasant news," or "I'm sorry I have to tell you..."
- Be prepared for an emotional reaction and try to detach yourself from it. If the person reacts badly—even if they take it out on you—remember that it has nothing to do with you. You are the messenger and sometimes messengers get the brunt of the reaction. If you are worried about a potential violent reaction, prepare in advance for your own safety and have a witness or alert security.
- Once the reaction has subsided, provide the resources the person will need, such as contacts or phone numbers. Help them focus on the positive.
- If you have to give bad news to a group, beware that you may get more negative feedback, as emotions may gain momentum.
- There is always a silver lining, and there are people who care— you, for one, who had the courage and empathy to deliver the bad news. Reassure the person that you are there for them. Help them prepare for what they must do next, beginning with a phone call or a ride.

A MANTRA TO TELL YOURSELF: *"A messenger is important."*

References:

Business consultant Bob Lewis, Bob_Lewis@csi.com or www.info world.com

Physician/writer Elizabeth Heubeck, eheubeck@physicianspractice.com

See: fear of showing emotions, fear of confrontation or conflict, fear of the unknown, fear of illness or pain, fear of death, serious worries, fear of ending a romantic relationship

Fear of Disorder or Untidiness

ataxophobia (fear of disorder)

mysophobia (fear of dirt or germs)

You know you have a problem when you fear your house will be burglarized and you worry you haven't had a chance to clean the place up. —ANONYMOUS

Characteristics: This condition involves an intense desire to keep everything proper, such as following a strict schedule, or a compulsion to arrange things in order. Some people may show displeasure with those who don't care about order as much as they do. Others fear dirt or contamination, some to the point that they constantly clean their fingernails or refuse to shake hands with people. At its most severe, this fear leads to obsessive-compulsive behavior, such as the repeated washing of hands.

Background: The desire or need to maintain control is inherent in many people, and in the big picture it helps create civilization and orderly societies. But this need could actually stem from a fear of dealing with others and their different styles and schedules. In moderation, the fear of disorder and untidiness can keep one clean, healthy and on time. Perfectionists can sometimes be compulsive with cleaning and may have self-esteem or ego issues to deal with. Fear of dirt or germs relates back to times when disease was more rampant.

Strategies:
- Without order, there is chaos. If you loathe dirt and lack of structure, however, you might want to examine whether your fears are obsessive and unwarranted.
- Sometimes there's a fine line between order and disorder. Consider your worries out of proportion if:
  - you treat scuff marks on your carpet like footprints to track down a suspect
  - you don't allow kids to play in your backyard
  - you are known only for your appearance and rarely for your spontaneity
  - your vacation plans are a strict itinerary

- Examine other areas of your life where a similar mindset may exist, such as inflexibility in relationships, fear of failure at work or trouble relaxing. Are you a perfectionist? Do you try to control things too much?
- Let go once in a while. Have a jeans-only day, or the audacity to be late for an appointment, and observe how life goes on and you don't get fired. At home, let someone else do the housework or schedule the appointments.
- Look upon your house as lived in. Leave cushions askew once in a while. Let glasses and cups have a living-room life of more than 30 minutes. What would happen if you didn't do the laundry for 24 hours?
- Go to other people's homes and see how they live. It might give you some perspective.
- If you laugh at yourself and your habits once in a while, the rigidity can loosen. Ask yourself, "Do I control my life or does my life control me?"

A MANTRA TO TELL YOURSELF: *"Do I want to live in a sterile world?"*

Reference:

Anxiety Disorders and Phobias by Aaron T. Beck and Gary Emery, Basic, 1985

See: fear of not having control, fear of change, fear of criticism, fear of what others think, fear of making mistakes, fear of embarrassment, fear of family get-togethers, fear of strangers

Fear of Solicitors and Telemarketers

hobophobia (fear of beggars)

If you get one of those pushy [telemarketers], just listen to their sales pitch. When they try to close the sale, tell them you'll need to go get your credit card. Then set the phone down and go do the laundry or something. —FROM WWW.FAKECRAP.COM

Characteristics: People with this fear are reluctant to answer the telephone or the door because they may have to confront someone who will try to sell them something or convert them to a religion. Some people may become irritable, even angry. Others are sheepish or intimidated when they walk past panhandlers.

Background: Most people are territorial by nature and habit, and suspicious of strangers coming onto their property. Some may feel their privacy has been trespassed when unauthorized people call or come to their door. A home is a person's castle and refuge. If we had no apprehension at all, we'd be letting everybody into our homes. Telemarketing has become more popular than door-to-door solicitation, but many people still see it as an invasion of privacy, especially at mealtime or late at night.

Strategies:
- Don't be so quick to shoot the messenger—solicitors usually work for a company or organization. Be kind—do you think they like setting themselves up for rejection or derision?
- Have a preset dollar figure in mind for your charitable contributions for the year and the type of charities you want to give to.
- If you are against solicitation, put a sign up: "No Solicitors Please," or "My Dog Doesn't Bite but My Spouse Does."
- Hard-sell tactics or tear-jerk stories could be a tip-off to an unscrupulous solicitor. Watch out for get-rich-quick schemes or company names that sound very close to the name of a well-known charity or brand name.
- At the door, ask for identification and perhaps a brochure on the group. (In some areas, door-to-door solicitors need a license.) You can read it and send a donation later.

- If you hire someone to do work around your house, ask for references. If you're unhappy with the work, call the Better Business Bureau.
- Pay by check. Don't give cash or your credit card number.
- Get a feeling for the *other side* by volunteering to go door to door or solicit over the phone for a charity.
- Try to be tolerant of religious groups. Remember that some religious groups believe one of their mandates is to go door to door to spread their message. If you want them to respect your beliefs, respect theirs. It doesn't mean you have to let them in.
- Telemarketers have developed a reputation for fast talk and con artistry, but people are buying; it's estimated that $230 billion in goods and services are sold over the phone each year in the U.S. If you are against telemarketers, keep a note near your phone, clearly stating your position. Screen calls and hang up on auto-dialers. Or get an unlisted number.
- If you consider buying something from a telemarketer, ask for written information on the product (or charity). Scammers will not send you written material.
- To avoid junk mail, think twice before entering sweepstakes and draws.
- To avoid solicitations, have your number placed on a do-not-call list in accordance with the Telephone Consumer Protection Act (in the U.S.).
- How to deal with panhandlers on the street is sometimes an ethical decision. Yes, you work hard for your money, but don't dismiss them as lazy bums; they may be mentally ill or destitute.

A MANTRA TO TELL YOURSELF: *"Be nice, but fair."*

References:

The Alliance Against Fraud in Telemarketing and Electronic Commerce, www.fraud.org

See: fear of strangers, fear of invasion of territory or privacy, fear of confrontation or conflict, fear of a break-in, fear of oneself, fear of embarrassment

Worry at Night and Sleeplessness

noctiphobia (fear of the night) *somniphobia* (fear of sleep)	*Sometimes I lie awake at night and I ask, "Where have I gone wrong?" Then a voice says to me, "This is going to take more than one night."* —CARTOON CHARACTER CHARLIE BROWN

Characteristics: Many people lie awake at night, tense or worrying about what happened during the day or what might happen tomorrow, or whether there is a burglar on the prowl. They may worry about getting to sleep and how that might impact their energy the next day. Some people fear sleepwalking. "The variability of their sleep drives people nuts—they [lie awake] and wonder, 'What's it going to be like tonight?'" says Jack Edinger, a professor of psychiatry and behavioral sciences at Duke University. "It's a crapshoot." Children may not sleep for a variety of reasons and fears, including bedwetting (I was an occasional bed wetter until age 11).

Background: We are vulnerable to anxiety when we lie in bed, with nothing to do but attempt to sleep. When we are fatigued or tense, issues are often exaggerated and turn into worries. Little wonder that prayer is so popular at the end of the day. Sleep disorders have been common throughout history; up to 10 percent of the population suffers from insomnia. Shift workers are particularly vulnerable to night worry and sleep problems. In some people, this condition relates to the fear of death; they are afraid they won't wake up.

Strategies:
- If you constantly have problems sleeping, limit the time you spend in the bedroom. Use the bedroom for sleep only.
- If you have issues or worries that need dealing with, tell yourself you will tend to them in the morning.
- If you have an active mind at night, worry about things over which you have some control, then sleep on it. Some research has shown that when you awake in the morning, you might have been thinking about an answer in your sleep.

- Keep a pad by your bed to write down ideas. Or talk to your partner about your concerns.
- "White noise" can calm you—turn on an air purifier, a house fan, an air conditioner or soothing music you wouldn't ordinarily listen to. If you have a tendency to look at the clock, turn it around or cover the face.
- If you really can't sleep, get up and do something. In the short term, getting only four or five hours of sleep won't hurt your performance the next day. Don't panic if you average only six or seven hours of sleep a night. Everyone is different in their sleep needs. As well, older people tend to sleep more lightly.
- Watch your lifestyle: drinking too much caffeine or having cat-naps during the day can keep you sleepless at night.
- Be aware that you might be suffering from depression, anxiety disorder or physical problems. See your doctor.
- In some cases, sleeping pills may be necessary. Consult your doctor. Many sleep experts argue against their use for more than a few weeks because they can increase the risk of auto accidents and memory or confusion problems.
- Nightmares may be expressions of waking fears. People who have nightmares tend to have other forms of sleeping disorders.
- If your child awakes from a nightmare, calm him or her. Later, draw the dream with the child, helping him or her see it from a different perspective. Then make up a happy ending for the dream. About 25 percent of children 6 to 12 have nightmares.

A MANTRA TO TELL YOURSELF: *"Count your blessings instead of sheep."*

References:

Sleep Thieves: An Eye-Opening Exploration into the Science and Mysteries of Sleep by Stanley Coren, Touchstone, 1998

Solve Your Child's Sleep Problems by Richard Ferber, Fireside, 1986

See: fear of the dark, fear of death, fear of the unknown, fear of not having control, sexual fears, fear of religion, fear of a break-in, fear of oneself, fear for your children's safety

Fear of Being Alone

isolophobia (fear of solitude) *monophobia* (fear of being alone)	*Many people become anxious or fearful if they are not always in a crowd of people, socializing…we might feel left out of something.* —LAUREN WOODHOUSE, AUTHOR OF *LAUGHING IN THE FACE OF CHANGE*

Characteristics: People with this fear may constantly feel the need to be around others, may easily get bored or sad being alone, or may not like their own company. Just thinking about being alone can cause anxiousness, vulnerability or even depression. When alone, their other fears tend to become exaggerated. Many children fear being alone because they feel helpless and worry their parents will never return. We tend to feel loneliness more when we get tired or when our resources are depleted.

Background: Humans are generally social creatures built and conditioned for interaction, so we often feel vulnerable alone. Many of us don't spend enough time alone to be comfortable with it (although this may be changing in our increasingly insular society). Some people don't like to be alone because they don't like themselves very much or they don't want to face the truth about themselves, which may involve mindsets and behaviors they have to change. This fear tends to affect women more than men, perhaps because of their sensitivity to or possible need for companionship. It also can increase with age, especially if a person's relatives or acquaintances die or are ill. Victorian author Charlotte Brontë wrote, "My mind has suffered somewhat too much; a malady is growing upon it—what shall I do? How shall I keep well? Sleepless I lay awake night after night, weak and unable to occupy myself."

Strategies:

- Learn to be your own best friend. If you don't like yourself enough to be in your own company, take steps (small ones, at first) to correct that. It's a great way to find out things about yourself. Don't be too dependent on others. Learn to entertain yourself. If you find yourself alone, talk aloud to yourself. Laugh with yourself.

- Write your feelings down or try to do something creative when you feel lonely. If you are lonely because you have lost a loved one, a job or a routine, help to fill that loss by connecting with something else.
- Don't mope or lull into self-pity—it may turn off others.
- Stay active. Exercise. Reading a book opens up another world with other characters. Get a pet. When you are engaged in something, it's hard to worry. Meet people with interests and needs similar to your own. Join a club or volunteer. Look up an old friend. Have a regular walking route and say hello to everyone you pass. Don't be afraid to strike up conversations.
- Use your favorite music to take the stillness out of silence. Music also can inspire you or put you in a state of flow, connecting you with ideas and with others, even though they are not there.
- Keep a journal. Briefly review your life and your plans and goals for the future. Tend to the things you might not do with others around: improving hygiene, thinking through complex issues and projects, writing, or tending to a pet's needs. Your most creative work may be done alone. Learn to treasure your time alone. Remember that other people are always close by through telephone, e-mail, letter or photo album.
- If you fill loneliness with drinking, drugs, aggression or overwork, it can make your situation worse.
- If you form intimate and nurturing bonds with others, you will feel inner support even when you are alone.

A MANTRA TO TELL YOURSELF: *"Hello, me."*

References:

The Tao of Music by John M. Ortiz, Weiser, 1997

Dr. Luann Linquist, psychologist
P.O. Box 13172
La Jolla, CA 92039
(858) 581-1122, DrLuann@deletestress.com

See: fear of intimacy or love, fear of oneself, fear of death, fear of the dark, fear of your children leaving home, fear of retirement, fear of aging

Fear of the Dark

achluophobia (fear of the dark)	*I overcame my fear of the dark and put it into my books.* —Tomi Ungerer
phasmophobia (fear of ghosts)	**Characteristics:** Sufferers may avoid dimly lit areas or even stop going out at night.

Children often confuse fantasy and reality and may be afraid to sleep for fear of monsters. Some adults may avoid being alone at night. Others are spooked by shadows or they fear that their mind will play tricks on them in the dark.

Background: This is a perfectly natural fear from our days as hunter-gatherers, when the real danger of predators lurked in the dark. Since we cannot see well in the dark, this is nature's way to help us to be more alert. This fear is closely related to the fear of the unknown. We are sometimes conditioned to fear the dark; remember the line from that childhood prayer, "If I should die before I wake"? Sometimes this fear surfaces after a traumatic event. The benefit to small children is that such fears keep them cautious at an age when they are vulnerable. Fear of the dark usually dissipates when the child is able to understand how the world works, but if the child continues to be afraid of going into a dark room, it could be that it has turned into a phobia, and may even spread to refusal to going into a basement or outside. On the positive side, this fear makes everyone more alert when visibility is not good.

Strategies:

• Understand that most of your fears of the dark are probably unjustified; trees do not turn into monsters after sunset and ghosts do not wait until then to appear in closets. Muggers usually do not target middle-class areas. However, use common sense in strange areas; stay out of high-crime areas at night.

• Desensitize yourself to the dark by sitting alone at home with most of the lights off, then all of them. If you feel anxious, breathe deeply, meditate, or listen to music.

- Talk about your fear or write about it, as author Anne Rice did in her novels about vampires.
- If you or your child has a fear of ghosts, remember that there is no proof they exist. Is it just a coincidence they are only seen in the dark or when we are half-asleep and our brains are not functioning 100 percent? If fear of ghosts persists, it could be you have an unresolved issue with a dead person.
- If you walk or jog after sunset, wear bright clothes. If you bicycle, have lights and take extra precaution with motorized vehicles. If you drive, be more cautious.
- If your children fear the dark:
  - let them know you are nearby and available to them
  - put a nightlight in their room or leave the door slightly ajar
  - don't make a big deal out of their fear of monsters; reassure them and don't tell them they're wimpy
  - some parents allow their kids to sleep in their bed under certain circumstances
  - offer the child some input on how to solve the problem; get them to talk about a monster and what it could do to them; if something in the room looks frightening, ask how to make it less so
  - limit scary movies and TV shows

A MANTRA TO TELL YOURSELF: *"I'm a night creature, too."*

References:

Keys to Parenting Your Anxious Child by Katharina Manassis, Barron's, 1996

See: worry at night and sleeplessness, fear of the unknown, superstition or fear of the supernatural, fear of being mugged, fear and stress in children, fear of enclosed spaces, fear of being alone

6

Fears in Social Settings

Fear of People

anthropophobia (fear of people)

scopophobia (fear of being looked at)

Man is a social animal. —ARISTOTLE

Characteristics: People with this condition are often shy and will avoid one-on-one situations, eye contact with others, eating in public, crowds, or gatherings at work, school or with family. They may be embarrassed or blush through self-consciousness or from fear of appearing silly or inadequate. Shyness can prevent people from making friends, especially close friends, and it can lead to depression or drug use and heavy drinking. Shy people may believe that no one is interested in them, and they may have a distorted view of relationships or feel lonely. Some shy people overcompensate for their feelings and are actually assertive or aggressive in public. Many become performers so that they can act out in a structured environment.

Background: Some 93 percent of people experience some sort of shyness from time to time. About 7 percent of North Americans have a type of person-related phobia. Some species of animals, including humans, use *staring* to intimidate. Many people fear being observed; in serious cases, this fear can be permanent unless treated. This form of shyness could be genetic (children with the same upbringing can have opposite reactions to people) or stem from bad experiences or lack of exposure to people. Such fears increase as our society becomes more insular and as we communicate more and more through computers. Social phobias usually peak in a person's late teens.

Strategies:
- Come to this quick conclusion: most people don't bite. And if they do, get a civil lawyer fast.
- If you are uncomfortable around people, try to establish why and come up with solutions. Do you sometimes have a low opinion of yourself, or are you very sensitive to criticism? Are you just lazy and don't want to talk or develop a relationship?

- If you or someone you know has such a social phobia, it can be treated by a therapist, perhaps by improving your view of the world and of yourself. Start by getting help from a family doctor or member of the clergy.
- Tips for developing communications skills: make eye contact, don't talk too softly, stand close enough to people to show confidence, don't apologize or belittle yourself, use open-ended questions, learn to be assertive and to be a good listener. Think about the good things you have to offer other people.
- Medications, such as Neurontin, are available to help treat intense shyness.
- A shy patient of Los Angeles psychologist Gary Emery developed the following strategies for meeting others:
  1. I look straight at the other person, eyes fixed.
  2. I hold my ground and let him move toward me, rather than rushing to him.
  3. I keep my body straight and balanced, projecting presence.
  4. I communicate openly, keeping my arms down rather than in a defensive position.
  5. I keep my head erect rather than nodding or looking away.
  6. I speak confidently in a clear, direct way, rather than qualifying excessively, apologizing or overexplaining.
  7. I ask questions about the person and call him by name.
  8. I'm friendly but quiet and sincere.
  9. I'm dressed in a way that allows me to feel good about myself.
  10. I'm really enjoying meeting the person.

  A MANTRA TO TELL YOURSELF: *"I'm important, too."*

Reference:

The Shyness and Social Anxiety Workbook by Martin M. Antony and Richard P. Swinson, New Harbinger, 2000

See: fear of strangers, fear of crowds, fear of what others think, fear of embarrassment, fear of criticism, fear of panic attacks in public, most fears in Part 4 and Part 6

Fear of Panic Attacks in Public

agoraphobia (fear of crowded public places)	*While a person cannot always immediately overcome the first level of fear, he can stop frightening himself over the anxiety itself.* —GARY EMERY, DIRECTOR OF

THE LOS ANGELES CENTER FOR COGNITIVE THERAPY

Characteristics: This is the fear of having a panic attack in what one considers an unsafe place. It is the fear of fear itself. At the same time, it is a complex and sometimes generalized fear that could pertain to a number of situations. Sufferers may avoid crowded highways or stores because they worry about panicking and being unable to escape, or bringing embarrassment upon themselves in their anxiety. They may shake, perspire, hyperventilate or even believe they are having a heart attack. Some people feel this way when at home alone, but it commonly occurs when people are far away from home. This condition is often accompanied by, or leads to, depression.

Background: This fear is often passed along in families. It can also begin if a person grows up with an overprotective or perfectionist parent. About 80 percent of agoraphobics are women (leading to the phrase *housebound housewife syndrome*), although this percentage has been dropping in recent times. The onset of panic disorder usually occurs between late adolescence and the mid-30s.

This fear is believed to be related to early humans' fear of being caught out in the open and vulnerable to attack. It served to keep vulnerable people close to their protectors. Charles Darwin described his occasional panic attacks as a "sensation of fear... accompanied by troubled beating of the heart, sweat and trembling of muscles."

Strategies:

- Gradually expose yourself to the situations that you fear and that tend to make you panicky. You might want to go with a trusted companion at first. Get used to crowds and trips to the country. Start by using visualization to imagine the situation, then do it in real life.
- Learn to make your thinking more realistic, and don't allow

your imagination to get the better of you. This situation cannot harm you, but your catastrophic thinking can make you tense and sick.

- Learn to relax by using breathing techniques, humor, music on a portable player or meditation. Say calming things to yourself both before and while you're in what you consider to be an unsafe place.
- Stop worrying about what others think of you. If you feel panic or embarrassment coming on, no one else knows but you. And no one else cares.
- Don't panic about your panic. If you become dizzy, calm yourself by remembering that agoraphobics rarely pass out. If you constantly feel threatened or tense, you may have a hair-trigger nervous system and need medication. See your doctor.
- Consider therapy. A study of people who suffered panic attacks revealed that only 19 percent who were treated for it subsequently suffered depression, compared to 45 percent of those who were not treated. Researchers concluded that detecting and treating panic disorder may reduce the risk of depression.

A MANTRA TO TELL YOURSELF: *"Slow and slower."*

References:

The Anxiety and Phobia Workbook by Edmund J. Bourne, New Harbinger, 2000

The Encyclopedia of Phobias, Fears and Anxieties by Ronald M. Doctor, Ada P. Kahn and Isaac Marks, Facts on File, 2000

Agoraphobic Foundation of Canada
P.O. Box 132
Chomeday, Laval, Quebec
Canada H7W 4K2

Agoraphobics in Action Inc.
P.O. Box 1662
Antioch, TN 37011
(615) 831-2383

See: fear of people, fear of crowds, fear of what others think, fear of strangers, fear of embarrassment, fear of not having control, fear of the unknown, fear of enclosed spaces, fear of doctors or dentists

Fear of Public Speaking

glossophobia

topophobia (stage fright)

The essence of public speaking is this: give your audience something of value, to walk away feeling better about themselves or some job they have to do. Even if you pass out, get tongue-tied or say something stupid, they won't care.
—PHYSICIAN, AUTHOR AND PROFESSIONAL SPEAKER MORTON C. ORMAN

Characteristics: Many if not most people suffer anxiety when speaking before a group of people or even when engaged in a social affair. Sufferers report dry mouth, stumbling voice, trembling fingers and loss of confidence. Some people are so fearful of being evaluated, looking silly or making a mistake, they never speak to a group or go to a party.

Background: As we have evolved into sensitive, self-conscious creatures, fear of public speaking has come to rival fear of death among humans. About 75 percent of North Americans report experiencing this fear; in some surveys, more people say they are afraid of speaking than say they are afraid of dying. This fear can set off your emergency fear system, with its increased heart rate, blood flow and adrenaline. Sufferers have included former presidents Ronald Reagan and Franklin Roosevelt and singer Barbra Streisand. On the positive side, some people say they actually perform better when anxious, because their fear gives them increased focus and a feeling of power.

Strategies:
- Get some experience with speaking to groups of people. Even if your first steps are small, you'll still grow in confidence.
- Use your nervous energy to help you organize and prepare for your talk. The extra effort will give you confidence in your knowledge of your topic. Know your audience as you prepare your content. Have a theme and structure to your presentation, but make only two or three major points.
- Keep things in perspective and don't become obsessed with an upcoming talk. If you see a presentation as too much of a threat, your emergency fear system will make you overly anxious and tense and you may not be able to control your nervousness.

- Look upon the talk as an information-giving session rather than as a performance. If you worry about how a performance will be perceived, you have a greater chance of letting your ego come into play and you may feel more anxious and defensive.
- Remember that the audience, even if it is just a few coworkers at an office presentation, wants one thing—the information you are giving them. They want you to succeed in giving it.
- Conceptualize your message. Don't memorize, because if you do, the moment one section is forgotten, your whole session could break down.
- When the time for your presentation comes, if you feel overly scared or tense, take a few deep breaths and visualize what you are going to do. If your mouth gets dry, drink water or press your tongue against the roof of your mouth.
- Use humor, especially self-deprecating humor, which releases endorphins into your system and relaxes you. Audience members want to laugh and like to know that you share their sense of humor. Laughter is a way of connecting.
- If you want to become a performer or a professional speaker, take a speaking course. And don't be afraid of being critiqued or of asking others' opinions about your stage presence.

Author's Two Cents:

In my first professional speaking engagement in 2002, I received a poor mark. My ego was bruised for 12 hours and I contemplated quitting. But the next day, I organized my speech better and added humor. At the next conference, two weeks later, I received the second-highest mark among 21 speakers.

References:

In the Spotlight: Overcome Your Fear of Public Speaking and Performing by Janet E. Esposito, Strong, 2000

See: fear of what others think, fear of failure, fear of embarrassment, fear of making mistakes, fear of criticism, fear of not being loved, fear of strangers

Fear of Crowds

enochlophobia (fear of crowds)

agoraphobia (fear of open or public places)

I hate crowds and making speeches.
—ALBERT EINSTEIN

Characteristics: People with this condition may avoid shopping malls, sporting events and theaters for fear of strangers, of what others think of them, of being crushed or trampled, of pickpockets or of contracting a virus. Some people may feel a loss of their identity or feel alone in a crowd, or they may fear getting lost. Others get very anxious or aggressive or feel like they are having a panic attack. Many people live in the country or suburbs because they are intimidated by the crowds and traffic in cities.

Background: Traditionally, humans tended to live in groups of no more than 75 people. Humans also have a history of sometimes getting caught up in mob mentality and acting differently, perhaps even violently, in large crowds. Women tend to suffer from fear of crowds more than men. If one of your relatives suffers from this condition, you are three times more likely than the average person to suffer from it as well. If you have low self-esteem or suffer from a traumatic disorder, you may feel insignificant or lonely in a group of people. Others may be afraid of crowds because they are in poor health and worry about falling and getting crushed.

Strategies:
- Go to a shopping mall, a sporting event, a movie theater or another crowded place—perhaps with someone you feel comfortable with—and gradually get used to rubbing elbows with people in crowds. Pin up photos of big crowds in your home.
- You may be simply shy. Talk to others more often. Go to group activities and interact with people. Consider taking a leadership role, even if it is just a small one at first.
- If you are physically afraid of groups of strangers, tell yourself that you're actually pretty safe in a crowd. That's why criminals (except for pickpockets) rarely try anything with others around. Too many witnesses.

- Avoid crowded situations in which intense emotions come into play, unless you can desensitize yourself to often noisy fans at sports stadiums. If you cannot, don't do anything to inflame your condition.
- Don't quickly dismiss or judge people who live in cities; you may do so out of a subconscious fear of crowds or traffic.
- Crowds can actually be fun! People at sports events or in theaters can enjoy doing the "wave" or singing together ("Take Me Out to the Ballgame") or giving a standing ovation at the opera or a rock concert.
- If you fear crowds, you're in some elite company—singer Frank Sinatra was uncomfortable being around a lot of people. And actor Clark Gable didn't like crowds.
- If you find yourself in a tight, claustrophobic situation around people, breathe deeply, think of your loved ones, use humor or music in a portable player or force yourself to keep perspective.

A MANTRA TO TELL YOURSELF: *"Blend in"* OR *"No one will harm me."*

Reference:

The Hidden Face of Shyness: Understanding and Overcoming Social Anxiety by Franklin Schneier, Avon, 1996

See: fear of people, fear of strangers, fear of other races, fear of the unknown, fear of illness or pain, fear of being mugged, fear of invasion of territory or privacy, fear of panic attacks in public, fear of enclosed spaces

Fear of Strangers

xenophobia (fear of foreigners or strangers)	*Fear makes strangers of people who should be friends.* —SHIRLEY MACLAINE

Characteristics: This fear often results in avoiding people one doesn't know. In serious cases, it keeps people housebound. Some people avoid crowds or parties. Some even avoid new jobs or moving to new regions or neighborhoods because they are apprehensive about talking to people they haven't met. Others won't ask directions from strangers on the street.

Background: There may be more fear of strangers in recent times because our society is becoming increasingly insular. Many people spend a lot of time on their computers and don't develop close relationships. Sometimes we make a snap decision about a person based on looks and decide we don't want to get to know him or her. This fear also relates back to primitive days, when strangers were potential attackers. When we're in strange areas, this fear keeps us alert.

Strategies:
- Keep an open mind and heart toward others. A stranger may be just a friend you haven't met, not someone out to fleece you.
- When approaching someone new, there's nothing to break the ice like a smile or a hello to encourage a conversation or to ward off confrontation. Take the initiative in conversation. Strangers don't have anything up on us; they're just as in the dark about us as we are about them, and perhaps just as apprehensive.
- If you rarely strike up a conversation with a stranger, it may be a sign that you are shy or that your confidence needs a boost. Volunteering or joining a club will help you deal with this fear.

- Go to a restaurant or bar in a region or section of town you are not acquainted with, perhaps with a person you know. Or take a cruise with new people you must mingle with for a week or two. Always try to make new friends. A relative of mine wondered how I could walk onto a playground and start playing pickup sports games with strangers (as I sometimes do); I told him you get used to it and sometimes you look forward to it.

- Don't be a couch potato, and don't conduct your relationships on the Internet. Get out more often. Remember that meeting new people introduces you to fresh ideas and styles. You may learn a different way of dancing, of tying a shoelace or of baking a cake.

- If your baby cries around strangers, don't panic. It's normal for infants to be afraid of strangers, especially when they're around eight months old. This is often just a sign that the baby feels comfortable with familiar faces.

A MANTRA TO TELL YOURSELF: *"I am a stranger to others."*

Reference:

Beyond Shyness by Jonathan Berent, Fireside, 1993

See: fear of other races, fear of the unknown, fear of terrorism, fear of intimacy or love, fear of religion, fear of crowds, fear of public speaking, fear of change

Fear of Other Races

| *xenophobia* (fear of foreigners or strangers) | *There can be hope only for a society which acts as one big family, not as many separate ones.* —FORMER EGYPTIAN PRESIDENT ANWAR EL SADAT |

Characteristics: This condition involves fear or dislike of people from a different region, culture, race, religion, age or color. Sufferers may avoid them, form stereotypical attitudes toward them, or even shun them or become hostile toward them. Some people believe other races are more violent or less worthy than their own.

Background: We are all programmed with a gene that makes us suspicious of other groups of people. This is sometimes called the us vs. them gene, which nature originally gave us to protect us from unknown tribes that may wage war against us. Nowadays, we know much more about other "tribes" and we are relatively good to one another, yet this fear still causes much grief in the world and was one factor in the tragedy of September 11, 2001. We often fear others and sometimes become angry toward them when we don't understand them. Real problems can occur if we start to consider others less human than us, or if we believe another race will contaminate our own. This fear, which appears more when we are under stress, is prevalent in politics, in which right-wing people may despise left-wingers and vice versa.

Strategies:

- Don't be so quick to assess or judge others who are not like you. When we oversimplify or stereotype other people, we open the door for resentment and fear.
- Educate yourself and get to know someone from another race. "When we have fear of the unknown, we kill the unknown. That is a natural instinct," said Randall Tetlichi, speaking to the Canadian Royal Commission on Aboriginal Peoples.

- Try to find common ground with others; you'll probably discover that you share similar hopes and attitudes. If put in a similar situation to yours, most people would probably react in a similar manner.
- Try to avoid raising your self-esteem by becoming part of a group, such as a winning team or a particular race, just to defeat or put down another group.
- Don't feel a sense of entitlement over new immigrants. Originally, we all came from someplace else. Should we close the door now that we are inside the gates?
- In politics, when you examine attitudes and beliefs, right-wingers are not that far apart from the left-wingers; don't always exaggerate the differences to prove a point. For example, don't assume that all conservatives are intolerant or that all liberals are undisciplined. You won't be able to defend yourself when presented with evidence to the contrary.
- Although 9/11 was an inexcusable attack on civilians, try to understand the mindset of radicals and the danger of lumping them together with others from their culture. Sheldon Solomon, a professor of psychology at Brooklyn College, points out: "For the radical Islam represented by Osama bin Laden, the West is evil and must be eradicated. On the other side, President George W. Bush declared this conflict a crusade, suggesting that our god is better than theirs."
- Practice tolerance. A tolerant society may be a higher form of society.

   A MANTRA TO TELL YOURSELF: *"They're more like me than I think."*

Reference:

Tolerance (Cultures of Peace) by Dominique Roger, UNESCO, 1995

See: fear of terrorism, fear of religion, fear of the unknown, fear of strangers, fear of rejection, fear of homosexuality

Fear of Singing or Dancing

phonophobia (fear of voices or speaking aloud) chorophobia (fear of dancing)	*I am terrified of dancing. Any social situation where I may suddenly be cajoled into strutting my self-conscious, inhibited, middle-class stuff scares me stiff.* —MICHAEL STEPHENS, GUITARIST AND MUSIC COLUMNS EDITOR AT WWW.POPMATTERS.COM

Characteristics: People with this condition avoid singing or dancing in front of others for fear of embarrassment, comparison or criticism. Even if they attempt it, they may experience dry throat, nausea, tension, sweaty palms, or lack of rhythm or confidence. At parties, people may drink heavily to lose their inhibitions before they have enough confidence to sing or dance.

Background: Fear of singing or dancing in front of others is one of the most common fears. People may worry that their voice will break or sound flat, or that others will think less of them if they fail. Or they may worry that others won't like their choice of music. Those who fear dancing may fear embarrassment or may have problems with balance and coordination.

Primitive man may have been less inhibited and may have had more rhythm than we have; social evolution has made some societies more rigid and self-conscious. Music could be more important to our society—if we allowed it to be, if we didn't keep it to ourselves. One theory is that there is a connection between social rhythm and physical rhythm. For example, Italian people tend to be rhythmic in dance and in their social connections. Music is good for your health; research shows that people who keep the beat or sing along in a 30-minute music session have a greater increase in antibody concentrations than people who only listen to it.

Strategies for singing:

• Host a party with people who like to sing; invite a friend experienced in playing piano or guitar. Buy a karaoke machine and practice alone, or go to a karaoke night where you are anonymous.

- Take singing lessons (I'm thinking about it) or buy an instructional CD or tape (I did). Practice will strengthen your vocal chords, which are muscles like those in your arms.
- If you must, have a few drinks to take the edge off your nervousness (but not too many!).
- Start out by humming or whistling. Let the rhythm and the harmony take you; focus on the words, and don't be distracted by other people in the room.
- Lower your expectations; others won't expect you to sound like Sinatra. But if you show the courage to sing, you could become a leader and discover that others want to sing along.
- Many people who became famous singers were initially afraid, such as Perry Como and Barbra Streisand. Others without strong voices made it big, including Madonna and Bryan Adams.

Strategies for dancing:

- Do you have two left feet? Who doesn't? Few people are great dancers because most of us don't dance enough to get really fluid at it. Dance at home to build up some rhythm and confidence.
- Surround yourself with fun people, particularly if they are not judgmental. Even if you are a bad dancer, they won't care that much, and they certainly won't see you as less of a person.
- Take dance lessons, perhaps with a partner, but be sure you are signing up for lessons that teach the type of dance you want.
- Let your defenses and inhibitions down and take your coat and tie off. To deny your inner rhythm is to inhibit yourself unnecessarily. This is a personality trait you may want to improve.
- Don't deny yourself one of life's joys.

A MANTRA TO TELL YOURSELF: *"Let my rhythm flow."*

References:

Learn to Sing Harmony by Cathy Fink, Marcy Marxer, Robin Williams and Linda Williams, Hal Leonard Publishing, 2001

Video: *Learn to Dance in Minutes* by Cal Pozo

CD: *Learn to Sing Like a Star* by Ava Tracht Landman

See: fear of embarrassment, fear of making mistakes, fear of criticism, fear of what others think, fear of showing emotions, fear of falling

Fear of Dating

| sarmassophobia (fear of love play) | A man can be short and dumpy and getting bald, but if he has fire, women will like him. —MAE WEST |

Characteristics: Many people experience this condition. They feel nervous about the social or sexual consequences of going on a date with someone, or simply fear being with a new person all evening. People can feel pressure to make a good impression or to have others like them immediately. The fear of rejection from a date can be powerful; we may react to it very personally. Multiple failures can result in a person becoming gun-shy and avoiding relationships, or he or she may start to feel inadequate or unattractive.

Background: Dating is always unpredictable because of the differences in people and their needs and motives. One person may want to have fun and the other to get married. Experts are still not sure what makes a perfect date, never mind a perfect match. Nature wants to keep us procreating, so the sexual desire in people who date remains strong. This can add to the fear and pressure of a date.

Strategies:

- It sounds geeky at first, but try going on a date with a relative to reduce your fear.
- Ask for advice from a parent, friend, teacher, relative or confidante, particularly someone with lots of dating experience.
- Be open and honest with your date. Admitting your fear and sensitivity often makes you more attractive to the other person.
- Always start dating slowly. The relationship may grow or it may not. Relationships are unpredictable. If you are too enthusiastic, you may scuttle your opportunity.
- If you want to start a relationship on the first date, don't go to a high-class type of venue just to impress because you may never go there again. You want to find somewhere you'll enjoy again and again. If you try to be someone you're not, the truth will eventually come out.

- Be wary of kissing on the first date, never mind jumping into the sack. Don't be so superficial as to endanger others' feelings or your future. Seek something more than sex, and let the other person know your attitude toward this issue.
- Be a good listener and try to have fun. It's just a date. Do not force yourself to determine feelings about the other person too quickly.
- What looks like a fear of dating may actually be a fear of the opposite sex, of intimacy, of having sex or even of other people in general. Analyze your fears and your motives.
- Remember that opposites may attract, especially in their personalities, but this kind of attraction can be superficial and temporary. People of similar values and interests are more likely to bond over the long haul. If you are looking for a long-lasting relationship, seek out someone you can be friends with.
- What is the worst that could happen on a date? Is your self-esteem so insecure you couldn't withstand rejection? Could your date bite off your nose?
- Go the cliché route: don't put all your eggs in one basket. There are lots of fish in the sea.
- Learn something from every date you have, and leave the other person with something.

A MANTRA TO TELL YOURSELF: *"At least for now, it's only a date."*

References:

Fearless Loving: 8 Simple Truths That Will Change the Way You Date, Mate and Relate by Rhonda Britten, E.P. Dutton, 2003

The Worst-Case Scenario Survival Handbook: Dating and Sex by Joshua Piven, David Borgenicht and Jennifer Worick, Chronicle, 2001 (careful, this book's a little in-your-face)

The Romance Page, ww2.best.vwh.net/romance.html

See: fear of commitment, fear of rejection, fear of intimacy or love, sexual fears, fear of the opposite sex, fear of embarrassment, fear of the unknown, fear of oneself

Fear of the Opposite Sex

heterophobia (fear of the opposite sex) *androphobia* (fear of men) *gynephobia* (fear of women)	*Men mistakenly expect women to think, communicate and react the way men do; women mistakenly expect men to feel, communicate and respond the way women do. We have forgotten that men and women are supposed to be different. As a result, our relationships are filled with unnecessary friction and conflict.* —JOHN

GRAY, AUTHOR OF *MEN ARE FROM MARS, WOMEN ARE FROM VENUS*

Characteristics: This condition creates discomfort, anxiety or even conflict about the opposite sex in social, professional or intimate situations. This fear may affect behavior and decisions in business, making some women feel discriminated against and some men feel threatened. Such fears may result in prejudices and stereotyping.

Background: Men and women have probably misunderstood each other since the beginning of time. We tend to fear things we don't understand, and until recently, we have not openly discussed the differences between men and women. In many areas, we've tended to treat men and women as identical, and we've often been frustrated when they've reacted differently. Heredity plays a part in this fear, but so does environment (for example, boys and girls are often warned by adults to stay apart). This fear may be related to the fear of sex, fear of a parent, or strong, repressed feelings.

Strategies:
- We need to better understand the trends and traits of the opposite sex: men tend to be more rational, objective and goal- and work-oriented. Women tend to be more emotional and subjective, eager to talk about their feelings and interested in developing relationships.
- The above having been said, men and women should be aware that they also display traits from the opposite sex, and they should try to develop the positive ones (men should be more open, cuddly and cooperative; women should think things through before relying on their emotions and shouldn't be afraid to compete).

- Be prepared to challenge stereotypes: are all men really unsentimental? Are all women really afraid of mice?
- Try to understand the evolution of the opposite sex. If you're a working woman, try to be dispassionate and see the Old Boys' Club as a natural progression of men's having long had most of the power in the world. If you're a man, try to examine why many women seem more drawn to spirituality, even to psychic and supernatural things. For a long time, many men didn't take such things seriously, but many women sought peace in them.
- Sit down and have a serious conversation, and don't be afraid to bring up these issues. Lack of communication is often behind fear and poor relationships.
- Don't criticize or judge someone of the opposite sex who reacts with different emotions than you. Says marriage counselor William F. Harley Jr., "The five most important emotional needs of men are usually the least important for women, and vice versa...the two sexes lack empathy."

Author's Two Cents:

My wife is from a family of boys. Our first date was to a Buffalo Bills game. Sometimes I ask her if we always have to watch football on Sunday. She wonders why I sometimes wear more jewelry than she does. I consider our relationship healthy because we allow each other to break gender stereotypes.

A MANTRA TO TELL YOURSELF: *"Understand a different way of thinking."*

References:

He Says, She Says: Closing the Communications Gap Between the Sexes by Lillian Glass, Putnam, 1993

Men Are from Mars, Women Are from Venus by John Gray, HarperCollins, 1992

You Just Don't Understand by Deborah Tannen, Ballantine, 1990

See: fear of intimacy or love, fear of not being loved, fear of rejection, sexual fears, fear of responsibility, fear of commitment, fear of becoming a parent

Fear of Commitment

gamophobia (fear of marriage)

We have to make a conscious decision for commitment. That means choosing not to have affairs, choosing not to make another person as important as our partner, choosing to talk to our partner rather than someone else when we're angry, choosing to listen, choosing to see things through.
—AUTHOR AND CONSULTANT REX BRIGGS

Characteristics: This condition keeps people from committing to others for such reasons as an inability to trust or to take responsibility. Those affected may not want to go steady or get engaged or married; they may even balk at having relationships. This fear can leave people with sad lives and few close friendships.

Background: We live in an increasingly fast society in which commitment often takes a back seat. Indeed, 50 percent of marriages fail. But without commitment, can there really be true love? Some people just won't take a chance to come out of their comfort zone. People who lack commitment in one area, such as romance, may not in another area, such as a job or an organization.

Strategies:

- Commitment may sound like a kind of straitjacket, but if both parties compromise, it won't be too tight or too foreboding. Talk openly about the relationship, and get to know what each person needs and expects from the other.
- Be aware that this fear may be a sign of immaturity. It may also indicate that you lack the patience, passion or discipline required in a healthy relationship.
- It may, however, simply be a sign that you don't want commitment with a certain person, or that you don't love them or don't see yourself developing love for them. Think it through. Maybe there is something about the other person you don't like, or would like to see improved. Talk to them about it.
- If someone is willing to make a commitment to you, consider taking it as inspiration to increase your own effort.

- How can you tell if he or she is Mr. or Mrs. Right? No one is ever completely sure of such things.
- Don't fool yourself: making a full commitment, especially to marriage and perhaps children, is a life-altering decision.
- Maybe you want to stay single. Who said there was anything wrong with that? Well, lots of people, but it doesn't mean they are right in every instance.
- If you don't get into a relationship because you don't trust others, consider the words of therapist Robert Epstein: "Yes, people sometimes cheat and lie, but they sometimes are also faithful and truthful. Trust is a matter of interpreting what people do positively. You decide—trust or live in isolation."
- If you have trouble committing to things in other areas, such as in work, family life or school, you might have to develop the same type of patience, passion or discipline required in a relationship. Sign up for a course or an organization in which you have to stay the course for at least several months; if you can't do it alone, do it with a friend.

A MANTRA TO TELL YOURSELF: *"I'll take a stand on taking a stand" (make a decision on whether to make a commitment).*

Reference:

Transforming Anxiety, Transcending Shame by Rex Briggs, Health Communications, 1999

See: fear of taking chances, fear of the unknown, fear of intimacy or love, fear of responsibility, fear of the opposite sex, sexual fears, fear of becoming a parent, fears for your marriage/partnership

Fear of Ending a Romantic Relationship

neophobia (fear of anything new)	*There are no cut-and-dried answers, merely accumulated feelings that show it is time to end a relationship.*

—BARRY LUBETKIN AND ELENA OUMANO, AUTHORS OF *BAILING OUT*

Characteristics: People with this fear often stay in stale or abusive relationships because of apprehension or guilt over a breakup, or through fear of hurting the other person's feelings. They may even fear physical reprisal or reprisal against friends or children caught in the middle. Others are just lazy or don't want to give up familiar surroundings.

Background: Breaking a bond, especially a long one, can be very difficult physically, emotionally and spiritually, particularly if people are married with children. We all form bonds that we are reluctant to break, out of concern for either our own needs or the other person's. We may be very needy and have emotional holes from a poor home life or an earlier relationship. And we may fear that we'll never get another relationship if this one ends. In general, most people are afraid of the type of confrontation a breakup can create. People may also be afraid of giving up the friends or the perks that came along with their partner. Many spouses of powerful people or celebrities stay in poor relationships because they don't want to give up the high life.

Strategies:

- Be certain that you want to end the relationship. Many bonds simply need more commitment, compromise and work.
- Look for warning signs that the relationship may be on the way out: Are you feeling disconnected from the person or have you stopped caring? Do you feel you can't trust him or her anymore? Are you being abused physically or emotionally? Have you become too critical? Are you looking for excuses to be apart? Have you been to counseling and decided it cannot help?

- Find the right time and place to break up. Usually, it's best to break up when no one else is around, but if you feel it may spark an emotional or physical reaction, you may want to do it in a public place or with witnesses.
- Once you have decided on ending the relationship, tell the person why. Don't blame one another. Breakups are complex and usually occur for more than one reason. Be respectful and kind, even after the relationship is over. Don't end it with a bad taste in your mouths. Anger is often a counterproductive emotion.
- Understand that the other person will likely feel hurt or sad. Perhaps you'll both feel that way and it may take some time to get over.
- If you are married, don't be so quick to end the relationship. You may later regret it and find it is hard to patch up. But if you do end it, protect your rights and see a lawyer.
- In the early days after the breakup, expect a range of emotions. Try to keep busy. And don't jump into another relationship right away. There may be chances for reconciliation.
- Don't stay around just for the sex.

A MANTRA TO TELL YOURSELF: *"I'll do what must be done."*

Reference:

Crucial Conversations: Tools for Talking When Stakes Are High by Kerry Patterson, Joseph Grenny, Ron McMillan, Al Switzer and Stephen R. Covey, McGraw-Hill, 2002

See: fear of not being loved, fear of what others think, fear of change, fear of failure, fear of the opposite sex, fear of delivering bad news

Fear of Homosexuality

homophobia (fear of homosexuality)	*The biggest problem we've got is the primitive, age-old fear and dehumanization of people who are not like us.*

—PRESIDENT BILL CLINTON, TO GAY AND LESBIAN SUPPORTERS IN 1999

Characteristics: This is the fear, anxiety, anger, discomfort or aversion that some heterosexual people feel toward gays and lesbians. Some people discriminate against or harass gays and lesbians; in extreme cases, people even commit acts of violence against them. Others fear they are attracted to members of the same sex or worry that they are perceived as gay or lesbian themselves.

Background: Homosexuality exists throughout the animal kingdom and is a natural phenomenon. But surveys show that up to 70 percent of the American public is homophobic. Many people fear what they don't understand or what they feel threatens them or their beliefs. Other factors accounting for homophobia include rigid gender roles, social pressure to fear and hate gays, institutionalized heterosexism and homophobic religious beliefs. Some research suggests that homophobia is sometimes the result of repressed homosexual urges that a person is either unaware of or denies.

Strategies:

- Ask yourself how open you are about others' sexuality and about your own. Think the issues through and don't be afraid of them.
- Keep an open mind and be receptive to new research. Much of what we have been taught has been colored by bias, stereotyping and misinformation or has been based on lack of information. We're still finding out new things, partly because gays and lesbians have been reluctant to come forward with information.
- Be aware that most serious research points to genetics and not environment as the cause of homosexuality, although this question remains open to debate. "Mental health professionals used to consider homosexuality a type of mental illness, but now it's seen as a normal condition that is at least partially determined by genes," says psychologist Robert Epstein.

- Get to know an openly gay man or woman and listen closely if they talk about their attitudes and life. Discuss yours with them.
- Refrain from hating homophobics. Understand that some people genuinely see homosexuality as a threat to procreation, world health (through AIDS) or their religious beliefs.
- If you discriminate against someone because of sexual preference, think of how you would feel if someone did the same thing to you.
- Understand that many men and women who appear to be gay are not.
- Some of the most creative, productive people are openly gay: Olympic gold medal swimmer Mark Tewksbury, singer kd lang, tennis legend Martina Navratilova, actors Ian McKellan and Ellen DeGeneres, to name but a few.

A MANTRA TO TELL YOURSELF: *"Understanding and tolerance."*

Author's Two Cents:

While conducting two major investigations into AIDS for newspapers, I found gay men to be generally nonthreatening, sensitive and caring. This discovery made me less intimidated by them.

References:

And the Band Played On by Randy Shilts, St. Martin's, 2001

Homophobia: How We All Pay the Price by Warren Blumenfeld, Beacon, 2002

See: fear of other races, sexual fears, fear of religion, fear of what others think, fear of the unknown, fear of the opposite sex

Fears at School

Fear of School

scolionophobia (fear of going to school)

sophophobia (fear of learning)

Nearly all children will have some reluctance and fear going to school. They eventually get over it with encouragement and support...stay calm and tell them you love them.

—FAMILY PSYCHOLOGIST MICHAEL G. CONNER

Characteristics: Up to 10 percent of children suffer from a mild form of fear of school, and about 1 percent have a serious form of it. Some children may fake illness or throw tantrums or have tension or stomach cramps. They may stay away from school or complain about the teachers, the principal, the curriculum, classmates or bullies, or they may fear being punished. Even children who like school may get stressed going back after summer vacation. Some children are afraid of getting undressed for gym or going to the bathroom. Healthy fear or respect can make some lazy students try harder.

Background: There may be many reasons for fear of school: some children are afraid of leaving home (separation fear); others are afraid of teachers, of having to work hard, of not living up to parents' expectations, of not being accepted or popular, or of other students or bullies. This fear can last an entire academic career, or it can come and go, depending on the circumstances of the student or the school. In some cases, fear may be related to not liking school—many children do not like structure or being told what to do. A British study of students 7 to 16 years of age showed that 46 percent of them were stressed about doing well at school, 43 percent worried about coming into contact with drugs and alcohol, 40 percent feared being bullied, 37 percent worried about future education and 34 percent worried about friendships at school.

Strategies:

- All children grumble about school occasionally, but be wary if your child constantly complains about school, teachers or classmates. Examine if the fear is specific—students may fear a certain teacher or course, they may fear bullies, peer pressure or the prospect of looking stupid, or they may fear the pressures of exams or competition, of speaking before a class, of hard work or of having to get a job when it's all over. Whew!

- Maybe the fear is academic, or the curriculum is not suited to the individual. Maybe the student believes he or she is not allowed to be expressive or creative. If this is the case, see a counselor or trusted teacher.
- Don't coddle your children too much—they'll become too dependent and fearful. On the other hand, if you pressure them too much academically, they may rebel or quit.
- If you believe your child suffers from separation anxiety, slowly desensitize her to the situation by going with her to class for a brief time, and then gradually decrease that amount. Talk about this condition with the teacher. If the child still refuses to go to school, find ways to help boost her confidence. Children will eventually adjust to school when they realize they can handle it by themselves.
- Encourage your child to join a club, a sports team or an activity. Consider becoming a volunteer. Motivation in one area can spill over to another, such as the academic field.
- It's possible that a health issue is involved. Perhaps the student is allergic to something or there is poor circulation in the building.
- In any type of serious case, get the teachers and school nurses or counselors involved. Counselors are there not only to guide students about education and career choices, but also to help them with lifestyle and stress issues.

A MANTRA FOR PARENTS: *"With my encouragement, my child will be fine."*

References:

The School Years by Benjamin Spock, Simon & Schuster, 2001

David A. Gershaw, psychologist, Arizona Western College, DAGershaw@aol.com

See: fear of change, stress and fear in children, fear of strangers, fear of religion (in some private schools), fear of bullies and all the school fears

Fear of the First Day of School

separation anxiety syndrome (children's fear of being separated from their parents, which can also occur the other way around)	*September finds more than one parent walking away from a preschool or elementary school classroom with misty eyes... for women, separation anxiety actually begins at birth and continues through various stages.* —PARENT EDUCATOR ELAINE M. GIBSON

Characteristics: Apprehension in children and/or parents about the first day of school is natural and common. Signs of nervousness may appear before or during that day, including dry throat, trembling or lack of confidence. There may be a lot of crying and clinging to parents for at least the first few days. Parents may feel guilty that their child is put into a situation where he or she is afraid.

Background: Nature creates a tight bond between parents and child to ensure the child's survival and care. When a young child's parents have always been close by, it can be traumatic to be suddenly without them and among strangers at school. Letting go of a lifeline is sad, but necessary to the development of both child and parents.

Strategies:
- At an early age, get your children gradually used to your occasional absences. Until the age of three, most children can't understand the concept of time. When you leave briefly, they may think you are gone forever.
- Improve your child's social and play skills. Get the child used to other relatives and visitors and make visits to others' homes. Show your children love and security, but teach them skills in getting along with others and give them some freedom.
- At first, ask to occasionally sit in on school activities and see how your child interacts with teachers and classmates.
- Make sure your child has sufficient verbal skills to communicate with others. Read age-appropriate books with them.
- Before the big first day, tell the child that he will be going to school and reassure him that it will be a good experience. Use role playing or puppets to act out the first day. Consider riding the bus with your child the first day. Let the child bring a security object (a stuffed toy) or your photo to class.

- Don't overreact if your child cries and refuses to leave your side. Most teachers will allow you to stay for a while. When you leave, don't sneak out; it may make the child feel abandoned.
- If you are anxious, don't show it in front of your child, who may pick up on it. Learn to deal with your own issues of separation and try to trust other adults with your child's needs.
- With each step, children gain freedom and independence on their way to growing up. And parents learn to relinquish some of their control for the benefit of the child.

Author's Two Cents:

We put our shy three-year-old Kevin in preschool too young. He accumulated a softball-sized clump of tear-soaked tissues and planned on stealing a tricycle to sneak home. We pulled him out, but even two years later, he was afraid when we dropped him off at kindergarten. Later in kindergarten, his mother and older brother had to stay with him in class through part of the morning for several weeks. Finally an understanding teacher got him through it. Kevin slowly developed his social skills and now shows leadership in groups.

A MANTRA FOR PARENTS: *"Take a deep breath, then go"* OR *"She's not a baby anymore."*

References:

My First Day of School by P.K. Hallinan, Ideals Children's Books, 2001

When You Go to Kindergarten by James Howe and Betsy Imershein, Mulberry, 1995

Life Advice, www.lifeadvice.com

See: fear of not having control, fear of school, fear of your children leaving home, fear of the unknown, fear of showing emotions, fear and stress in children, fear of being alone, fear of strangers, fear of panic attacks in public

Fear of Appearing Stupid

asthenophobia (fear of weakness)

catagelophobia (fear of ridicule)

Zeal will do more than knowledge.
—AUTHOR WILLIAM HAZLITT

Characteristics: Nobody wants to look stupid or inadequate. But some students suffer from serious anxiety or withdrawal because they believe others—classmates, friends, teachers or smart students—think of them as academically inferior. Some students may lose motivation, exaggerate their prowess or even cheat because of this condition. In extreme cases, this fear can lead to depression, antisocial behavior and substance abuse.

Background: In an education center such as a school, much of the focus is on intelligence and the ability to learn; hence, the popularity of tags such as nerd, geek, brain, dumbbell, clueless and professional student. A healthy fear of appearing inadequate can sometimes motivate a student through a school career that may span 15 years or more. A student's home environment and circle of friends can have a heavy influence on this fear. If people are constantly told they are stupid, they might start to believe it. In our society, we are constantly aware of how we measure up to others, and we worry if they look down on us. This fear can make one try hard, but it can also make one try *too* hard.

Strategies:

- Step back and gain some perspective. Just because you think you appear stupid to others doesn't mean others actually feel that way. If you have this mindset, it may be that your family or friends continually talk down to you.
- We all have an inner critic—a little voice in our head that is constantly giving us advice and often judging us. Challenge the inner voice if it keeps putting you down. Ask yourself where it comes from and how much credence you should give it.
- Upgrade yourself through study and discipline. The best revenge against critics is living well, or in this case, learning well. Examine your level of academic competence and ask yourself if you are where you want to be.

- Don't be afraid to ask for a tutor. A little extra help, or just bouncing your thoughts and ideas off a tutor, can take you to another level academically and boost your confidence.
- Remember that everyone is different. People peak and learn at different ages; boys, especially, tend to be late bloomers academically.
- Don't hang around with negative people who constantly run others down. Praise others for their knowledge. While alone, praise yourself.
- If you worry too much about what others think or if you constantly compare yourself with others, maybe you need to develop your confidence and determination.
- If you're a parent, don't put all your emphasis on the three Rs. Encourage your kids to think for themselves and to understand ideas, to learn cooperation and empathy for others, and to familiarize themselves with the behaviors of other cultures as well as their own.
- If you flunk out, try to bounce back. But remember, Joan of Arc was illiterate, comedian Jack Benny was expelled from high school after failing, and Benjamin Franklin attended school for just a few years and was largely self-taught.
- If nothing else, establish some structure and discipline; you'll need it as an adult.

  A MANTRA TO TELL YOURSELF: *"I might not become Einstein, but I am intelligent, and I can develop it."*

Reference:

Test Taking Secrets by Steve Frank, Adams Media, 1998

See: fear of embarrassment, fear of failure, fear of criticism, fear of rejection, fear of what others think, fear of what friends think, fear of exams, fear of teachers, fear of your appearance, fear of dating, fear of the opposite sex

Fear of Exams

testophobia	*Pressure can be a good thing in small doses.* —JAY BAGLIA, TEACHING ASSISTANT, UNIVERSITY OF FLORIDA

Characteristics: Some students freeze or perform poorly when they write tests. Others feel anxious, tense or depressed about exams right from the first day of school—even good students who prepare well for them. Some are so afraid of failing, they cheat. A track record of low marks can add to the fear.

Background: For just about everyone, it's natural to be apprehensive about being tested or evaluated, whether at home, at work or at any level of school. Up to 25 percent of college students have what has been termed *math anxiety*. Students might fear failure, loss of job opportunity, or what their parents, teachers, family or friends might think. Indeed, upbringing has a large effect on a student's apprehension toward tests; demanding mothers or fathers can push children to great heights, but can also burden them with too much pressure. On the other hand, overly casual parents may leave students without the respect for curriculum and exams they need to be successful. Teachers' expectations also provide pressure, or lack of it.

Strategies:
- When approaching an exam, try not to put too much pressure on yourself; keep your goals realistic. A test may be important, but it won't be the end of the world if you don't attain the mark you seek. Show respect to the wishes of your parents and teachers, but make your goals your own. Some students set their own academic standards too high or are too hard on themselves.
- Test yourself prior to the exam, or have someone test you, then mark you critically. Simulating a type of pressure in advance allows you to get used to the feelings of tension and anxiety. Then, when the exam day comes, you'll feel as if you've been through it already. Some schools give test-taking practice; check to see if *your* school does.

- Study intensely over an extended period, but don't cram. Conceptualize the work, the theories and the ideas. Don't memorize: if you do, you take the risk of your structure breaking down if you forget one section.
- Before an important test, make sure you get the right amount of sleep and exercise and eat a balanced diet.
- Remember that a *manageable* amount of pressure and intensity can actually bring out the best in you, as long as you are well prepared. You don't want to be too casual or you might not be mentally sharp. The hormones released by your nervous system can help you concentrate at a higher level if you remain calm or direct the energy into your work.
- The start of a test is important. Take a few deep breaths and do the easier questions first. If possible, take short breaks. Close your eyes and relax. Even 30 seconds of deep breathing can reduce distress.
- Put yourself on automatic pilot and let your subconscious and your knowledge take over. If you try too hard, you'll get in your own way. Focus on the process, not the potential results. After you receive your marks, review and analyze everything, including your strategies. Think of your errors as an opportunity to grow and learn.
- If these strategies don't work, it's possible that your daily anxiety levels are too high. You may have too many pressures in your life, or may not be managing your pressures properly. You might want to see a school counselor.
- Parents, monitor the attitudes and tension levels of your children throughout the year and especially at exam time.

A MANTRA TO TELL YOURSELF: *"I'm not perfect, but I'm ready."*

References:

Take the Anxiety Out of Taking Tests by Susan Johnson, Publishers Group West, 1996

Sylvan Learning Center, (866) 732-3438, www.educate.com

See: fear of the unknown, fear of not having control, fear of failure, fear of making mistakes, fear of criticism, fear of appearing stupid, fear of what friends think, fear of not having or getting a job, fear of losing status, dealing with deadline pressure

Fear of Teachers

tyrannophobia (fear of tyrants)	*When you make peace with authority, you become authority.* —ROCK STAR JIM MORRISON
dikephobia (fear of justice)	**Characteristics:** Nowadays we often hear about lack of respect for authority and teachers. Yet many students still fear

teachers, or at least worry about going to school or a class because a teacher is harsh or unfair, or makes students look foolish in front of the class or work hard. Some students worry that a teacher will give negative appraisal to their parents.

Background: Fear of authority is common among children, especially those who have harsh, overprotective or argumentative parents. It's natural for a child, even a teenager, to be in awe of someone with so much knowledge and power. If a child feels the teacher is not meeting his or her needs, this awe could turn into distress. But *healthy* fear of or respect for a teacher can boost student production and discipline and make going to school challenging, even pleasurable.

Strategies:
- Realize that if a teacher seems critical, it's probably not personal; teachers are human and have different personalities and even prejudices. Some teachers are more authoritarian than others. They also have lots of pressure with increasing workloads and class sizes. What a job! One day, try to volunteer for sessions in which you are given authority, or pretend you are the teacher and put yourself in their shoes.
- Don't engage in anti-teacher talk with other students. This will lower class morale, could erode your relationship with the teacher and may make you more cynical.
- Understand the changing climate; society has less respect for authority than it had in the past. This can cause frustration in teachers who grew up in a different era. Do your small part by trying to foster more mutual respect.
- Consider the possibility that you are more afraid of the subject than of the teacher. Let the teacher know if you need special

help. Talk through problems and issues with the teacher one-on-one, or involve your parents or counselor.

- Do something nice for your teacher, even if he or she isn't nice to you. Volunteer on a class trip or clean up after a group experiment.
- If you constantly blame a teacher for your failures, chances are you will blame authority figures in other stages of your life. Learn to take responsibility.
- If you continue to be a good student, chances are you will eventually develop a good relationship with the teacher. You are together every day; why not try to get along?
- Parents, don't allow an issue between you or your child and a teacher to rob the child of a proper education. If you suspect that legitimate problems exist between your child and a teacher, initiate a meeting and volunteer to be a go-between to deal with the issues. Consider becoming a volunteer at the school.

A MANTRA TO TELL YOURSELF: *"The teach is human."*

Author's Two Cents:

As a sports coach and school volunteer for 20 years, I found that any problems I had with children under me and their parents usually had to do with communication. I occasionally held group and individual meetings to get the issues out in the open; I also encouraged the children to come to me one-on-one. If the kids were afraid of me, I wanted to find it out from them.

Reference:

www.teachers.net

See: fear of not having control, fear of criticism, fear of embarrassment, fear of failure, fear and stress in children, fear of strangers, fear of school, fear of appearing stupid, fear of the boss, fear of confrontation or conflict, fear of responsibility

Fear of What Friends Think

peer pressure

Peer pressure can be frightening for kids and parents in adolescence when the young are challenging so many basic values: demanding the right to sexual freedom at younger and younger age periods and becoming involved increasingly in pregnancies, experimenting with drugs and alcohol.
—DR. BENJAMIN SPOCK

Characteristics: This condition involves excessive concern for the esteem of friends. People who change their behavior or appearance to suit their friends—for example, by smoking, drinking or disrespecting teachers—could be overly afraid of what their friends think. Some students become depressed. Sometimes, though, peer pressure can be a positive thing and can result in people upgrading their marks or getting involved in school activities.

Background: Friends are very important to a young person, especially in the teenage years when identities are being molded. Youths sometimes rebel against their parents and look for independence and, ironically, acceptance from others at the same time. The people they get involved with could have a major impact on them and they make take on their mannerisms, even if only subconsciously. Students are particularly impressionable in the first years of middle school, high school and college, when they don't fully have their bearings at a school. Students who develop confidence and a strong sense of identity at home have less chance of being heavily influenced by peer groups.

Strategies:

- Assess how much influence your friends are having on your schoolwork, your personal life and your attitude, and ask yourself if it is positive. At what expense do you want to be liked? If you're a student, school is pretty much your job. Are you willing to let others screw it up, or screw up your future?
- Five years from now, the people you are trying to impress likely won't be involved in your life. But the decisions you make could still be affecting you. In reality, your friends probably don't care as much about what you do as you think they do.

Most people are focused more on themselves, or worried about what *you* think of *them*.

- As pals, influence one another in a productive way; join a school club or a sports team or study together.
- We all want to be liked and accepted by our friends, but we should also try to win the respect of our other classmates, our parents and our teachers.
- Be wary of "friends" who want to try borderline things and justify their own behavior by getting other kids (perhaps ones with stronger values) to go along. But don't forget to have a blast once in a while, as long as it is not at others' expense.
- Don't stay in a negative relationship for fear of what friends and family might think if you break up.
- If you are a parent, listen with compassion, not judgment, when your child talks about friends, but don't back down from your values. Look upon this as a time to solidify your relationship with your children, while understanding that they also need others to balance their lives. Get to know the parents of your child's friends. Monitor TV and telephone time.
- You can't avoid the media hype and consumerism, but if you refuse a request for a peer-pressure item or clothes, explain your reasons. Maybe you can't afford it, or you think your child is too young, or you think it's dangerous or mean-spirited. Don't give in just because you feel guilty about not spending enough time with your child.
- Teach your children to stand up for themselves in disagreements with friends and praise them for doing the right thing.

A MANTRA TO TELL YOURSELF: *"I'm me"* OR *"Real friends will accept me for me."*

References:

The Complete Idiot's Guide to Surviving Peer Pressure for Teens by Hilary Cherniss and Sara Jane Sluke, Alpha, 2001

Parent Guidance Workshops, New York, founder Nancy Samalin, www.samalin.com

See: fear of what others think, fear of not being loved, fear of rejection, fear of cliques, fear of appearing stupid, fear of confrontation or conflict

Fear of Cliques

enochlophobia (fear of crowds)   *Everybody sticks together in these dirty little goddam cliques. The guys that are on the basketball team stick together, the goddam intellectuals stick together, the guys that play bridge stick together. Even the guys that belong to the goddam Book-of-the-Month Club stick together. —*HOLDEN CAULFIELD, IN J.D. SALINGER'S *CATCHER IN THE RYE*

Characteristics: Individuals or groups may be suspicious or antagonistic toward other groups who may not share their attitudes, dress, music or behavior. This may appear as a dislike of another group, but deep down it might be a fear that stems from mutual intimidation.

Background: This fear is similar to the fear of other races or any people who are different from us. We are all hardwired with an us vs. them gene, which protected us from strange tribes when we were primitive people. This fear can be potent because students are confined in the same building every day. Of course, joining a group can have benefits when it gives a student some positive direction. Students often join subcultures such as the hip hop, punk, skater, raver, goth, metalhead or alternative scenes because they want to become accepted by others or join a common cause. Although such group affiliation can be healthy, it can sometimes cause rivalry with other groups.

Strategies:

* Fear of other cliques often comes from lack of understanding. Start by communicating with students or groups of students who are different from you. Encourage communication; perhaps start with the most approachable member of a group or, if the climate is acceptable, hold a "clique party." At one point in my newspaper career, I brought together numerous subcultures in a high school for an article and, after they had openly discussed their attitudes and desires, they went away with a better appreciation and understanding of one another.

- On the other hand, be suspicious of groups who are always negative or destructive. You won't change them, but they may change you.
- Examine your attitude; it's possible that you dislike people only out of arrogance. You may look down on them and believe they are not worthy of your attention.
- If you are part of a clique, be conscious of it and don't make others feel like outsiders. Don't provoke other cliques or try to accentuate your differences from them.
- Don't judge individuals who are part of a group. They may not even agree with the group they are associating with; rather, they may be lonely and just want to be accepted.
- If you are a parent or teacher, monitor the student's situation, but always remember that children are looking to develop their identities, and that means associating with people other than adults. Sometimes it's hard for parents to accept that.

A MANTRA TO TELL YOURSELF: *"Deep down, they're probably like me."*

References:

Cliques: 8 Steps to Help Your Child Survive the Social Jungle by Charlene C. Giannetti and Margaret Sagarese, Broadway, 2001

Cliques, Phonies and Other Baloney by Trevor Romain, Free Spirit, 1998

See: fear of what friends think, fear of rejection, fear of other races, fear of confrontation or conflict, fear of strangers, fear of homosexuality, fear of your appearance, fear of bullies

Fear of Your Appearance

obesophobia (fear of gaining weight)

Not being beautiful was the true blessing... it forced me to develop my inner resources. The pretty [person] has a handicap to overcome. —GOLDA MEIR

Characteristics: Worry about body shape, facial looks or clothes can lead to anxiety, stress, missing school, ill health and even eating disorders. Some people develop distorted views of their appearance, believing they are ugly or fat when they're not. Many are afraid of how they look in their gym clothes. Plastic surgeons report instances of children as young as 14 coming in with their parents to request surgery. A mild form of this fear can encourage people to take pride in themselves and their appearance.

Background: Everyone wants to impress others to some degree and to put on the best possible face while covering up their weaknesses. It seems a sad indictment of our society (indeed, of our history as human beings), but the pretty people often get more attention, while some others retreat and even suffer self-esteem problems. The fashion industry taps into society's obsession with looks; many ads now have teenagers in sexual poses.

How you feel about yourself, your shape and your appearance has a lot to do with how you were raised and how your parents felt about themselves. The teen years are filled with self-discovery and self-doubt. As we grow older, we realize that appearance is just a small part of who we really are.

Strategies:
- Keep this fear in perspective. Intense focus on your appearance can lead to a superficial, distorted attitude. You can start worrying more about your clothes than your intelligence, personality, skills or other things you have to offer.
- Do you feel you are inadequate because you don't have a perfectly round face or Michael Jordan basketball shoes? Get your priorities in order—it's who you are as a human being that counts. Being a nice person and helping and inspiring others is a lot more important than looks or shoes.

- Make the most out of what you've got while being as natural as possible. Be yourself, but don't be sloppy. When you dress in a "presentable" way, you look professional, even if you're still young. But be cautious about buying expensive clothes just because your friends have them. If they have a hang-up with materialism, that's their problem.
- Have fun with your look! Overload with jewelry one day, or wear jeans if appropriate. Having a fun attitude might take the pressure off trying to keep up with your peers.
- Eating a balanced diet and staying in shape have many benefits, but if you are concerned about your physique, don't go overboard. Metabolism is an individual thing; some people retain fat more than others, while others burn their blood sugar more quickly.
- If students continually tease you about the way you look, beat them to the punch by poking fun at yourself. This can take the sting out of their comments. If you are afraid of losing friends over your looks, those may be friends not worth having.
- If you fret about your body shape in gym class, look around; people come in different shapes and sizes. Would you look down at someone with a body shape you didn't like? Then don't look down at yourself.
- If you believe you have an eating disorder, see a trusted teacher or school counselor. And, of course, talk to your parents about it.
- Parents, talk to your teenagers about the importance of appearance, but do a lot of listening and don't try to impose your standards on them.
- If you continually try to prove yourself through your appearance, you might have an inferiority complex. Remember the words of former first lady Eleanor Roosevelt: "No one can make you feel inferior without your consent."

A MANTRA TO TELL YOURSELF: *"I'm cool."*

Reference:

Smart Eating: Choosing Wisely, Living Lean by Covert Bailey and Ronda Gates, Houghton Mifflin, 1996

See: fear of what others think, fear of what friends think, fear of criticism, fear of rejection, fear of not being loved, fear of embarrassment, fear of having a photo taken, fear of getting a compliment

Fear of Bullies

scelerophobia (fear of being hurt by a wicked person) *For a lot of years I've taught at the university, and I always ask my classes how many felt an impact from bullying, and probably a third raise their hands and say, "You know I'm still carrying with me a sad or frightened memory about someone doing something to me."* —CHILD SAFETY EXPERT DAVIE SCRATCHLEY

Characteristics: Fear of bullying is widespread. Students may become anxious or depressed and avoid situations or classes because they fear physical or verbal harassment or robbery. If bullying continues, it could have a long-term effect on self-esteem and confidence and result in physical injury.

Background: Bullying is a worldwide problem that has lately received more attention. Bullies, often victims themselves, know that psychological intimidation can be as fierce as physical force. Bullies may be jealous of others, insecure, afraid of being unpopular or unable to show their feelings. They may act out because they are trying to "find themselves," to prove something to others or to themselves, or to get the attention of a group they want acceptance from. Boys tend to bully with force while some girls engage in sophisticated forms of aggression such as gossip, backbiting and social isolation. These days, however, girls are increasingly getting involved in physical bullying. A Gallup poll revealed that 47 percent of parents feared for their children's safety at school.

Strategies:

- Whenever possible, try to ignore teasing, nasty comments or getting drawn into an argument. If you show you're upset, it may spur the bully on. If someone insults your appearance, abilities or race, ignore it. Resist the temptation to meet force with force. The law of the jungle where only the strongest survive is not the law of civilized society.
- If you are afraid, hang out with people you trust.
- If the bullying is a sudden, isolated incident, assess the situation and respond accordingly. Simply walk away or stand up for your rights or possessions—but don't do it at the expense of a beating. Learn to shout "No!" and walk confidently.

- If you are harassed for your possessions by someone who may become aggressive, give them up without fighting back, then report it to teachers and the police.
- If bullying continues, talk to a trusted teacher or your parents about it. In certain cases, you might want to confront the bully yourself. Some kids who are nice to your face may pick on you when they're in a group. Get them alone or on the phone and ask them why they gang up on you.
- Consider taking a self-defense course, or gain physical confidence through sports.
- Parents, be aware of signs that your child is being bullied. If a child is unhappy or gets stressed at the same time every week, hates going to certain places, has mysterious cuts or bruises, has become sullen or nervous, cries at night or when alone, or keeps losing possessions, he or she may be a victim of bullying.
- Make sure your child is not worsening a situation by countering bullying with insults or abuse. Teach your children to avoid bullies, explaining that the bullies are the ones with the problem, but also teach assertiveness and positive self-talk. If nothing helps, get involved through the teacher or even the police.

A MANTRA TO TELL YOURSELF: *"Don't get even, get help."*

References:

The Bully, the Bullied and the Bystander by Barbara Coloroso, HarperResource, 2003

Kids Help Phone (in Canada, a 24-hour phone counseling and referral service for children and youth), (800) 668-6868, www.kidshelp.sympatico.ca

National Association of School Psychologists, Bethesda, MD, (301) 657-0270, www.nasponline.org

See: fear for your children's safety, fear of being mugged, fear of illness or pain, fear of embarrassment, fear of cliques, fear of strangers, fear of confrontation or conflict, fear of invasion of territory or privacy, fear and stress in children

Fear of Not Having or Getting a Job

There are no wrong jobs. Every job is a learning experience and there is no one clear path to glamour and happiness.
—HEIDI MILLER, CHIEF FINANCIAL OFFICER OF CITIGROUP

Characteristics: Many people worry about not having a job. Students may feel pressure to get a good job—even one that can buy them a house—right out of school. This fear can affect their work habits, and add pressure during exams. Adults feel pressure to maintain their standard of living. This pressure can lead to overwork and distress, even depression and broken families. Many laid-off workers get distressed or depressed.

Background: There are few things more important to humans than providing for themselves, their future and their family. Until recently, many men were defined by their job and became depressed if they were out of work. Now women have joined the workforce in droves and have similar concerns. "It's a complicated topic, but many men still haven't been taught the skills of coping," said management consultant Jane Baddeley. "Women deal with things differently and express their feelings more. And, if a woman loses her job, she may look on it as an opportunity to stay home with her children." A fluctuating economy and unemployment rates and the specter of downsizing all add to fears and uncertainty. But many people have become motivated by this fear and have used it to make a better life.

Strategies:
- There are probably more ways to find a job now than ever before—through the Internet, newspapers, headhunters, professional journals, trade magazines, unemployment offices, cold calls and word of mouth (not to mention relatives).
- Here's how to write an effective resume: before you begin, assess your skills, abilities and goals, and jot these down on paper. Put your contact information (telephone, e-mail address and mailing address) at the top of your resume. Be specific about the job you want, but tailor your objective to each employer. Using action words, give your work experience and responsibilities. Indicate you will give references upon request. Have your resume reviewed by a career counselor.

- Develop a relationship with your school's career counselor and be sure to look out for trends or openings. Keep an open mind about your career choice.
- Keep your education and training upgraded. It's a competitive world and others are looking for the same job you are.
- When starting out, toss a wide net and don't be too choosy; you may have to work in entry-level positions before you get the job you want. Gradually try to become good at one thing. Plan your schedule of looking for work, but don't let it take over your life. Make sure you balance things with recreation, and keep taking care of your health.
- When career planning, determine the things that constitute your dream job, pinpoint companies that fit and don't allow discouraging economic news to temper your enthusiasm.
- Be open to change and trends in the workplace.
- If you have just lost your job, don't fall into anger or resentment. It happens to thousands of people. If you've left a job you didn't like, you'll eventually feel a sense of relief. Seek friends and family to support you emotionally or see a counselor.
- Losing a job or changing jobs are two of life's most stressful events. But if it is done properly, career transition can be one of life's biggest learning opportunities, a time for self-exploration and reflection. You can come out of it with a better perspective and a hungrier attitude.
- Don't let your job—or lack of a job—define who you are. It's an important part of your life, but so is being a son or a mother or a volunteer or a friend.

A MANTRA TO TELL YOURSELF: *"I will land on my feet."*

References:

The Resume Handbook by Arthur Rosenberg and David V. Hizer, Adams Media, 1995

What Color Is Your Parachute 2003 by Richard Bolles, Ten Speed Press, 2002

See: financial fears, fear of downsizing, fear of the unknown, fear of what others think, fear of failure, fear of exams, fear of losing status, fear of a job interview, fear of quitting

Fears at Work

Stress at Work

ponophobia (fear of overworking)

karoshi (Japanese for death by overwork)

If you don't have a job without aggravation, you don't have a job.
—MALCOLM FORBES, ART COLLECTOR, AUTHOR AND PUBLISHER

Characteristics: Who hasn't felt stressed at work, at least occasionally? While some stress is normal, some people feel stretched thin physically, emotionally and spiritually; others feel tense, irritable and unproductive; and others feel dizzy, grind their teeth or have chest pains. Some workers even burn out, particularly people in service jobs, because they are often empathetic towards others and don't take time for themselves. On the other hand, pressure can also be a positive force: we can use it to increase our passion, our physical and mental skills and our efficiency.

Background: Stress, pressure and fear at work can be double-edged swords, at times helping with production and focus through eustress but more often causing tension, poor focus and fatigue through distress. It's estimated that the U.S. economy loses $300 billion annually through worker absenteeism related to distress. This problem seems to have grown in recent years as many companies and workers have been asked to do more with fewer resources, partly because of government cutbacks. And the pace of business has accelerated. Many workers feel powerless and uncertain about their jobs. Peoples' reactions to bureaucracy and office politics are also major contributors to distress. All of these factors combine to create cumulative distress, which may take some time for workers to defuse. The No. 1 stressor in many studies is interruptions; the average interruption experienced by a manager lasts six to nine minutes, and it takes three to 23 minutes to recover. People with physical jobs are generally not as prone to distress because they are able to channel their nervous energy into their work.

Strategies:

- Identify how you react to pressure at work—do you generally focus better under the gun or do you choke, letting your emotions interfere with your production? Understand that you may do both at various times, depending on the circumstances and your energy levels. Try to improve in the areas in which you most often perform poorly.

- Examine whether you are putting too much pressure on yourself by setting expectations too high.
- Without overdoing it, lose yourself in your work by focusing on the task and your skills, not on results.
- Talk with your coworkers or superiors about having more input and power in your job.
- See to your needs. Keep your energy levels up with a balanced diet and enough sleep. Exercise, breakfast and a shower before work are beneficial.
- Keep your commute to work manageable by rising a little earlier in the morning and using relaxation techniques while driving home, such as music and positive self-talk. Carpooling is a great idea.
- When hassles and tension appear, it's how you react that defines whether you are an effective worker. Find one or more "letting go" techniques that work for you: music, meditation, daydreaming, humor, exercise, stretching or taking breaks. Your mind and body need recovery after intense periods of work.
- "Master your breathing and you'll be able to find calm sanctuary in even the most stressful work environments," writes Paul Wilson in his book *Calm at Work*. "Take air through your nostrils and expel it through your mouth. Breathe slowly, six to eight breaths a minute."
- Don't drink more than two cups of coffee or tea in a day. Try herbal tea or hot water with lemon.
- Make good use of your time. Some surveys show that holding too many meetings is the No. 1 time waster and a cause of distress in many businesses. Another problem is too much socializing. Consider using a headset for the phone, allowing you to do other things with your hands. Don't feel that you have to answer all e-mails immediately.
- Sharpen your focus and streamline your tasks: prioritize, stay on schedule, reduce paperwork and cut down on distractions by telling coworkers if you don't have time to socialize or you

really can't help them with a question. Organize your work station so that you feel you have more control.

- Allow time to think; for conceptual thinking, you need quiet. Set aside an hour or more daily when you will not be reached by phone. Keep a private e-mail address for the more important notices and make it available only to a select few. If possible, do some work out of the office.

- Pace yourself. If the workload becomes too heavy, prioritize, delegate and learn to say no. Balance your expectations with the hours and resources you have; people who work more than 50 hours a week usually are not efficient. Don't be on call unless it's necessary. Learn to identify the signs of burnout: lack of incentive, energy or ideas.

- Take regular recovery breaks. Connect with a coworker for lunch, exercise or chill out. Take enough time off throughout the year. Don't take your work or your problems home with you.

- Many offices have found that production improves when music is played—music can even regulate the employees' heart rates. However, musical tastes are subjective, so you might want to use a headset.

- Take care of your posture and make sure your work station is ergonomic. Physical tension leads to more distress.

- If you get distressed through boredom, try to be more creative, but also consider the words of M.C. McIntosh: "Every job has drudgery. The first secret of happiness is the recognition of this fundamental fact."

- If you make mistakes, choke or have occasional spats with others, welcome to the club. Everybody does. Laugh at yourself. The average child laughs 300 times a day, the average adult only 17 times. We're too serious! Encourage periodic dress-down days.

- Be sure to have stress control on Sunday nights and Monday mornings; research shows that Mondays are the most stressful day, triggering more strokes and heart attacks than other days of the week.

- We live in a job-based culture. In the big picture, assess how much of your identity and time goes into your work and how much balance you have with your personal life.

Most Stressful Jobs: teacher, U.S. president, police officer, stockbroker, secretary, laborer, air-traffic controller, inspector, office manager, administrator, waiter, farmer, physician

Less Stressful Jobs: scientist, architect, programmer, librarian, civil engineer, professor, lineman

> A MANTRA TO TELL YOURSELF: *"Balance everything, including pressure."*

> QUOTABLE: *"Oh, you hate your job? Why didn't you say so? There's a support group for that. It's called EVERYBODY, and they meet at the bar."*—comic Drew Carey

Author's Two Cents:

At two jobs I had, I was able to find a group of noon-hour basketball players at the local YMCA. After a 30-minute sweat, we went back to work not only more relaxed, but with more "calm" energy. After the games, I had a light lunch with no alcohol. If such games become too competitive, however, they can be counterproductive and kick in your ego defense system and cause more distress.

References:

Stress Management for Dummies by Allen Elkin, IDG Books, 1999

Surviving Job Stress by John B. Arden, Career Press, 2002

See: fear of not having control, fear of the unknown, fear of failure, fear of making mistakes, fear of what others think, fear of criticism, financial fears and the other work-related fears

Financial Fears

peniaphobia (fear of poverty)	*Robber: "Your money or your life."*
	Comedian Jack Benny: "Let me think
chrometophobia (fear of money)	*about it."*

Characteristics: Insecurity or worry about having enough money to pay the bills, to keep up a certain lifestyle or to send children to school is common in our society. Many people lie awake at night worrying about income and bills. Some even get ulcers over it. One survey of 1,000 Americans showed that 57 percent feared the Internal Revenue Service, while just 30 percent feared God. People who've lived through troubled economic times may develop a mindset of thriftiness or deny themselves gifts and pleasures. Some people work two jobs or become workaholics. Others may hoard their money.

Background: Because financial matters are related to powerful human needs, they produce substantial pressure and fears. Even many successful people remain insecure; comedian Jackie Gleason always kept $10 in the pocket of each suit he owned in case his riches suddenly collapsed. Personal bankruptcies hit an all-time high of 1.5 million families in 2002. Research shows that women tend to get stressed by financial fears and men by work. Despite these fears, the quality of life in North America remains high. Some people believe they are afraid of never having enough money or material goods when their *real* fear is over what others think of their lifestyle ("keeping up with the Joneses").

Strategies:

- Have regular family discussions about money. It is not talked about enough. Teach your kids how to save and budget. Get into the habit of saving. Stash money aside regularly in a variety of mutual funds and stocks or in a savings plan.
- Ease up on credit card purchases, using them only for safety and convenience. Be cautious about using them for online purchases; your identification number can be vulnerable to theft.
- Unless it is an emergency, don't borrow money from friends or family. It could later cause problems in your relationship.

- Don't let money, or lack of it, define who you are as a person, especially if you must sacrifice family life for it. People with self-doubt often fill the void with materialism.
- Cut back on take-out food and eating out. Last year, those sucked up 46 percent of American families' food budget. Pack a lunch for work.
- Prepare for your retirement by checking what pension benefits you may be eligible for. Social security will provide only about 40 percent of your total retirement income. Save in advance. When you get a raise, save it.
- Watch out for the effect of taxes; take advantage of tax-deferred and tax-exempt investment opportunities.
- Teenagers should try to save their summer cash. Bankrate.com has a test to see how good teenagers are with money.
- Get insurance coverage for your home, even if you are renting.
- If you have problems motivating yourself to work, or to make extra cash, think of your loved ones, who would benefit from it, or target something you want to buy and work toward paying for it.
- Don't panic or make drastic decisions if you face money problems; there are enough social safety nets in our society to catch you until you can get back on your feet.

A MANTRA TO TELL YOURSELF: *"It's only money...if you have enough."*

QUOTABLE: *"To be satisfied with what one has, that is wealth. As long as one sorely needs a certain additional amount, that man isn't rich."*—Mark Twain

Reference:

Consumer advocate Clark Howard, www.clarkhoward.com

See: fear of not having control, fear of the unknown, fear of asking for a raise or promotion, fear of downsizing, fear of retirement, fear of quitting, stress at work

Fear of a Job Interview

testophobia (fear of being tested)	*The only difference between a date and a job interview is that there are not many job interviews where there's a chance*

you'll end up naked at the end of it. —JERRY SEINFELD

Characteristics: Fear of job interviews is very common. This fear can make a candidate appear less qualified than he or she is for a job. A candidate may be nervous or sweat before an interview, stammer, or show lack of concentration or confidence. Some people may avoid an interview entirely or show up late. Others, however, "turn on" for such an event with heightened personality, confidence and focus, bringing out the best in themselves.

Background: Being tested or evaluated in any way usually makes people nervous, if not downright scared. Apprehension over a job and your future is quite understandable. Someone who doesn't get a little nervous may not be that interested in the job and may not be alert enough to make a good impression on the potential employer. There is more pressure on an applicant these days because of increasing competition in a declining workforce. You know that if you flub, someone else is probably waiting in the wings.

Strategies:
- Research the company you are applying to. Familiarize yourself with what the employer wants from you, as well as with its goals, such as a plan to increase mergers, to expand sales or to solidify a market. Just as importantly, know yourself and what you want. Many people are not clear about what they want to do, or even about what they *currently* do for a living.
- Prior to the interview, get proper diet, exercise and sleep. That sounds simple, but your health can affect your performance and your mood. Practice the interview at home by simulating pressure and having someone play the part of the interviewer. Try to anticipate the type of questions that will be asked.
- On the day of the interview, visualize the entire process. Imagine yourself driving to the appointment, sitting down and presenting yourself well. Imagine the interviewer reacting well to you and offering a second interview or the job.

- It's natural to be keyed up for an interview; if you aren't nervous at all, you may come off flat, and the employer may not see the enthusiasm and passion he or she is seeking.
- Wear clothes that make you feel good but that won't offend anyone. You may want to bring a favorite piece of jewelry that you can touch from time to time if you get nervous.
- Tell yourself that you will deliver. If you're troubled by nervousness during the interview, use cue words to snap into focus ("Get it done!") or get mad at yourself briefly without showing it, then focus on the interview again.
- Get off to a confident, but not aggressive, start. Interviewers usually make up their minds about a candidate in the first five minutes. But don't try to be perfect. It's your expertise, ideas and work ethic that employers are looking for. Make sure you don't look too anxious or eager (by sitting on the edge of the chair, for example).
- Look the employer confidently in the eye and explain why you are a good candidate and how you will contribute to the company.
- If you don't get the job, don't take it personally. As psychotherapist Susan Britt says, "It may have little to do with you and a whole lot that you look like the interviewer's ex-wife or perhaps you worked for a company which once turned down the interviewer for a loan." And it's not the end of your world. Allow yourself disappointment, but quickly pick yourself up and get back at the job search. Write down the good and bad points of your last interview and learn from both. Perhaps ask the interviewer what he or she thought of you.

A MANTRA TO TELL YOURSELF: *"Prepare."*

Reference:

Best Answers to the 201 Most Frequently Asked Interview Questions by Matthew J. Deluca, McGraw-Hill, 1996

See: fear of failure, fear of making mistakes, fear of the unknown, fear of what others think, fear of embarrassment, fear of the boss, financial fears, fear of rejection, fear of confrontation or conflict, fear of losing status

Fear of Downsizing

the pink slip syndrome

Downsizing creates a whole new set of dynamics in a company. Workplace survivors *feel a deep sense of loss, a severing of close friendships and a fear of the future.*
—AUTHOR AND CAREER DEVELOPMENT COUNSELOR BARBARA BOWES

Characteristics: Many workers feel worry, doubt or anger that they or fellow employees will be let go. This fear can cause anxiousness, nausea, tension and many health problems, including migraines, ulcers, and even disease and heart problems. Some workers worry they will be replaced by a computer. Even the word *downsizing* can cause distressful symptoms. Seeing coworkers get laid off can cause uncertainty and resentment with the remainder of the staff and can be demoralizing and hurt productivity. On the positive side, this fear can spur greater productivity and commitment.

Background: What makes downsizing doubly hurtful to workers of the new millennium is that, not so long ago, there was job security in our society and a person might stay at the same job for life. Many companies were good to their employees and protected them with benefits. Now the focus of many companies is on the bottom line. Some firms treat their workers impersonally, said Larry More, an engineering designer, who blamed his ulcer on a layoff: "They treat employers like used toilet paper and put pressure on them to quit or they just throw them out. You get dejected if you think you got a raw deal."

Strategies:
- If you keep doing a good job with an honest effort, chances are that if downsizing comes, you will be a valuable commodity and your firm will try to keep you. But you might have to find ways to become more versatile.
- Don't expect a lot from big companies, even good companies. Even those people who perform long and well can be susceptible to cutbacks these days. Downsizing can be used as a strategy to make a firm's bottom line more attractive to a prospective buyer or to increase profits for shareholders.

- If you feel daily anxiety, use a calming method that works for you—perhaps a combination of deep breathing, meditation or prayer, music, humor and exercise.
- Find out if your company has support groups, counseling or job-search services. If you have a union, keep on top of issues through your local representative.
- If you are released, don't ask "Why me?" but "What's next for me?" and don't let the experience embitter your future. This is an opportunity to reassess your goals. It might be the trigger to make that career change you've always thought about, or to gear down to part-time. Allow yourself a transition period, perhaps starting with a vacation and a funny book. Millions of people are unemployed; why not start your own support group?
- Getting released is also a chance to become what Harvard professor Juliet Schor has termed a *downshifter*, a new breed of professional who trades income and long hours for more leisure and a better quality of life.
- Managers, reduce uncertainty by letting employees know ASAP if downsizing will affect them. For those remaining, give them a vision of where your company is going and ask them for ideas on how to cut costs and create more efficiency.

A MANTRA TO TELL YOURSELF: *"It if happens, I'll be ready."*

References:

Are You a Corporate Refugee? A Survival Guide for Downsized, Disillusioned and Displaced Workers by Ruth Luban, Penguin, 2001

Career development counselor Barbara Bowes, barb@bowes-group.com

For senior executives, team leaders, HR directors and consultants: *Charging Back Up the Hill: Workplace Recovery After Mergers, Acquisitions and Downsizings* by Mitchell Lee Marks, John Wiley and Sons, 2003

See: fear of the unknown, fear of change, financial fears, fear of not having control, fear of failure, fear of losing status, fear of the boss, fear of rejection, stress at work, fear of retirement, fear of embarrassment

Fear of Retirement

gerascophobia (fear of aging)

The harder you work, the harder it is to surrender. —LEGENDARY FOOTBALL COACH VINCE LOMBARDI

Characteristics: People approaching retirement age often feel anxious, restless, irrelevant, or even depressed or ill. Their reasons are many and complex, ranging from concern over not having enough pension money to losing their colleagues at work to fear of getting bored to worry about suddenly being at home all the time. Some people may put retirement off. After retirement, some people become isolated and depressed, but others feel rejuvenated and free.

Background: It's common to feel a big letdown at retirement after spending 40 hours or more a week at something for all of one's adult life. If a person's self-esteem has been largely wrapped up with who they are at work, as is often the case with men, they will likely have problems after the work is finished. The goal of retiring early has become ingrained in our psyche, leaving many with lots of free time. Many retirees take part-time jobs or continue to lead active lives. Seniors and baby boomers are generally more fit than they've ever been—more than 250,000 people annually take part in U.S. regional competitions for the Senior Olympics (for those over 55).

Strategies:
- Before you retire, get your finances in order: start saving early and don't expect to keep up the same lifestyle you have had if you rely only on social security. Participate in your employer's retirement plan. Save in a tax-deferred account. Diversify your investment portfolio.
- Also prior to retirement, while you are still fully covered by health insurance, get a thorough checkup at the doctor's, have your eyes examined and your teeth cleaned and checked.
- Write down your retirement goals and strategies. There were probably some things you wanted to do while you were working, but didn't have the time for, such as starting a garden or taking up golf. Now is the time.

- Take part in the gray-power revolution. You'll only be "put out to pasture" if you allow society to do it to you. There are lots of opportunities for volunteering, part-time work or getting involved in community activities. If you were not in a leadership role at work, perhaps try one now. Don't worry about being bored—there is as much to do as you want to do.

- Develop your spirituality by making new friends and keeping in touch with old friends and work colleagues through golf, cards, church groups, volunteering and simple get-togethers. Take part in your children's lives (without interfering) and develop your career as a grandparent.

- Don't underestimate what seniors' residences have to offer, especially in terms of social contact with people of your generation. It's fun being around other people who might share your interests and experience.

- Look back on the work you did! If you are not happy with it, examine other ways you can still make a contribution. You've got lots of time left yet—life expectancy is near 80. You can do more!

- Moderate exercise is necessary to maintain your health in retirement. While you were working, the demands of your job probably helped keep you fit. A balanced diet, low in fat and with plenty of fruits, protein and vegetables, is recommended.

- This is a good time to reflect and document your life and that of your family. Talk to relatives and put together a written family history or organize photo albums.

- You're never too old for anything, except maybe bungee jumping.

A MANTRA TO TELL YOURSELF: *"Free to do as I wish."*

References:

The Ultimate Safe Money Guide: How Everyone Over 50 Can Protect, Save and Grow Their Money by Martin D. Weiss, John Wiley and Sons, 2002

Analyze Now (for retirement planning), www.analyzenow.com

See: fear of the unknown, fear of change, fear of not having control, fear of aging, fear of death, fear of success or happiness, fear of being alone, fear of losing status

Fear of Technology

cyberphobia (fear of computers)

I don't fear computers, I fear the lack of them. —ISAAC ASIMOV

mechanophobia (fear of machines)

Characteristics: Many people feel intimidated about learning to operate new machines, particularly computers. Others—especially older people, who tend to experience a decline in short-term memory, focus, processing speed and problem solving—may feel frustration, anxiety and difficulty concentrating with an overload of technology. Some people fear health problems from electromagnetic fields associated with computers and monitors. Others feel that computers will take their jobs. Some fear that by getting caught up in the Information Age, we risk neglecting ideas and overlooking more meaningful aspects of life.

Background: It isn't surprising that technological advances make some people uneasy. Things are changing so rapidly, it's hard to keep pace these days. More than 50 percent of the workforce uses high-tech equipment—e-mails, faxes and cell phones. Employees of Fortune 1,000 companies send and receive on average 178 messages each day through technology. Our brains have difficulty with such overload. If we are older, we may have trouble being flexible and attempting new things. If our cave ancestors could see the amazing things we are doing at such a fast pace, the hairs on their backs would stand up.

Strategies:

- Don't panic, but if you don't keep up with the changes in technology, you'll be left behind. The good news is, there is lots of help out there, and computers are getting simpler to operate every day. And they'll help you do your paperwork quickly and allow you to communicate with others across the globe.
- If you are having trouble adjusting to computers, use your tech-support person at work. Ask him or her to format your desktop with shortcuts to the programs and files you use on a regular basis.

- If you are having problems learning, practice using your computer and upgrade your training. Don't be afraid to ask someone younger than you; children pick up technology fast.
- Make sure you take periodic breaks at your computer to keep your stress at a manageable level. Organize yourself and go at your own pace, not at the machine's pace; otherwise, your metabolism may speed up and your attention span could shorten. Try to alternate repetitive computer tasks with other jobs that are unrelated.
- Improve your lighting (it should be over the computer, not behind you) and reduce neck and back problems by having your screen at about eye level.
- If you get headaches, attach an anti-glare shield to your screen.
- Keep your work environment as quiet and as undistracted as possible.
- Elderly people may want to consider using eyeglasses while using a computer.
- Beware of getting preoccupied (perhaps subconsciously) by the rush of information that comes across your desk or computer. Don't let technology crowd out creative, philosophical and ethical considerations. It's easy to get caught up in the cyber rat race and to become more superficial in one's thinking. If things become a blur, stop and get off for a while!

A MANTRA TO TELL YOURSELF: *"Machines will help me."*

References:

TechnoStress by Larry D. Rosen and Michelle M. Weil, John Wiley and Sons, 1998

The Internet for Dummies, Eighth Edition by John R. Levine, Carol Baroudi and Margaret Levine Young, John Wiley and Sons, 2002

See: stress at work, fear of change, fear of the unknown, fear of not having control, fear of embarrassment, fear of making mistakes, fear of taking chances, fear of appearing stupid

Fear of Asking for a Raise or Promotion

doxophobia (fear of expressing opinions or receiving praise)

Asking for a raise ranks up there with getting a tooth pulled. —DETROIT JOURNALIST JENNIFER BOTT

Characteristics: Many people are reluctant to ask for a raise or promotion. They may work themselves into a tizzy just worrying about what to say or how the boss will react. They may feel unworthy or believe that the company can't afford it. But if workers can't bring themselves to at least ask, their incentive can decline and their work might suffer.

Background: Many people are afraid to blow their own horn, even when it's warranted, partly because our society teaches us to be humble. Others may be afraid of getting turned down or being exposed as inadequate at their job. Paradoxically, some workers refuse to ask for a raise out of arrogance, because they believe they are worth much more and that their employer won't give it to them.

If you are reluctant to ask for a raise or promotion, it could mean that your skills or work ethic need improving or that you're afraid of your boss or that you lack initiative or courage.

Strategies:

How to ask for a raise:

- If you think you're worth a raise, take a stand. If you don't stick up for yourself, who will? Very few of us have agents or public relations representatives.
- Research what others in similar jobs are getting and be reasonable in your request. Know your company's policy on incentives and raises. And find out if your company tends to give raises at certain times of the year. Make an appointment with your boss a day or two in advance and treat it like an important meeting. Close the door and discourage distractions.
- Don't come right out with, "I deserve a raise." You might deserve one, but sometimes the world isn't fair. And don't say *why* you need the extra money; it doesn't mean much to your employer. Probably most people in your company also believe they deserve or need a raise.

- Make a case for your job performance by outlining how you've benefited the company. Your boss may not recall all of your achievements. Many firms have no tools in place to measure performance.
- Negotiate rather than ask for a raise. You have a service to offer and you are simply asking a good price for it.
- If your company has just had a poor quarter, consider other things you can negotiate—incentive compensation, stock options, an extra vacation week, personal days or education benefits.
- If you don't get the raise, be grateful for what you have, and let the boss know it—not only with words but with continued good performance. The boss may remember your grace and the raise may come a little later.

How to ask for a promotion:
- It may be easier to ask for a promotion than a raise because, if you are turned down for the promotion, you can then ask for a raise.
- If you believe you are ready to take on more responsibility, make it clear to your employer. It shows him or her you are ready to grow with the company.
- Always make it seem like you are offering something rather than requesting something. In other words, the company will be getting something more in return for your promotion.
- Try to come up with a new initiative in which you serve the company. Employers like initiative and are always eager to reduce middle-management tasks.
- If you are passed over for a raise or promotion, don't take it personally. Put things in perspective by talking to a trusted friend or relative.

A MANTRA TO TELL YOURSELF: *"I'm worth something."*

Reference:
How to Say It at Work by Jack Griffin, Prentice Hall, 1998

See: fear of not having control, fear of rejection, fear of confrontation or conflict, fear of the boss, fear of success or happiness, fear of taking chances, fear of responsibility, fear of losing status, fear of what others think, stress at work, fear of competition

Dealing with Deadline Pressure

choking (letting your emotions negatively affect your work)

flow (being in the zone of optimal performance)

Coffee is only for closers. —ALEC BALDWIN'S CHARACTER TO UNDERACHIEVING REAL ESTATE SALESMEN IN *GLENGARRY GLEN ROSS*

Characteristics: The pressure of deadlines and important tasks can make people tense or excited. Pressure often leads to shaking fingers, flustered concentration and apprehension, as well as decreased productivity. On the other hand, pressure can lead to increased focus, drive and efficiency. A person may deal with pressure well on some days, while on other days, their wheels may fall off. Some people avoid jobs with intense deadline pressure, while others seek them out.

Background: Some people are hardwired for good production under pressure and are adrenaline sensitive. They may produce seven hours of work in just four. Others are not able to control their adrenaline production. Age, upbringing and experience all come into play.

If you have your ducks in a row physically and mentally, you can actually perform better under pressure because your "arousal hormones" can add to your concentration and your energy levels. If you can get into the zone at work, time seems to slow down and everything seems to be happening smoothly in a type of flow.

Strategies:

- Keep your pressures from reaching unmanageable levels. Prior to a task, prepare yourself physically and mentally.
- If you keep your desk uncluttered, with resources at hand, you'll have a feeling of control. Organize your time and, if possible, allocate a certain amount of time to a certain amount of work.
- See the job as a challenge, not a fearful situation. If you feel nervous, see it as a sign that you are geared up for the challenge and your emergency fear system has kicked in. Let it help you.
- Don't worry too much. Trust your skills, stop resisting the pressure and get out of your own way. Your subconscious and your muscle memory, which you've trained, will come through.
- Visualize what you want to do and imagine yourself doing it successfully and on time.

- Make sure your posture is good, particularly if you're at a computer.
- Don't get too keyed up. Try to keep a level of arousal that you can control. If you begin to lose control, take deep breaths, use cue words such as "Easy does it" or get up and take a break. If you lose motivation, remind yourself of the importance of the job and use cue words like "Just do it!"
- With confidence and focus, it's possible to redirect high arousal directly into your work. Stay in the present, focusing not on the end result but on the task. Check on the time periodically, but not every few minutes or you'll get distracted.
- Take breaks and allow recovery time after an intense session.
- If you miss a deadline or are not satisfied with a job, learn from it and move on.

> **How Physiological Arousal and Your Emergency Fear System Affect Skills:**
>
> The average heart rate is 70 beats per minute. When engaged in fine motor skills (those involving dexterity or hand-eye coordination), you can perform well at low to medium levels of arousal, with up to 115 heartbeats per minute, but this will lessen the dexterity of your fingers. When engaged in complex motor skills (those involving a series of muscle groups and movements requiring hand-eye coordination, precision, tracking and timing), skills begin to deteriorate at 145 heartbeats per minute. Gross motor skills (those involving the large muscle groups and strength and speed activities) actually improve as your level of arousal rises.

A MANTRA TO TELL YOURSELF: *"Focus and get out of your own way."*

Reference:

Intelligent Fear by Michael Clarkson, Key Porter, 2002

See: fear of failure, fear of making mistakes, fear of what others think, fear of criticism, financial fears, fear of not having control, fear of the boss, fear of choking in sports, fear of exams

Fear of the Boss

tyrannophobia (fear of tyrants) *poinephobia* (fear of being punished)	*In apologizing for accidents and errors, never tell your boss how he or she should feel about it.* —COMMUNICATIONS EXPERT JACK GRIFFIN

Characteristics: Most people probably have some apprehension about their boss. They might fear the power he wields or what he might do if they fall out of favor. Some people are so anxious that they rarely talk to or challenge their boss, and that can be bad for everyone. Some people even quit because they don't like or fear their superior.

Background: Most employees have always feared, respected or hated their superiors because of the power they wield. Some people fear authority figures because of their own insecurity or self-esteem issues. In this age of downsizing, the boss may seem more formidable than ever. Because of human nature, bosses can sometimes condescend to their subordinates, and workplace relations can turn into a type of class system. However, a healthy fear of authority can keep a workplace running effectively. Some people actually fear or hate their work and turn their angst toward their boss. People who suffer from this fear may have had argumentative parents.

Strategies:

- If your boss is critical, try to put a positive spin on it. She may be right. Thank her and find ways to improve.
- If you goof, admit it. Show your superior that you actually learn from your mistakes.
- If a compliment comes, accept it with gratitude and grace. Perhaps share it with others who helped you.
- If things are never good enough for your boss, see it as an opportunity. If you want to prove something, focus your energy on your work, not in belittling your boss.
- When talking with your boss, always keep eye contact and be confident.
- To show you are a team player, when talking to your superior, use the words "we" or "us" rather than "I."

- If given an assignment you don't like, don't grumble, but tell him you'll approach it with a good work ethic. If it is an important task, ask if it's possible to take some time to digest it and get back to him ASAP.
- Keep small and big communications lines open; for important issues, ask for a closed-door meeting. You probably shouldn't be buddy-buddy with your boss, but develop an open relationship by occasionally going for coffee or lunch with her.
- If she is unreasonable, talk to your employee-assistance rep or a trusted colleague about it, but don't gossip. It may get back to her.
- If your boss is a monster, his bad attitude is probably not personal. Cut him down in your mind by imagining him as a child acting out his fantasies. Smiling at him could improve his demeanor with you. Try to get something positive out of your situation—having a disagreeable boss is a good way for you to raise your tolerance and toughness levels.
- If your boss is an empire-builder, he may be impossible to deal with, so try looking the other way. As anthropologist Michael Maccoby writes in his book *The Productive Narcissist: The Promise and Peril of Visionary Leadership*, "Don't invest your ego in the relationship. Don't look for empathy, interest in your life or praise. You won't get it...you may have to let him or her take credit for all of your good ideas and accept blame for all his bad ones. It's the bargain you make working for a visionary."

A MANTRA TO TELL YOURSELF: *"Fe, fi, fo, fum..."*

References:

Competitive Strategy: Techniques for Analyzing Industries and Competitors by Michael E. Porter, Free Press, 1998

Awesome and Awful Boss Hall of Fame,
www.meaningatwork.com/boss/awfulpage3.html

See: fear of not having control, fear of failure, fear of criticism, fear of making mistakes, fear of downsizing, fear of confrontation or conflict, fear of teachers, stress at work, fear of asking for a raise or promotion, fear of quitting

Fear of Quitting

| neophobia (fear of anything new) | *Tell people that you have an opportunity more in line with your goals and one that you cannot pass up.* —BEVERLY RILEY, |

HUMAN RESOURCES REPRESENTATIVE, TEXAS INSTRUMENTS

Characteristics: Leaving a job can be traumatic and complex. It can also make people nervous, anxious and even ill with headaches, stomach problems or ulcers. Some people quit inappropriately and suddenly because they are afraid of confrontation with bosses or coworkers.

Background: Most people want security and are afraid of change, especially in today's uncertain job climate. The larger a person's family, the more reluctant he or she may be to quit even a bad job. Some people feel too loyal to quit, or too tied to their coworkers or the job itself. Those reasons, however, are not always poor ones. Fear of quitting can inspire people to try harder and to try to make their job more tolerable.

Strategies:

- If you decide to quit, be sure that you *want* to quit. Think about the reasons and write them down. Can you live with the issues that trouble you at your present job? Give it a fair chance because you don't want to jump from job to job. Perhaps you just need to put in a bit more effort to like your job more, or perhaps you should talk to your superiors about nagging issues, and they may do something about them.
- Be certain that you have other irons in the fire before you quit. Have another offer, or a resume and references ready to go.
- If you are certain you want to leave, write a resignation letter, then make a formal appointment with the boss. Keep the meeting respectful, but friendly.
- Keep things positive and progressive. Even if you can't function in your job anymore, you have learned from the experience and from your employers. Write down these positive lessons and leave with a good taste in your mouth.

- If you have an offer from another company, tell your boss the money you will get and the conditions that make the potential job attractive. If he makes a counteroffer, tell him you want to think about it overnight.
- Check your rights and conditions with the company you are leaving. Will you lose retirement funds? Vacation? Will your new employer offer security?
- Give plenty of notice, if possible, and allow for your transition to go smoothly. Don't go out in a tantrum. Remember that if you burn your bridges behind you, the swim back will be difficult. "First impressions may be important," says career counselor Jean Ann Cantore. "But your last few weeks in a position are what really shape employers' and coworkers' opinions of you. Remember to handle the situation tactfully. Leave your work and files organized and don't tell coworkers you will be back to visit often if you can't keep the promise."
- Make good use of your exit interview. Offer constructive criticism to your employer. Start with what you liked about your job, discuss problems briefly and then end with a positive remark about the job or coworkers.

A MANTRA TO TELL YOURSELF: *"I'll do what's best."*

References:

It's a Job, Not Jail by Robert M. Hochheiser, Fireside, 1998

Quit Your Job and Grow Some Hair: Know When to Go, When to Stay by Gary N. Rubin, Impact Publications, 2003

See: financial fears, fear of the unknown, stress at work, fear of change, fear of the boss, fear of asking for a raise or promotion, fear of confrontation or conflict, fear of failure, fear of what others think, fear of delivering bad news

Fear of Firing an Employee

Firing someone with dignity takes thoughtfulness, sacrifice and skill. It's never, ever easy, but it can be done well. —Diane Tunick Morello, an official with the research firm Gartner

Characteristics: Unless they're cold-blooded, who relishes the idea of terminating someone? Just the thought of it can make an employer anxious or tense. Some bosses may be too sensitive or forgiving to do it, and that doesn't necessarily make them a good boss.

Background: Just like employees, most bosses like to be accepted and liked. Being up in an ivory tower is not much fun, and they don't pay enough for this kind of task. It's a painful chore to fire someone when you know their livelihood is in your hands. A boss may avoid giving a worker the ax for fear of triggering a harsh reaction, a lawsuit or fallout with the rest of the staff, or for fear of hurting the company's image. But it may be bad for the company and bad for morale to keep someone who is dragging his or her feet or is incompetent. Not many people are cut out for, or have the experience for, such a confrontation.

Strategies:
- Closely examine why you feel the employee might be terminated. It's a big decision. Consider all the ramifications, including the fact that if a poor employee is not released, it could affect the performance and morale of some of the staff.
- Firing someone usually takes several steps and may not come as a surprise to the employee. But before it comes to that stage, you may want to put the employee on warning and perhaps discipline him or her.
- Prepare well for the firing with valid reasons and perhaps evidence of the employee's inadequacy or offense.
- Treat the employee with fairness and respect. Don't make it personal. You are disappointed with the performance, not the person.
- Have the employee leave on the best terms possible. Give positive remarks to help the person the next time, such as, "I know

it didn't work out here, but I liked some of the things you did [detail them] and I'm sure you will improve upon them with another firm."

- A letter informing the employee of the termination and the effective date of the discipline is the most usual method of telling the employee about the organization's decision. If possible, let the employee go immediately, with two weeks of added pay to ease the blow and to avoid worker's compensation difficulties.

- See this confrontation as a chance to grow as a boss or manager. Don't take it personally if the fired employee takes it out on you. He or she may be embarrassed and not want to admit failure or be worried about the family consequences.

- If you are the one being fired, try not to discuss the issues immediately with the boss, except to get all the relevant details. Tell the boss you want a few days to digest the news. If you feel that the firing is unjust, seek your union representative or a lawyer. It may not be personal, but merely a matter of downsizing. Ask under what possible conditions you might stay with the company.

A MANTRA TO TELL YOURSELF: *"Do what's best."*

References:

From Hiring to Firing by Steven Sack, Alliance House, 1995

www.hrzone.com (human resources guide)

See: fear of confrontation or conflict, fear of quitting, fear of taking chances, fear of downsizing, fear of responsibility, fear of criticism, fear of delivering bad news, fear of ending a romantic relationship

Fear of Harassment

With harassment or discrimination, explore all your options; you have more power than you think.
—JOHN B. ARDEN, AUTHOR OF *SURVIVING JOB STRESS*

Characteristics: People may become nervous at work if they are harassed, offended, intimidated or humiliated by a coworker or a boss. It's not uncommon for people to face discrimination based on race, age, religion or sex. Some people are offended by wolf whistling, stereotyping and off-color jokes. People get upset if malicious rumors about them are spread around the office. At the very least, such problems create workplace distractions and may lead to high rates of absenteeism and employee turnover.

Background: Sexual harassment is quite common in workplaces, where people get much of their regular social contact. Many relationships begin at work, but others are thwarted. Many people don't complain about harassment for fear of embarrassment, for fear of being seen as a complainer or for fear that nothing will be done about it. Harassment is sometimes about a person or a group of people using power inappropriately over another person or group. This can cause poor morale or poor employee relations and give the company a bad reputation. Companies are not permitted to discriminate, but it does happen. In North America, most governments have antidiscrimination and equal opportunity laws that protect people in the workplace, but these often differ from region to region.

Strategies:
- Before you take any official action against someone at work, make your displeasure known to the person who is harassing or offending you or discriminating against you.
- With sexual harassment of a minor nature from an older person, consider the age and background of that person, who may be from an era in which offhand sexual comments were common and often laughed off. In other words, remarks such as "Aren't women supposed to be the ones making coffee?" may not have been personal. This doesn't make the person's attitude right, but it may make it easier to understand. You might want

to respond, while you are chuckling, "Aren't men supposed to be the only ones working outside the home?" Don't be politically correct to the point of losing your sense of humor.

- Make sure you don't create a possible opening for sexual harassment by flirting with a person, perhaps even subconsciously. Learn to read other colleagues' body and verbal language and respond accordingly.
- Examine your company's policies on harassment. Follow them and make sure you document an incident, preferably with witnesses.
- If someone verbally bullies you, ask for him or her to repeat it, especially in front of witnesses. The person, forced to hear his or her own tone again, may then realize what has been said and back off.
- Try to avoid bullies at work whenever possible. Giving them a taste of their own medicine often escalates a situation.
- If a supervisor orders you to do a task a certain way and you know it doesn't work, ask him or her to show you the way. If it fails, don't rub it in.
- Employers should remember that it is in their interest to promote a safe, healthy and fair environment for their workers.

A MANTRA TO TELL YOURSELF: *"I'll get protection when I need it."*

Reference:

Workplace Sexual Harassment by Anne C. Levy and Michele Antoinette Paludi, Prentice Hall, 2001

Note: Complaints can be lodged with the (U.S.) Employment Equal Opportunity Commission, which investigates cases of harassment and discrimination. The Labor Commission oversees labor law and ensures that nonunionized employers abide by basic labor standards.

See: fear of invasion of privacy or territory, fear of solicitors and telemarketers, fear of bullies, fear of not having control, fear of confrontation or conflict, fear of being mugged, sexual fears, fear of enclosed spaces, fear of embarrassment, fear of the opposite sex

Fear of Competition

kakorrhaphiophobia (fear of defeat)	*The best way to motivate people is to pit them against one another.* —J. WATSON JR., FORMER CEO OF IBM
testophobia (fear of being tested)	

Characteristics: This condition involves anxiousness or avoidance of jobs or projects that have goals or quotas. It also involves fear of comparisons or competition with other employees or business rivals. It can lead to lack of confidence and even illness or depression prior to a project or event. It can also drive people to great heights as they improve themselves and try harder and prepare better for fear of losing.

Background: A competitive nature is inbred in humans, who have had to struggle for survival of the fittest. (At the same time, early humans survived partly through teamwork and cooperation.) Partly because of this drive, humans have conquered the world. Our competitive nature can show itself even before birth—twins have been photographed fighting for space in the womb. In a society that often values status, becoming No. 1 is important. This fear can be related to fear of rejection or failure—some people won't even play Scrabble for fear of losing—and the fear of being on a team. But some people avoid competition because they don't want to belittle or defeat others.

Strategies:
- Be competitive in the areas you need to be and let go in others. If you are fighting for a contract, you will need to give it a full effort. If you are competing for attention from a coworker or a relative, you might want to assess how far you want to go.
- Compete with yourself first, challenging yourself to make improvements, even if they are small but continual.
- If you have an intense fear of looking silly when losing a competition, examine your ego and self-esteem issues. Maybe you take losing too personally. False pride is not worth it.
- Maybe you are more cooperative than competitive; there's nothing wrong with that, as long as it isn't affecting your job.
- If you must compete intensely, learn teamwork and respect for others. If you are part of a team, praise others to raise

collective pride. And learn to be a good loser; for one thing, you learn a lot about yourself and your character.

- Be sure to compete only to get ahead at work or to have fun in your hobbies, not to prove something or diminish somebody. Unfortunately, many high achievers take this route; it may lead to improved job productivity, but it also harms their personal lives and keeps them from forming many close relationships. On the other hand, don't judge people who are ultra-competitive. While their attitudes and personal lives may not be what you seek, such people can create a lot of progress and good in the world.
- Think positively. Research showed that optimists sold 29 percent more insurance in their first year than their more pessimistic peers and 130 percent more in their second year.
- If you want to get to the top in any profession, you must embrace competition, because your competitors certainly will.
- Remember that healthy competition usually produces a better product and a tougher and smarter person.

A MANTRA TO TELL YOURSELF: *"What am I afraid of?"*

From Another Angle:

"Life for us has become an endless succession of contests. From the moment the alarm clock rings until sleep overtakes us again, from the time we are toddlers until the day we die, we are busy struggling to outdo others. This is our posture at work and at school, on the playing field and back at home. It is the common denominator of American life."—Alfie Kohn, in his book *No Contest: The Case Against Competition*

Reference:

Michael Porter on Competition by Michael E. Porter, Harvard Business School, 1998

See: fear of failure, fear of what others think, fear of success or happiness, fear of losing status, fear of not having control, fear of confrontation or conflict, fear of choking in sports, fear of embarrassment, fear of getting a compliment, fear of exams, fear of a job interview

9

Serious Worries and Ways to Relax

Serious Worries

It makes no difference how deeply seated may be the trouble,
How hopeless the outlook,
How muddled the tangle, how great the mistake.
A sufficient realization of love will dissolve it all.
—EMMET FOX, IN *THE GOLDEN GATE*

Characteristics: Most people experience moderate to serious symptoms when they are faced with life-changing events such as illness, death or divorce. These symptoms can include anxiety, withdrawal, aggression, anger, denial, grief, sleeplessness or too much sleep, depression, ulcers, hypertension, high blood pressure, disease and even thoughts of suicide. But many people overcome such symptoms to show leadership in times of crisis.

Background: Some worries are legitimate and unavoidable. These include serious illness and death, job loss, divorce, massive change, problems with family, and general worries over issues like terrorism, global warming or the spread of AIDS. Fear of death is hard to cope with because we live in a repressed society when it comes to grieving and worrying about our demise. At first, these worries may seem overwhelming, but we do have resources to deal with them, beginning with our own character and our support network of family, friends and coworkers.

Strategies:
- If you have a serious problem, don't allow yourself to add chronic worry to your burden. You can choose to put your worry to good use by planning strategies and finding solutions, or you can allow yourself to slide into depression or self-pity.
- If you develop your sense of well-being and your self-esteem, large problems will not be overwhelming. If you practice love and compassion in your daily life, you will feel less pain when something bad happens.
- Be open to your pain and face it. But then let it go, even laugh at it. It helped me deal with my uncle Gordon's tragic death when my last words to him in hospital were: "You look like s——." And his reply, through a chuckle, was "I feel like s——."

- Sometimes it is hard to reduce mountains to molehills, but dwelling on a big problem can make it even more ominous.
- A big worry is important, but it is only part of your life. Your life remains complex, with numerous issues, people and responsibilities, including the responsibility to yourself. Don't throw them all aside for one component. "The most important thing to remember is that life is a gift," says author Richard Carlson. "Despite the pain, the troubles, and all the big stuff, life is still a magical experience."
- If you have a serious illness, don't look for someone to blame. Says clinical psychologist Hap LeCrone, "As an alternative to thinking, 'My pain is all the fault of my employer, doctor, family, etc.,' one might instead consider, 'Unexpected things sometimes happen in life, but I am confident that I can learn to deal effectively with unexpected events.'"
- It's impossible not to spend at least some time worrying about the future, but stay in the present and enjoy it as much as possible.
- If someone close to you dies, allow a grieving period, but don't allow yourself to become a victim of self-pity. Nature gave you grief partly to get you to focus on the deceased and all the issues that need attending to when someone dies (such as funeral arrangements).
- For big worries, seek help and advice from others. "Trouble is a part of your life, and if you don't share it, you don't give the person who loves you a chance to love you enough," singer and philanthropist Dinah Shore once said. Consider professional help, spiritual help or medication. Also consider a support group for people with similar problems. In fact, share other people's real problems. It's an opportunity to grow stronger together.
- Try to remain optimistic. Studies show that optimists who suffer setbacks attribute them to external causes that are temporary and can be changed. When Mozart suffered the deaths of four children, serious illness and repeated financial disasters, his optimism actually rose.
- Understand that everyone has serious worries. As Ann Landers said, "When life's problems seem overwhelming, look around and see what other people are coping with. You may consider yourself fortunate."

MANTRAS TO CONSIDER: *"My family loves me"* OR *"Thankfully, my life will go on."*

Author's Two Cents:

My wife, Jennifer, is an inspiration to all around her. In 2002, she had a knee replacement, suffered three dizzy spells a day, and discovered she had an incurable blood disorder. Using mental toughness, humor and compassion for others, she made it easier for the rest of us to support her. Rather than quitting work, she set a record for sales. On one occasion, I tried to get depressed about her condition, but how could I?

References:

What About the Big Stuff? by Richard Carlson, Hyperion, 2002

Clinical psychologist Hap LeCrone, hlecrone@aol.com

See: fear of illness or pain, fear of death, fears for your marriage/partnership, fear for your children's safety, fear of delivering bad news, fear of retirement, fear of downsizing

How to Relax

- Examine and manage the pressures in your life so that your nervous system does not constantly kick in. Try to avoid overloading yourself with responsibilities at home and work.
- Identify and eliminate exaggerated thinking. You may be an obsessive thinker and make mountains out of molehills.
- Raise your "anxiety threshold" so that you don't become anxious over unimportant things.
- Learn to express your feelings without constantly bottling them up.
- Get regular aerobic exercise, eat balanced meals and get as much sleep as you need.
- If you have a phobia, slowly expose yourself to what you fear.
- Cope with worry by focusing only on the problems you can control.

- When you feel anxious, breathe deeply from your abdomen, or use mantras such as "Relax" or "Stop it now!"
- Learn to relax through meditation and spirituality. Think about things beyond yourself. Volunteer.
- Build a good network of family, friends and coworkers.
- Get a pet and talk to it. Pet owners have fewer visits to the doctor.
- Change things once in a while. Routine and boredom can make you anxious.
- Prescription medications can help. See your doctor.

Note: More serious anxiety disorders not covered in this book include panic disorder (although we've discussed agoraphobia, the fear of having a panic attack, on pages 154–55), post-traumatic stress disorder and any generalized anxiety disorder that persists for over six months. If you feel that you or someone you know has one of these disorders, see a doctor or therapist.

A MANTRA TO TELL YOURSELF: *"What is going to hurt me?"*

Author's Two Cents:

I was not good at recognizing my own anxiety until one day, in my 30s, I got numb all over my body for two weeks. I went to my family doctor and his diagnosis was that I had too much pressure in my life and that I needed to manage it more effectively. After that, I stopped worrying about some of the things I couldn't control and my numbness left.

References:

The Anxiety Disorders Association of America
11900 Parklawn Drive, Suite 100
Rockville, MD 20852-2624
(301) 231-9350
www.adaa.org

The National Institute of Mental Health (offers pamphlets and a list of resources)
(888) ANXIETY (269-4389)
www.nimh.nih.gov

See: Most of the fears and phobias in this book have at least some anxiety as a symptom.

How to Cope with Pressure

- Control your external pressures before they become unmanageable by keeping your resources high. Keep your energy up through proper diet, sleep and exercise. Upgrade your job skills: if you can type only 50 words a minute and the job calls for 60, you will feel pressure unless you upgrade.
- Control your internal pressures by keeping your goals in perspective.
- Don't worry so much about what others think, unless you can channel your worry into motivation.
- Learn to delegate some of the pressures.
- Be aware that these days, women generally feel more pressure than men because of the duties they take on at work and at home. Women must learn to delegate and not feel guilty when everything doesn't get done. Men must learn to help take some of the pressure off them by pitching in with the children and relationship issues.
- By performing more under pressure and by training with pressure, you can raise your threshold and learn to feel comfortable when under strain.
- Stay cool under pressure or your emotional reaction may cause more pressure.
- Music and humor can keep pressure at a manageable level.

Reference:

Positive Under Pressure by Gael Lindenfield and Malcolm Vandenburg, Thorsons, 2000

See: how to deal with stress, dealing with deadline pressure, fears at school and fears at work

How to Deal with Stress

It's not stress that kills us, it's our reaction to it.
—PIONEER STRESS RESEARCHER HANS SELYE

Strategies:

* Keep stress levels manageable by keeping your life and your work in perspective. Taking on too many challenges sets off strong reactions from your emergency fear system.
* Examine the things in your life that you see as a threat and that thus set off your nerves. Some of them may create healthy challenges.
* When we feel nervousness or tension, we can defuse this energy or, if we are working, we can try to redirect it into whatever it is we are doing. In most situations, we will want to defuse it and calm down our fear reaction.
* Situations in which we may want to defuse our stress: when talking to people, when worrying, when reacting to a putdown or when a pressure situation is too much for us to handle. Situations in which we may want to redirect our nervous energy or tension: during an intense project or deadline pressure, during a sports competition or theatrical performance, when faced by a physical challenge, or anytime we feel confident that we can perform better with adrenaline in our system.
* To defuse stress, find one or more of the traditional methods that help you wind down: deep breathing from the abdomen, meditating and putting your issues into perspective, listening to music or talking to and laughing with someone you trust.
* If stress buildup is too high, you may want to walk away from whatever it is you are doing and take a break. Our bodies need a recovery period after too much fear reaction. Exercise also eases the stress buildup.

- To redirect stress energy, focus intently on whatever you are doing. If the stress distracts you, change your mindset briefly to anger or look upon the situation as a challenge, using a cue phrase such as "Go for it!" This will change your emotional chemistry to a more proactive mix of hormones. Then focus intently again.
- Remember Hans Selye's words on the previous page. Reacting negatively to stress can make you ill and ruin your efficiency. Up to 70 percent of visits to doctor's offices are stress-related.
- If you have chronic stress, you may want to examine problems with your job, your home life and how you view yourself and the world.

References:

Don't Sweat the Small Stuff by Richard Carlson, Hyperion, 1997

The American Institute of Stress
124 Park Avenue
Yonkers, NY 10703
(914) 963-1200
stress124@earthlink.net

www.stress.org

The Canadian Institute of Stress
P.O. Box 665, Station U
Toronto, ON
Canada M8Z 5Y9
www.stresscanada.org

See: Stress is a component of most if not all fears in this book. Especially see how to cope with pressure, fear of the unknown, fear of change, fear of embarrassment, fear of failure, stress at work

How to Deal with Anger

- If you are angry, analyze what has triggered this reaction and think about whether your anger is justified. Anger is not a force you want to unleash for every situation. If you are angry over a situation that legitimately threatens you, such as someone giving facts that misrepresent you, you might feel justified. But if you snap at someone just to protect your pride or reputation, your anger can be counterproductive, especially if the facts don't support you. In the long haul, anger can seriously hurt you. You might be using it as a defense mechanism to cover up your deficiencies. Ask someone you trust if you get angry too much; it's hard for you to be objective.

- If you're faced with a real danger and you feel justified in using anger, you can still be civilized about it. If you just explode in a primitive tantrum, your anger can be like an acid that erodes everything nearby, and your message can lose its effectiveness.

- On rare occasions, you may *have* to show primitive, visible anger—if it's hard to get your message across in any other way. In a pickup hockey game, if someone constantly hits you with a stick and the referee is not protecting you, you might have to show anger to ward your opponent off. You might face a similar situation in a relationship if a person keeps harassing you and doesn't heed warnings to back off. But don't hold onto anger longer than necessary.

- If you have an anger problem, don't look on it as an issue of *anger management*. It's really about *anger production*. You are the one who is activating your emergency fear system. Monitor and manage your anger production. There are probably just a few circumstances in which you need to produce anger. Stop seeing so many things as threats; there's no need to get upset if the driver in front of you is too slow or if someone criticized you over something unimportant. Do you really want to produce cortisol and testosterone to get revenge on a faulty computer?

- Be wary of the short-term, feel-good symptoms of anger. Yes, anger can intimidate others or make them respect you for standing up for yourself, and it can give you a sense that you are doing something about what stresses or frustrates you.

However, it can also make you seem out of control to others.

- If you consider using anger as a performance tool from time to time, be certain that you have mastery over your skills. During the job, use anger as a very short-term fuel to jump-start your task, then focus intently on your skills. For example, if you are failing at deadline work, briefly get angry with yourself (perhaps using a cue phrase like "Stop letting yourself down!") and focus the extra energy into beating the clock.

- If anger is affecting your life or health, learn to relax. Don't take things personally. Get a better perspective on life and use deep breathing, humor or your favorite music to defuse the emotion. Raise your anger threshold by driving behind the slowest truck or hanging around someone who annoys you. It will also raise your tolerance and patience thresholds.

- If you are constantly angry, identify and deal with your feelings. Perhaps there is an unresolved issue you must approach. On a larger scale, examine your confidence and feelings of self-worth. You might want to talk to someone, perhaps a counselor, about it.

A MANTRA TO TELL YOURSELF: *"Is this worth getting angry about?"*

References:

Anger: The Misunderstood Emotion by Carol Tavris, Touchstone, 1989

Stress Management for Dummies by Allen Elkin, CDG Books, 1999

See: how to deal with stress, how to relax, fear of oneself, fear of not having control, fear of downsizing

When Nothing Works

You know you need professional help when nothing has worked, when you feel depressed, anxious or agitated, when you are unable to carry out your obligations. But the most important point is to select someone with professional credentials and experience, referred by a reputable person or organization.
—DR. TERRY MIZRAHI,
PRESIDENT OF THE NATIONAL ASSOCIATION OF SOCIAL WORKERS

If the strategies in this book don't help you, and if discussing your fears, phobias and problems with family, friends and peers haven't helped, you may want to seek further help, perhaps starting with your family doctor or a therapist. Group therapy—sharing your concerns with people like you—can also be effective.

There is no shame in seeing a psychologist or a psychiatrist (I've been to both). Why should we go to doctors for physical issues only? Check in your yellow pages for psychologists or mental health centers, especially if you suffer from depression. Sadly, less than 25 percent of Americans with anxiety disorders receive any kind of treatment.

"There is a wide range of warning signals that could indicate the need for therapy," says Dr. James Morris, president of the American Association of Marriage and Family Therapy. "That includes marital or family relationship dissatisfaction or distress, alcohol or drug abuse, loneliness, depression, sexual problems, unexplained physical problems, employment difficulties, or an inability to set or attain goals."

Counseling can be helpful for phobias you cannot shake on your own. Counselors can also help you face a transition period in your life or your job, or deal with the pain of separation or loss.

You may need medication from time to time to balance your biochemicals, especially if you suffer from depression (I was on the antidepressant Paxil and it worked). In certain situations, it is healthy for children and teenagers, especially those with generalized anxiety disorder, to receive anxiety medication.

Therapists can deal with your phobias by tailoring their strategies specifically to you, or they may use elaborate or high-tech methods such as virtual reality programs that provide simulated exposure to your fears.

Psychotherapy can change your life, not only by teaching better techniques to cope with your pressures, fears and stresses, but by increasing your self-esteem and improving your view of yourself and the world, which is often at the root of such issues.

References:

The American Psychological Association
For referrals to psychologists, call (800) 964-2000, www.apa.org

Be Your Own Therapist, www.psychologyhelp.com

When You Don't Fear Enough

hypophobia (absence of fear, or a fear of not being afraid)

Those without normal levels of anxiety may lack basic caution and end up losing jobs and getting into fights where others simply sidestep trouble.

—HELEN SAUL IN *PHOBIAS: FIGHTING THE FEAR*

Characteristics: Some people actually don't worry or become anxious or alert enough about real threats or the future. People who don't worry about the consequences of their behavior may get into trouble when they speak up. Others have problems getting inspired for exams or important projects, and their lack of focus or effort can scuttle relationships. Children who fear too little are prone to accidents. Some adults with this condition are called apathetic.

Background: This lack of fear may result partly from an underactive nervous system or from attitudes and beliefs developed in childhood. Not much is known about this condition because "sufferers" don't come forward for help and may not even realize they have a problem. If we didn't have a certain amount of fear for what others thought of us, we'd probably walk around like slobs with poor work habits.

Strategies:

- Take notice if you are continually getting into trouble at work or in relationships for speaking before you think or for not considering the consequences of your actions.
- If you often get injured, you may suffer from lack of fear rather than from lack of coordination or other physical problems.
- Find something you like to do and develop it. The passion could rub off in other areas of your life.
- Network with others, especially enthusiastic people. They can introduce you to mindsets and activities that could light your spark.
- Set goals and stick by them. Look upon them as a challenge.
- Exercise and become physically passionate about life. Get involved in sports or an aerobics class. Play more with your kids.
- Realize that if you are rarely active, if can affect others around you.
- Learn to recognize life's real challenges and threats: your family's health and welfare, financial security, close relationships, career issues, spirituality and the chance you could fall into apathy.

A MANTRA TO TELL YOURSELF: *"Heads up."*

QUOTABLE: *"Nerves provide me with energy. It's when I don't have them, when I feel at ease, that I get worried."—film director Mike Nichols*

Reference:

Fears, Phobias and Rituals by Isaac Marks, Oxford, 1987

Other Phobias

alektorophobia: fear of chickens
anthrophobia: fear of flowers
arithmophobia: fear of numbers
ballistophobia: fear of missiles or bullets
bibliophobia: fear of books
caligynephobia: fear of beautiful women
cibophobia: fear of food
coulrophobia: fear of clowns
deipnophobia: fear of dining or dinner conversations
dishabilliophobia: fear of undressing in front of someone
eleutherophobia: fear of freedom
ephebiphobia: fear of teenagers
frigophobia: fear of cold or cold things
heliophobia: fear of the sun
homilophobia: fear of sermons
hoplophobia: fear of firearms
koniophobia: fear of dust
liticaphobia: fear of lawsuits
macrophobia: fear of long waits
maniaphobia: fear of insanity
methyphobia: fear of alcohol
misophobia: fear of being contaminated with dirt or germs
novercaphobia: fear of your step-mother
nudophobia: fear of nudity
ommetaphobia or *ommatophobia:* fear of eyes
panophobia or *pantophobia:* fear of everything
paraskavedekatriaphobia: fear of Friday the 13th
peladophobia: fear of bald people
phalacrophobia: fear of becoming bald
psellismophobia: fear of stuttering
pyrophobia: fear of fire
rhytiphobia: fear of getting wrinkles
scoleciphobia: fear of worms
tridecaphobia: fear of the number 13
vitricophobia: fear of your step-father
xenoglossophobia: fear of foreign languages

Acknowledgments

I have tried to make the complex subject of fear as simple and understandable as possible by writing in layman's terms. Some of the research I have done myself since 1988, including thousands of interviews with psychologists, psychiatrists, researchers, phobics and people caught or working in pressure situations. But much of the background and strategies have come from other sources, such as the publications and reputable websites mentioned throughout this book.

I would like to thank some specific people whose research and studies have brought us to this point in our quest to understand fears and phobias, beginning with pioneers in psychology such as the father of psychoanalysis, Sigmund Freud (1856–1939); stress researcher Hans Selye (1907–1982) of McGill University in Montreal; psychologist Abraham Maslow (1908–70), who studied the hierarchy of needs; psychologist Maxwell Maltz (1899–1975) for his work on the mind-body connection and visualization; and Norman Cousins (1915-90), whose work on positive thinking and health was groundbreaking.

In recent years, universities, colleges and health centers have been doing wonderful research, which is available to writers like me. Thank you to Redford Williams, M.D., head of psychiatry and behavioral sciences and medicine at Duke University, for his research on hostility and anger control; Herbert Benson, M.D., Harvard Medical School, for his theories on the relaxation response; psychiatrist Edward Hallowell, M.D., founder of the Hallowell Center for Cognitive and Emotional Health in Sudbury and Andover, Massachusets, for his work in several fields, including worry; Massad Ayoob, director of the Lethal Force Institute in Concord, New Hampshire, for his cutting-edge work on emergency fear; David H. Barlow, Ph.D, professor of psychology at Boston University, for his research on anxiety; Julian Hafner, Ph.D, associate professor of psychiatry at Flinders University in Adelaide, Australia, who studies the effect of anxiety on relationships; Graham Davey, Ph.D, professor of psychology at the University of Sussex in England, who has found that cultural beliefs contribute to things like fear of spiders; and Robert Thayer, Ph.D., professor of psychology at California State University, who studies emotions.

Thanks also to psychologist Jaylan Turkkan, Ph.D, for her work on behavioural biology at the Johns Hopkins University School of Medicine; S.J. Rachman, Ph.D, in the department of psychology at the University of British Columbia, for research on the biology of emergency fear; psychologist Steven Berglas, Ph.D, for his work at Duke University on success-induced burnout; Richard Earle, Ph.D, director of the Canadian Institute of Stress, for his work on workplace fears and stress; British psychotherapist Frances Wilks for her work on using emotions intelligently; Michael Davis, Ph.D, professor of psychiatry and behavioral sciences at Emory University School of Medicine in Atlanta, who led his department's research to find medicine to help deal with phobias; Mihaly Csikszentmihalyi, Ph.D, an expert in concentration and the flow state at Claremont Graduate University in California, who conducted earlier work at the University of Chicago; clinical research psychologist Steve Fahrion, Ph.D, who studies biofeedback at the Life Sciences Institute of Mind-Body Health in Topeka, Kansas; Sue Johanson, R.N., a founding member of the Planned Parenthood Federation of Canada, for her work on sexual fears; and evolutionary psychiatrists Randolph Nesse, M.D., at the University of Michigan and Isaac Marks, M.D., at London University, who have researched fear as a survival instinct.

Thank you to Clare McKeon and Meg Taylor at Key Porter Books; to my unflappable agent, Robert Mackwood of Seventh Avenue Literary Agency; to my booking agents at the National Speakers Bureau/Global Speakers Agency; and to my editors at the *Toronto Star*.

On a personal note, thanks to my immediate family for their love and support—my wife, Jennifer; my sons, Paul and Kevin; my daughter-in-law, Tanya; my granddaughter, Skye; my mother, Irene Clarkson; my late father, Fred Clarkson; and my in-laws, Tony and Kathleen Vanderklei, and their family, along with my brother, Stephen, and his family.

And thank you to the many other people who have contributed to this book over the years, from people I have interviewed and worked with to the writers, psychologists and researchers who have inspired me. It is their book, as well.

Index

Sources of fears are in **boldface** type.

abandonment, 63, 124, 146
accidents, 81, 88
accidents, 58–61, 78, 98
dystychiphobia, 58–59, 80–81
adrenaline, 4, 16, 21, 120, 216
affection, 40–41
aging (gerascophobia), 68–69, 210–11
agoraphobia, 6, 154–55, 158–59
airplanes, 52–53
anger, 9–10, 59, 116, 237–38
anger (angrophobia), 80, 116–17
animals (zoophobia), 82–83, 124
anxiety, 5–6, 233, 239
attackers, 54–59, 78, 148
attention, need for, 40–41, 104–5
attention (scopophobia), 108–9, 152–53
lack of (athazagoraphobia), 104–5
authority figures, 186, 218–19

bad news, delivering, 138–39, 222–23
bathing (ablutophobia), 86–87
bats, 83
bedwetting, 144
bees, 83
beggars (hobophobia), 142–43
behaviorism, 11–12
birds (ornithophobia), 82
blood (hemophobia), 7, 58–61
blushing (erythrophobia), 94–95, 106, 114, 152
body image, 118, 192–93
boredom, 210
boss, 218–19
break-ins, 136–37
breakup, 172–73
bullies, 178–79, 194–95, 224
burglars, 144
harpaxophobia, 56–57
scelerophobia, 136–37, 194–95
burial alive, 72
burnout, 200, 202

cameras, 118–19
cars, 78–81
cats, 82
change (tropophobia), 32–33, 212–13
childbirth (lockiophobia), 130–31

children, 99. *See also* parenting; teenagers
fear and stress in, 124–25, 145, 161, 186
and school, 178–81
children
leaving home, 128–29
safety of, 126–27, 194
choking (anginophobia), 120–21
claustrophobia, 72–73
cliques, 190–91
commitment, 170–71
comparison, 164
competition, 178–79, 226–27
compliments, 106–7
computers (cyberphobia), 212–13
conditioning, 11–12
confidence, 107
confinement, 72–73
conflict, 38–39
confrontation, 38–39, 114, 172, 220, 222
control, 48–49, 99, 216
control, loss of, 80, 90, 96, 140
physical, 68–69, 76, 86
cortisol, 4, 10, 16
counseling, 239–40
criticism (enissophobia), 80, 102–3, 152, 164
critics (criticophobia), 102–3
crowds, 72, 78, 120
enochlophobia, 158–59, 190–91
crushing, 158

dancing (chorophobia), 164–65
darkness (achluophobia), 124, 148–49
dating, 166–67
deadlines, 216–17
death from overwork (karoshi), 200–203
death (thanatophobia), 62–63, 68–69, 144, 148, 230
defeat (kakorrhaphiophobia), 112–13, 226–27
defense mechanisms, 14, 102–3
dentists (dentophobia), 60–61, 66–67
depression, 239
destiny, 48–49
dirt and disease
mysophobia, 140–41
suriphobia, 82
discrimination, 224
disorder (ataxophobia), 140–41

distress, 8–9, 16, 200
doctors, 64
doctors (iatrophobia), 60–61, 66–67
dogs (cynophobia), 82–83
dopamine, 14–15, 21, 44, 59
downsizing, 208–9, 218
driving, 80–81

ego, 13, 140, 226
ego defense, 108–9
embarrassment, 88, 94–95, 106, 116, 154, 164, 224
emergencies, 58–59
emergency fear, 3, 4, 7–9
emergency fear system, 7–8, 10, 16, 56, 217
coping with, 20–21, 237
emotions, 120–21, 138
emotions, showing, 116–17
empty-nest syndrome, 128–29
enclosed spaces (claustrophobia), 72–73
endorphins, 15, 157
enemies, 56–57
eustress, 8–9, 16
exams. *See* tests

failure (atychiphobia), 96–98, 100, 125, 141, 184
in sports (anginophobia), 120–21
falling (basophobia), 68–69, 74
down stairs (climacophobia), 76–77
fate (Zeusophobia), 44–45, 48–49
fatness (obesophobia), 192–93
fear. *See also* emergency fear
awareness of, 24–25
in children, 124–25, 145, 161, 186
coping with, 2–3, 15–21
lack of, 75, 240–41
physical effects of, 8, 14–15, 60, 217
reactions to, 4, 14–15
sources of, 10–15
specific, 6–7, 18–19
types of, 3, 13
uses of, 20, 120–21
fear, 154
fear defense system, 4, 108–9
fearful situations (counterphobia), 116–17
fight-or-flight response, 8, 56, 59, 120
fires, 58–59
firing an employee, 222–23
flying (aviaphobia), 52–53, 78, 79
foreigners (xenophobia), 28–29, 46–47, 54–55, 160–63
friends' opinions, 188–89
future, 28–29, 231

gays, 174–75
generalized anxiety disorder, 233, 239
genetics, 11, 12
germs
mysophobia, 140–41
suriphobia, 82
getting lost, 158
ghosts (phasmophobia), 44–45, 124, 148–49
gods (theophobia), 46–47
good news (euphobia), 100–101

happiness (cherophobia), 100–101
harassment, 224–25
health, 64, 231
heights (acrophobia), 74–75
helplessness, 146
high objects (batophobia), 74
homosexuality (homophobia), 71, 174–75
hormones, 14–15, 120
horses, 82–83
hospitals, 60–68
humiliation, 56–57, 96, 182–83, 224
hypochondria, 64–65
hypophobia (lack of fear), 75, 240–41

ideas (ideophobia), 34–35
illness, 62–65, 124, 158
imperfection (atelophobia), 96–99, 108
inferiority complex, 107, 125
injury, 56–57, 60–63, 68–69, 80, 124
in-laws (soceraphobia), 134–35
insecurity, 108, 121
insomnia, 144
interviews, 206–7
intimacy, 42–43, 70–71, 167
invasion of privacy, 110–11, 136, 142
isolation (autophobia), 114–15

jinxes, 44–45
jobs
interviews for, 206–7
losing, 196–97, 208–9, 220
quitting, 220–21
jumping (catapedaphoiba), 74–75
justice (dikephobia), 186–87

karoshi, 200–203

laughter (geliophobia), 116
lawsuits, 58–59, 222
layoff, 208–9
leadership, 36–37, 114, 138, 158, 211
learning (sophophobia), 178–79
lesbians, 174–75

lizards, 82
loneliness
    autophobia, 68–69, 114–15, 124
    monophobia, 146–47
looking stupid, 178–79, 182–83, 226
looking up (anablepophobia), 74
love, 40–41, 133, 170, 230
love (philophobia), 42–43
    lack of, 40–41, 70–71
love play (sarmassophobia), 166–67
luck, 44–45, 49, 101

machines (mechanophobia), 212–13
marriage (gamophobia), 170–71
    breakdown of, 132–33
masturbation, 71
medical situations, 60–61
medications, 19, 153, 239
memory loss, 68–69
men (androphobia), 167, 168–69
menopause, 68–69
menstruation, 70
mice, 82
mistakes, 96, 98–99
money (chrometophobia), 204–5
muggers, 56–59, 148
music (musicophobia), 88

narrow places (stenophobia), 72–73
needles, 67
new things (neophobia), 172–73,
    220–21
night, 144–45
nightmares, 124, 125, 145
noises (acousticophobia, ligyrophobia),
    88–89
noradrenaline, 21

obesity (obesophobia), 192–93
observation, 108–9, 152–53
obsessive-compulsive disorder, 96, 140
old people (gerontophobia), 68–69
open places (agoraphobia), 6, 154–55,
    158–59
opinions
    of friends, 188–89
    of others (allodoxaphobia), 108–9,
        158, 184
opposite sex (heterophobia), 167, 168–69
other people, 108–9, 158, 162–63, 184,
    188–90
other races, 162–63, 190
overwork (ponophobia), 200–203

pain, 6, 230, 231

pain, 58–59, 80, 124
    algophobia, 64–65
panhandlers, 142–43
panic attacks, 154–55, 158
panic disorder, 233
parenthood, 130–31
parenting, 124–27, 180–81, 184, 187, 189,
    194–95
parents-in-law (soceraphobia), 134–35
peer pressure, 178, 188–89
peer pressure, 178–79
people (anthropophobia), 124, 152–53, 167
perfectionists, 96, 98, 108, 140–41
performing (topophobia, stage fright),
    156–57
phobias, 3, 6–7, 242
    dealing with, 7, 18–19
photography, 118–19
pickpockets, 158
pink slip syndrome, 208–9
pleasure (hedonophobia), 100
post-traumatic stress disorder, 12, 233
poverty (peniaphobia), 68–69, 204–5, 210
powerlessness, 30–31, 48–49, 200
praise (doxophobia), 106–7, 214–15
pregnancy, 131
pressure, 8–9, 120, 216–17
    coping with, 234–35
    from peers, 178, 188–89
pride, 10, 112, 113, 192, 226–27
    as ego, 8, 14, 20, 94, 103, 108
privacy, loss of, 110–11, 136, 142
promotion, asking for, 214–15
public places (agoraphobia), 6, 154–55,
    158–59
public speaking (glossophobia), 156–67,
    178–79
punishment (poinephobia), 178, 218–19

quitting work, 220–21

racism, 11–12. *See also* tolerance
raise, asking for, 214–15
rats, 82
rejection, 40–41, 96, 104–5, 166, 214–15
relationships, 152, 166–71
    breakdown of, 132–33, 172–73
relatives (syngenesophobia), 134–35
relaxation, 232–34
religion (theophobia), 46–47
responsibility (hypegiaphobia), 36–37, 170
retirement, 210–11
revenge, 109, 182
ridicule (catagelophobia), 182–83
riding in cars (amaxophobia), 78–81

risk, 34–35, 126
road travel (hodophobia), 78–79
robbers (harpaxophobia), 56–57, 136–37,
    194–95

school (scolionophobia), 178–81
seasickness, 86
self, 114–15, 146
    appearance of, 192–93
    in mirror (eisoptrophobia), 118–19
self-consciousness, 118
self-esteem, 118, 194, 210, 230
    and ego, 13, 140, 226
self-esteem, loss of, 96
self-image, 118, 192–93
separation anxiety, 124, 178–81
seratonin, 20
sex, 133, 166–67, 173–75
sex (erotophobia), 70–71, 110, 167
sexual harassment, 224–25
sexual inadequacy, 68–71
shyness, 152–53, 158
singing, 164–65
singlehood (anuptaphobia), 40–41
sinning (peccatophobia), 46–47
sleep, 144–45
snakes (ophidiophobia), 84–85
snow (chionophobia), 90–91
social harm, 124
solicitors, 142–43
solitude (autophobia, isolophobia, mono-
    phobia), 114–15, 146–47
sounds (acousticophobia, ligyrophobia),
    88–89
speaking (phonophobia), 114–15, 164–65
    in public (glossophobia), 156–67
spiders (arachnophobia), 84–85
spotlight effect, 94
stage fright, 156–67
status, loss of, 96, 112–13
stereotyping, 162, 168–69, 174, 224
storms, 90–91
strange places, 124
strangers (xenophobia), 28–29, 46–47,
    54–55, 158, 160–63
stress, 8, 9, 16
    in children, 124–25
    dealing with, 124, 235–36
    at work, 200–203
success (successophobia), 100–101, 106
suffocation, 86
supernatural, 44–45, 124, 148–49

superstition, 44–45
swimming, 86–87

teachers, 184, 186–87
teamwork, 226
technology, 212–13
teenagers, 188, 205
telemarketers, 142–43
terrorism, 54–55, 78
testosterone, 59
tests (testophobia), 38–39, 184–85, 206–7,
    226–27
therapy, 18, 19, 239–40
thinking too much (phronemophobia), 5
thunderstorms (astropophobia), 90–91
tolerance, 143, 224–25, 238
    racial, 46–47, 55, 111, 163
touch (aphenphosmphobia), 42–43, 110–11
trampling, 158
trauma, 12–13, 15, 57, 136
travel
    airplane (aviaphobia), 52–53, 78, 79
    road (hodophobia), 78–81
trembling (tremophobia), 94–95
tyrants (tyrannophobia), 186–87, 218–19

ugliness, 192–93
unemployment, 196–97, 208–9, 220
unknown, 28–29, 44, 148
untidiness, 140–41

vasovegal reaction, 60
virginity, loss of (primeisodophobia), 70–71
visualization, 18
voice, own (phonophobia), 114–15, 164–65

water (hydrophobia), 7, 86–87
weakness (asthenophobia), 30–33, 182–83
weather, 90–91
weight, gaining (obesophobia), 192–93
witchcraft (wiccaphobia), 44–45
women (gynephobia), 167, 168–69
work, 178–79
worry, 2–3, 4–6
    coping with, 17–18
    financial, 210
    health, 64
    at night, 144–45
    serious, 230–32

xenophobia, 28–29, 46–47, 54–55, 160–63